Studies in Perception and Action XI

SIXTEENTH INTERNATIONAL CONFERENCE ON PERCEPTION AND ACTION

EDITED BY
Eric P. Charles and L. James Smart

Ψ Psychology Press
Taylor & Francis Group

New York London

Psychology Press
Taylor & Francis Group
711 Third Avenue
New York, NY 10017

Psychology Press
Taylor & Francis Group
27 Church Road
Hove, East Sussex BN3 2FA

Version Date: 20110617

International Standard Book Number: 978-0-84872-976-6 (Paperback)

Visit the Taylor & Francis Web site at
http://www.taylorandfrancis.com

and the Psychology Press Web site at
http://www.psypress.com

Table of Contents

Chapter 1: Perception (Theoretical and Dynamic Perspectives)

Chapter 2: Coordination & Action

Chapter 3: Affordances

Chapter 4: Posture

Chapter 5: Human Factors

vi   *Contents*

Preface

We live in interesting and exciting times, even in terms of the growth of academic psychology. This volume contains a record of the posters presented at the Sixteenth International Conference on Perception and Action, which for the first time was held in South America (Ouro Preto, Minas Gerais, Brazil). It showcases the broad range of innovative and thought provoking research being performed literally all around the world concerning perception and action. The Studies in Perception and Action series provides a means of sharing research as it is happening, and thus in many ways reflects the state of the field better than any other publication. Indeed, having examined the previous volumes in preparation for this one, it is easy to see how the field has evolved from the first meetings: never ignoring previous work, but continuing to expand the scope and implications of Gibson's "radical ideas". It was interesting from an editorial standpoint to be able to look at the body of work being performed by our colleagues and notice both the diversity in design and analyses, and at the same time, recognize the commonality in purpose and interpretation. We believe the ideas and research presented in these pages well represent the continued energy and growth in both theoretical and applied domains.

However, the variety of ideas is also challenging when trying to organize volumes such as this. As with the editors of the previous volumes, we found that much of the work crossed many boundaries and so we opted to use broad categories for the five chapters in this volume: Perception (Theoretical & Dynamic approaches), Coordination and Action, Affordances, Posture, and Human Factors. As with past volumes we have included a meeting history, contributors list, and author index. As with previous volumes we converted color figures/photos to grayscale when necessary, and have done our best to make sure that the information depicted in them remains detectable.

We would like to thank Bill Mace for giving us the opportunity to work on this volume and providing much needed support and advice throughout the process, and Paula Silva for her leadership in organizing the conference and serving as the contact point for the authors. We would also like to thank the scientific organizing committee for performing a large number of insightful reviews in an extremely short time frame. We would also thank the editors of the previous volumes for making our job easier by providing excellent templates and advice.

L. James Smart
Department of Psychology, Miami University, Oxford OH, USA

Eric P. Charles
Department of Psychology, The Pennsylvania State University, Altoona PA, USA

Meeting History

1. 1981 – Storrs, CT, USA

2. 1983 – Nashville, TN, USA

3. 1985 – Uppsala, SWEDEN

4. 1987 – Trieste, ITALY

5. 1989 – Miami, OH, USA

6. 1991 – Amsterdam, THE NETHERLANDS

7. 1993 – Vancouver, CANADA

8. 1995 – Marseilles, FRANCE

9. 1997 – Toronto, CANADA

10. 1999 – Edinburgh, SCOTLAND

11. 2001 – Storrs, CT, USA

12. 2003 – Gold Coast, QLD, AUSTRALIA

13. 2005 – Monterey, CA, USA

14. 2007 – Yokohama City, JAPAN

15. 2009 – Minneapolis, MN, USA

16. 2011 – Ouro Preto, MG, BRAZIL

Contributors

Mohammad Abdolvahab
CESPA-University of ConnecticutHaskins Laboratories, New Haven, CT

Yousuke Akatsu
Nissan Motor Co., Ltd, Japan

Bruno Nascimento Alleoni
Sao Paulo State University, Brazil
Escola Superior de Tecnologia e Educação de Rio Claro, São Paulo, Brasil

Eric L. Amazeen
Arizona State University, USA

Dilip N. Athreya
Center for Cognition, Action & Perception, Department of Psychology,
University of Cincinnati

Benoît G. Bardy
Movement to Health, EuroMov, Montpellier-1 University, Montpellier, France

Antonio Barrientos
Grupo de Robótica y Cibernética, Universidad Politécnica de Madrid

Simon J. Bennett
Research Institute for Sport and Exercise Sciences, Liverpool JM University

Anjana Bhat
Department of Kinesiology, University of Connecticut
Center for Ecological Study of Perception and Action, University of Connecticut
Center for Health Intervention and Prevention, University of Connecticut

Julia J. C. Blau
Center for Ecological Study of Perception and Action, University of Connecticut

F. Nienke Boonstra
Bartiméus Institute for the Visually Impaired, Zeist, The Netherlands

Reinoud J. Bootsma
Institut des Sciences du Mouvement E.J. Marey (UMR 6233), Université de la
Méditerranée, Marseille, France

A. M. T. Bosman
Behavioural Science Institute, Radboud University Nijmegen, the Netherlands

Alain Boyadjian
CNRS UMR 6196, Marseilles
Université du Littoral

Blandine Bril
Groupe de Recherche Apprentissage et Contexte, École des Hautes Études en Sciences Sociales, France

Franck Buloup
Institut des Sciences du Mouvement E.J. Marey (UMR 6233), Université de la Méditerranée, Marseille, France

Claudia Carello
Center for Ecological Study of Perception and Action, University of Connecticut

Thierry Chaminade
Mediterranean Institute for Cognitive Neuroscience (INCM), Aix-Marseille University – CNRS, Marseille, France

Chih-Hui Chang
National Kaohsiung Normal University, Kaohsiung, Taiwan

Eric P. Charles
Department of Psychology, The Pennsylvania State University Altoona

Anthony Chemero
Franklin & Marshall College, Lancaster, Pennsylvania, USA

Chung-Yu Chen
National Taiwan College of Physical Education

Fu-Chen Chen
Department of Kinesiology, University of Minnesota

Hyun Chae Chung
Kunsan National University, Republic of Korea

Peter Coppin
University of Toronto

Thelma Coyle
Institut des Sciences du Mouvement E.J. Marey (UMR 6233), Université de la Méditerranée, Marseille, France

Ralph F. A. Cox
Behavioural Science Institute, Radboud University Nijmegen, the Netherlands

Sarah E. Cummins-Sebree
University of Cincinnati – Raymond Walters College

Frédéric Danion
Movement Science Institute, Université de la Méditerranée & CNRS, FRANCE

Tehran J. Davis
Department of Psychology, Center for Cognition, Action, & Perception, University of Cincinnati

Dirk De Clercq
Dept of Movement and Sports Sciences, Ghent University

Alex Díaz
Facultad de Psicología, Universidad Autónoma de Madrid

James Dixon
Department of Psychology, University of Connecticut
Center for Ecological Study of Perception and Action, University of Connecticut

Dobromir G. Dotov
Center for Ecological Study of Perception and Action, University of Connecticut

Øyvin Engan
Developmental Neuroscience Laboratory, Department of Psychology, Norwegian University of Science and Technology, N-7491 Trondheim, Norway

Justin Fine
Arizona State University, USA

Arturo Forner-Cordero
Laboratório de Biomecatrônica, Escola Politécnica, Universidade de São Paulo

T. D. Frank
CESPA, University of Connecticut, Storrs, Connecticut

Nobuhiro Furuyama
Tokyo Institute of Technology
National Institute of Informatics

Enora Gandon
Institut des Sciences du Mouvement E.J. Marey (UMR 6233), Université de la Méditerranée, Marseille, France

Valéria Duarte Garcia
Laboratório de Informação, Visão e Ação, Faculdade de Ciências, Universidade Estadual Paulista - Bauru, Programa de Mestrado em Neurociências e Comportamento, Instituto de Psicologia, Universidade de São Paulo

Timothy Gifford
Department of Psychology, University of Connecticut
Center for Ecological Study of Perception and Action, University of Connecticut
Center for Health Intervention and Prevention, University of Connecticut

Jason M. Gordon
Department of Psychology, University of Connecticut

Jacqui Haas
Cincinnati Ballet Company

F. Hasselman
Behavioural Science Institute, Radboud University Nijmegen, the Netherlands

A-M. Heugas
Univ Paris-Sud, Laboratoire C.I.A.M.S (UPRES EA 4532), Orsay, France

Akiko Hibiya
Mitsubishi Estate Building Management Co., Ltd., Japan

Magnus Holth
Developmental Neuroscience Laboratory, Department of Psychology, Norwegian University of Science and Technology, N-7491 Trondheim, Norway

Chia-Chun Huang
Department of Physical Education, National Taiwan Normal University

Chia-Pin Huang
National Taiwan Normal University

Bianca Huurneman
Behavioural Science Institute, Radboud University Nijmegen, The Netherlands,
Bartiméus Institute for the Visually Impaired, Zeist, The Netherlands.

Makoto Inagami
Department of Information Processing, Tokyo Institute of Technology, Japan

Hiroshi Inou
DENSO Corporation, Japan

Johann Issartel
Dublin City University, Dublin, Ireland

David M. Jacobs
Facultad de Psicología, Universidad Autónoma de Madrid

Brasil-Neto Joaquim
Universidade de Brasilia. Laboratôrio de neurociências e comportamento

Hank Jwo
National Taiwan Normal University

Hirohiko Kaneko
Department of Information Processing, Tokyo Institute of Technology, Japan
Vivek Kant
Center for the Ecological Study of Perception and Action, University of
Connecticut

John M Kennedy
University of Toronto

Adam W. Kiefer
Department of Cognitive, Linguistic & Psychological Sciences, Brown
University

Takayuki Kondoh
Nissan Motor Co., Ltd, Japan
Tokyo Institute of Technology, Japan

Ding-Liang Kuo
Department of Physical Education, National Taiwan Normal University

Julien Lagarde
Movement to Health (M2H), EuroMov, Montpellier-1 University, France

Matthieu Lenoir
Dept of Movement and Sports Sciences, Ghent University

Stacy M. Lopresti-Goodman
Marymount University, Arlington, Virginia

L. Majed
Univ Paris-Sud, Laboratoire C.I.A.M.S (UPRES EA 4532), Orsay, France

Ludovic Marin
Movement to Health, EuroMov, Montpellier-1 University, Montpellier, France

Leonard S. Mark
Department of Psychology, Miami University (Ohio)

Kerry L. Marsh
University of Connecticut

Anthony M. Mayo
Department of Kinesiology, University of Minnesota

Benjamin R. Meagher
University of Connecticut

Audrey van der Meer
Developmental Neuroscience Laboratory, Department of Psychology,
 Norwegian University of Science and Technology, N-7491 Trondheim,
Norway

Claire F. Michaels
Center for the Ecological Study of Perception and Action, University of
Connecticut

Hiroyuki Mishima
Waseda University, Tokyo, Japan

Yoshihiro Miyake
Tokyo Institute of Technology, Japan

Miguel Moreno
Texas A & M University, Corpus Christi, Texas
Haskins Laboratories, New Haven, Connecticut

Kazuki Nakai
Department of Biomedical Engineering, Osaka Institute of Technology

Lin Nie
University of Connecticut, USA

Tetsushi Nonaka
Research Institute of Health and Welfare, Kibi International University,
Japan

Maria Ntolopoulou
Movement to Health (M2H), EuroMov, Montpellier-1 University, France

Ryuzo Ohno
Department of Built Environment, Tokyo Institute of Technology, Japan

Kinga Palatinus
Department of Psychology, University of Connecticut
Center for Ecological Study of Perception and Action, University of Connecticut

Zsolt Palatinus
Center for Ecological Study of Perception and Action, University of Connecticut

Ana Maria Pellegrini
Sao Paulo State University, Brazil

Frédéric Pous
Institut des Sciences du Mouvement E.J. Marey (UMR 6233), Université de la
Méditerranée, Marseille, France

Michael A. Riley
Department of Psychology, Center for Cognition, Action, & Perception,
University of Cincinnati

Sérgio Tosi Rodrigues
Laboratório de Informação, Visão e Ação, Faculdade de Ciências, Universidade Estadual Paulista - Bauru

Lee Rudolph
Department of Mathematics and Computer Science, Clark University, Worcester, MA, USA

Robin N. Salesse
Movement to Health (M2H), EuroMov, Montpellier-1 University, France

Marcelo Santos
University of Toronto

Geert J.P. Savelsbergh
Inst for Biomedical Research into Human Movement and Health, Manchester Metropolitan University
Research Inst MOVE, Faculty of Human Movement Sciences, VU University Amsterdam

Mamoru Sawada
DENSO Corporation, Japan

Richard C. Schmidt
Department of Psychology, College of the Holy Cross, Worcester, MA, USA

Joyce Schurink
Behavioural Science Institute, Radboud University Nijmegen, The Netherlands
Bartiméus Institute, Zeist, The Netherlands

Hiroki Seki
The University of Tokyo

Sadahiro Senda
Department of Biomedical Engineering, Osaka Institute of Technology

Kevin Shockley
Department of Psychology, Center for Cognition, Action, & Perception, University of Cincinnati

Isabelle A. Siegler
Univ Paris-Sud, Laboratoire C.I.A.M.S (UPRES EA 4532), Orsay, France

Michael E. Singer
Department of Psychology, The Pennsylvania State University Altoona

Karan Singh
University of Toronto

Nigel Stepp
HRL Laboratories
Center for the Ecological Study of Perception and Action, University of Connecticut

Thomas A. Stoffregen
Department of Kinesiology, University of Minnesota

Nanase Takata
Department of Biomedical Engineering, Osaka Institute of Technology

Ming-Young Tang
National Kaohsiung Normal University, Kaohsiung, Taiwan

Pieter Tijtgat
Dept of Movement and Sports Sciences, Ghent University

Di Tong
Department of Psychology, Miami University (Ohio)

Seiji Totsuka
DENSO Corporation, Japan

David Travieso
Facultad de Psicología, Universidad Autónoma de Madrid

Katsuyoshi Tsujita
Department of Biomedical Engineering, Osaka Institute of Technology

Micheal T. Turvey
CESPA-University of Connecticut, Haskins Laboratories, New Haven, CT

François Tyč
CNRS UMR 6196, Marseilles
Université du Littoral

Guy Van Orden
Center for Cognition, Perception, and Action, University of Cincinnati

Jenna E. Urbain
Department of Kinesiology, University of Minnesota

Manuel Varlet
Movement to Health, EuroMov, Montpellier-1 University, Montpellier, France

Daniela V. Vaz
Center for the Ecological Study of Perception and Action, University of Connecticut
Department of Physical Therapy, Universidade Federal de Minas Gerais

Julie A. Weast
Department of Psychology, Center for Cognition, Action, & Perception, University of Cincinnati

Ruud van der Weel
Developmental Neuroscience Laboratory, Department of Psychology, Norwegian University of Science and Technology, N-7491 Trondheim, Norway

M. L.Wijnants
Behavioural Science Institute, Radboud University Nijmegen, the Netherlands

Marta Wnuczko
University of Toronto

Chih-Mei Yang
Department of Physical Education, National Taiwan Normal University

Lin Ye
Motorola Corporation

Ken Yoshida
Department of Kinesiology, University of Minnesota

Studies in Perception & Action X
E. Charles & L.J. Smart (Eds.)
© 2011 Taylor & Francis Group, LLC

Chapter 1

Perception
Theoretical and Dynamic Approaches

Studies in Perception & Action X
E. Charles & L.J. Smart (Eds.)
© 2011 Taylor & Francis Group, LLC

Higher-Order Invariants Underlying the Perception of Emotion in Heider-Simmel Tasks: A Preliminary Report

Eric Charles[1], Mark E. Singer[1], Lee Rudolph[2]
[1]The Pennsylvania State University, Altoona, USA [2]Clark University, Worcester, MA, USA

Heider and Simmel (1944) showed *emotion attribution* in very minimal displays (stop-motion moving triangles and circles). Many modern studies use this effect to investigate neural correlates of affect perception, and to assess deficits therein, particularly autism-spectrum disorders (e.g. Abell, Happe, & Frith, 2000; Bowler & Thommen, 2000; Castelli et. al, 2000, 2002; Kiln, 2000; Kiln & Jones, 2006; Salter, et. al, 2008; Schultz, 2005). But the motion dynamics critical for emotion attribution have never been determined – displays are made intuitively and arbitrarily, and are not adequately validated.

The lack of research in into display properties is, at least partially, a result of the dualistic view that assumes the information available in the world is insufficient to explain behavior and cognition. Even the label for the phenomenon, attribution, implies a dualistic process in which the mind projects onto the perceived objects quality that cannot be detected. Several areas of research, however, take as their *raison d'être* relating the structure of stimuli to behavior and cognition, including psychophysicists' study of psychophysical constants (e.g., Kruskal & Wish, 1978; Manning & Rosenstock, 1968), ethologists' study of releasing stimuli (e.g. Lack, 1943, Tinbergen, 1948), and ecological psychologists' study of higher-order invariants (e.g., McBeath, Shaffer, & Kaiser, 1995; Lee, 1976). The success of these disciplines suggests we should be able to determine what, exactly, people are responding to when they attribute emotional content to actors in minimal displays. That is, we should be able to treat what seems on the surface to be a quintessentially cognitive task, as a perceptual task.

While our initial methods rely heavily on simple ANOVA and regression analyses of self-report ratings, we believe proper identification of the crucial display variables will eventually require the use of low-dimensional topological methods (finite topological spaces and finite stratified manifolds) in combination with multivariate scaling (e.g. Rudolph, 2006, 2008). Thus, this research will also serve as a test case for the incorporation of new mathematical methods in the identification of higher-order invariants.

Our research methodology entails an iterative cycle of mathematical modeling, computer implementation, and data collection and analysis. Reported here are the first three cycles of this process.

Method and Results

Overview

Using *NetLogo*, (Wilensky, 1999) an agent based modeling platform, we create 4, 20 sec. videos for each parameter set (see below). Movements are random, but within the limits of pre-specified approach / avoid parameters. Using *Inquisit*, participants viewed displays and rated them on a series of 1-7 rating scales. They rated how "angry," "curious," and "playful" the approaching shape was, and how "scared," "annoyed," and "playful" the avoiding shape was. Our overall goal for this preliminary research was to identify at least one higher-order variable and at least one variable that seemed as if it should be important, but was not.

Iteration 1

In Iteration 1, the triangle always initiated, the circle always reacted, color of actors varied randomly. The three variables we manipulated were: 1) Size of the actors (small or large). 2) Waggle dance (present or absent). 3) A complex variable that co-varied speed and acceleration (slow-decelerating vs. fast-accelerating). This resulted in 64 videos. 3 people were tested.

In fast/accelerating videos were rated higher on triangles-angry, circles-scared, and circle-annoyed. Judgments of playfulness were generally the inverse of the scared/aggressive judgments, but were not as clean.

We believed a large actor picking on a small actor would be viewed as more aggressive, but size had little to no effect, even for circle-scared and triangle-angry

The effect of presence or absence of the waggle-dance was surprising: Data was very clean when the circle performed waggle dances, but became quite messy without them. That is, in conditions where the waggle occurred there was much less variation between the 4 versions with the same parameters, and in particular, the effect of speed/acceleration was much more stable.

Because the results were most clean for the circle-scared and triangle-angry ratings, we will concentrate on those factors for the immediate future. Speed and acceleration must be separated to determine whether each contributes individually to the observed effects. Because size had no effect, we can randomize in future iterations. Because the waggle made the data cleaner, we will have all displays use the waggle in the immediate future.

Iteration 2

In iteration 2, size and color varied randomly, and we allowed actors to switch starting position. All videos had "waggle" on. The three variables studied were: 1) shape of the actors (either could be a circle or a triangle, 2) speed (slow, medium, fast), and 3) acceleration (accelerate, constant speed, decelerate). This resulted in 144 videos. 5 people were tested.

As desired, our cleanest results were again for circle-scared and triangle-angry. We had expected that a pointy actor initiating with a round actor would be viewed as more aggressive. However, across all results, shape had surprisingly little effect. Speed and Acceleration both had main effects (see Figure 1). Speed appeared to have a non-linear effect, while acceleration appeared to have a linear effect.

Estimate of Progress. As a simple means of estimating of our progress thus far, we ran a linear regression entering all manipulated variables. For "triangle-angry?", acceleration, speed, and shape resulted in $R^2 = .222$. Dummy coding subject

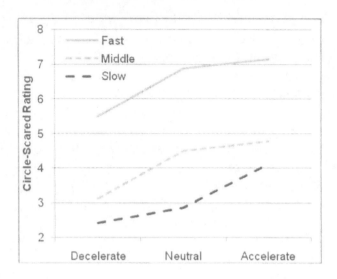

Figure 1: Iteration 2 data, compressed to show relationship between speed and acceleration.

and entering that as well, $R^2 = .438$. For "circle-scared?", acceleration, speed, and shape resulted in $R^2 = .308$. If we dummy coded subject number and enter that as well, $R^2 = .398$.

Summary. We confirmed that speed and acceleration have independent effects on participant experiences of actor anger and fear, and we were surprised to find another variable that we can vary freely in the next iteration (shape). Results up to this point were presented at the International Society for Developmental Psychobiology (Charles, Singer, & Rudolph, 2010)

Iteration 3 (In progress)

In iteration 3, shape was added to the random variable list. Our main goal in this iteration is to create a sophisticated higher-order variable composed of speed and acceleration. This requires a more careful mapping of the parameter space for those two variables. Hence, our three variables manipulated are: 1) Acceleration, 5 levels. 2) Speed, 7 levels. 3) Proportion of the movement accelerated or decelerated (.2 or .5). This produced 280 videos. We have tested 25 participants, each viewing 70 videos.

Expected Outcome. This iteration will produce a much more detailed version of Figure 1, which will allow us to construct our first formally-derived higher-order variable. Starting with Iteration 4, we will have the option of using a compound speed/acceleration slider. For whatever setting the slider is adjusted to, our simulation will pick a combination of speed and acceleration that produces displays with that expected value. For example, if a researcher wanted a video that (all else equal) received a triangle-angry rating of "4," the program would select among the corresponding combinations of speed and acceleration. Using the Figure 1 data, this could be a middle-speed display with mild deceleration, or a slow-speed display with full acceleration.

Discussion

Needless to say, accounting for approximately 40% of within-subject variance at after only two iterations is encouraging. We are on our way to successfully identifying a higher-order variable underlying emotion attribution, and implementing it into an agent based models. Rather than validate individual displays, we are validating a means of producing novel displays with pre-normed emotional valences. Customizable display production will advance basic research on affective processes and applied research on autism-spectrum disorders.

References

Heider, F., & Simmel, M. (1944). An experimental study of apparent behavior. *American Journal of Psychology, 57*(243-259).

Wilensky, U. (1999). *NetLogo (Version 3.0)*. Evanston, IL: Northwestern University.

Abell, F., Happe, F., & Frith, U. (2000). Do triangles play tricks? Attribution of mental states to animated shapes in normal and abnormal development. *Journal of Codnitive Development, 15*, 1-20.

Bowler, D. M., & Thommen, E. (2000). Attribution of mechanical and social causality to animated displays by children with autism. *Autism, 4*(147-171).

Castelli, F., Frith, C., Happe, F., & Frith, U. (2002). Autism, Asperger syndrome and brain mechanisms for the attribution of mental states to animated shapes. *Brain, 125*, 1839-1849.

Castelli, F., Happe, F., Frith, U., & Frith, C. (2000). Movement and mind: A functional imaging study of perception and interpretation of complex intentional movement patterns. *NeuroImage, 12*, 314-325.

Klin, A. (2000). Attributing social meaning to ambiguous visual stimuli in higher-functioning autism and Asperger syndrome: The social attribution task. *Journal of Child Psychology and Psychiatry, 41*, 831-846.

Kruskal, J. B., & Wish, M. (1978). Multidimensional Scaling. *Newbury Park, CA: Sage Publications.*

Klin, A., & Jones, W. (2006). Attributing social and physical meaning to ambiguous visual displays in individuals with higher-functioning autism spectrum disorders. *Brain and Cognition, 61*, 40-53.

Lack, D. L. (1943). The Life of the Robin. *London: Witherby.*

Lee, D. N. (1976). A theory of visual control of braking based on information about time-to-collision. *Perception, 5*, 437-459.

Manning, S. A., & Rosenstock, E. H. (1968). Classical Psychophysics and Scaling. *New York: McGraw-Hill.*

McBeath, M. K., Shaffer, D. M., & Kaiser, M. K. (1995). How do outfielders determine where to run to catch fly balls? *Science, 268*, 569-573.

Rudolph, L. (2006b). Spaces of ambivalence: Qualitative mathematics in the modeling of complex fluid phenomena. *Estudios de Psicologia*, 27, 67-83.

Rudolph, L. (2008b). A unified topological approach to Umwelts and life spaces, part II: Constructing life spaces from an Umwelt. In J. Clegg, (Ed.), *The Observation of Human Systems: Lessons from the History of Anti-Reductionistic Empirical Psychology.* (pp. 117-140). Transaction Publishers, New Brunswick, N.J.

Salter, G., Seigal, A., Claxton, M., Lawrence, K., & Skuse, D. (2008). Can autistic children read the mind of an animated triangle? *Autism, 12*, 349-371.

Schultz, R. T. (2005). Developmental deficits in social perception in autism: The role of the amygdale and fusiform face area. *International Journal of Developmental Neuroscience, 23*, 125-141.

Tinbergen, N. (1948). Social releasers and the experimental method required for their study. *Wilson Bull*, 60, 534-560.

Wilensky, U. (1999). NetLogo (Version 3.0). Evanston, IL: Northwestern University.

Studies in Perception & Action X
E. Charles & L.J. Smart (Eds.)
© 2011 Taylor & Francis Group, LLC

Vibrotactile Flow and the Detection of Step-on-Places with a Sensory Substitution Device

Alex Díaz[1], Antonio Barrientos[2], David M. Jacobs[1], & David Travieso[1]

[1]Facultad de Psicología, Universidad Autónoma de Madrid
[2]Grupo de Robótica y Cibernética, Universidad Politécnica de Madrid

The use of vibrotactile stimulation is increasing rapidly, and prominent examples of this increase can be found in the domain of sensory substitution (Dakopoulos & Bourbakis, 2010; Visell, 2009). The conceptual cornerstones of the ecological approach are crucial to research on sensory substitution: Whether perception occurs through normal vision (or other sense modalities) or with a sensory substitution device, the apprehension of environmental properties can be veridical only if information is detected that is specific to the properties to be perceived. For vision, specific information can often be identified as higher-order properties of the optic flow. As a consequence, the concept of optic flow has received wide attention in research on vision (Lee, 1980).

Given that optic flow is crucial to vision, one might hypothesize that vibrotactile flow is crucial to vibrotactile sensory substitution. Which properties of the environment can be specified in vibrotactile flows? And which properties of vibrotactile flows can users detect? Our claim is that such questions are useful guidelines for research in the domain of sensory substitution (in line with several previous efforts; e.g., Mizuno, Ito & Okamoto, 2009). To illustrate our claim we designed a simple sensory substitution device. The present paper reports an experiment performed with the device. The experiment determines the detection threshold of step-on-places for blindfolded users.

Method

Twelve male volunteers participated. All of them had normal or corrected to normal vision.

The used sensory-substitution device consisted of a 24-element array of actuators (0.9-cm diameter vibrating coin motors) placed vertically on the torso, attached to it with an elastic orthopedic waistband. The free space between the actuators was 0.2 cm. We registered the position of participants, and hence of the actuators, with a 4-camera motion capture system (Qualisys, Sweden). These

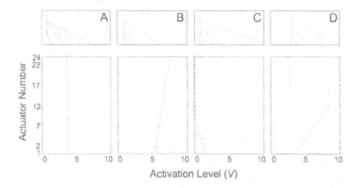

Figure 1. Schematic representation of the relation between body position and vibratory intensity. Upper panels show a participant standing straight up (A), leaning forward and backward (B and C), and standing in front of a step-on-place (D). Lower panels give corresponding intensities of vibration. The actuators are numbered from 1 (lowest) to 24 (highest). Intensities are given in driving voltages (V). Preliminary psychophysical experiments indicated that the vibration of a row of motors on the torso begins to be detectable at 2.63 V (SD=.13), and that perceived intensity gradually increases with increasing voltage. With our motion capture system we registered frequencies and amplitudes (maximal amplitude in one of the three spatial dimensions) of 62.9 Hz (SD=3.3) and 0.43 mm (SD=.23), for simultaneous stimulation with 10 V of motors included in the device but not placed on the body.

positions were used to compute the distance of each actuator to the nearest object in the environment in a particular direction. The distances were translated into voltages that were used to activate the actuators. Hence, the intensity of vibration of the actuators was a function of the distance to the nearest object: the nearer the object, the more intense the vibration.

The functioning of the device is explained in more detail in Figure 1. The dashed lines indicate the direction of sensitivity of the actuators. In a standard exploration position on a flat surface, a vibration baseline with the same vibration for each actuator was provided (Figure 1a). With forward leaning the distance to the ground surface diminishes for all actuators, especially for the higher ones, leading to more intense vibration (Figure 1b). The opposite occurs with backward leaning; in Figure 1c the distance between the upper actuators and the ground is so large that, with the current specifications of the device, these actuators do not vibrate at all. Figure 1d gives an activation pattern for a participant in front of a step-on-place. Changes in the position of the participant were translated to changes in the activation with an update frequency of about 20 Hz.

The experimental procedure was as follows. After a short familiarization phase participants were blindfolded and presented

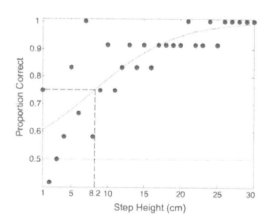

Figure 2. Proportion correct as function of step height.

with 30 trials that each consisted of two phases of 30 s, with a 5-s period without vibration between the phases. A virtual step-on-place was present either in the first phase of the trial or in the second phase. In each trial a different step height was used, ranging from 1 to 30 cm in steps of 1 cm. Participants were allowed to move as they wished in a 2-m long by 80-cm wide space that ended 1 m before the step-on-place. At the end of each trial participants judged in which phase of the trial the step-on-place was present. The responses of participants and their exploratory movements were recorded.

Results and Discussion

Figure 2 gives the proportion of correct responses for each step height. Also shown is a logistic curve fitted to the data. As indicated by the dashed segments, the logistic curve reaches the proportion of .75, which can be interpreted as the detection threshold, at a step height of 8.2 cm.

We computed the correlations between the proportion correct per participant and several kinematic measures, averaged over all trials per participant. These measures were, for each trial, the mean, standard deviation, range, minimum, and maximum of the horizontal and vertical movement and of the angle of inclination of the body. Most noteworthy of these correlations were the ones of .57 and .53 for the mean and minimum of the angle of inclination ($p<.10$ for both): The further participants leaned back, the higher the probability of a correct response. The experimenter (Alex Díaz) observed that several of the better participants kept their back straight up or inclined slightly backward and then slowly moved forward and backward during parts of the trials. This led to downward and upward movements of the activation pattern illustrated in Figure 1d. This upward-downward movement along the array is apparently one of the more useful vibrotactile flow patterns for this task.

In sum, participants were reasonably successful in detecting the presence or absence of the step-on-place, with a 75%-detection threshold of about 8.2 cm. We expect that this threshold can be improved with further developments of the device, increasing, for instance, the number of actuators. Many questions remain in this regard (cf. Visell, 2009). For instance, how many actuators are needed? Which inter-actuator distances are optimal? Or, what distance-vibration relation should be used? It would also be of interest to relate this work to studies that address how observers learn to detect informational variables (e.g., Jacobs & Michaels, 2007). Because of the many open questions, the present study should mainly be considered as a confirmation of the usefulness of our device, and similar ones, as a tool for future research, and as an illustration of how ecological concepts concerning flow variables can be applied in the domain of sensory substitution.

References

Dakopoulos, D. & Bourbakis, N. G. (2010). Wearable obstacle avoidance electronic travel aids for blind: A survey. *IEEE Transactions of Systems, Man and Cybernetics – Part C: Applications and Reviews, 40*, 25-35.

Jacobs, D. M., & Michaels, C. F. (2007). Direct learning. *Ecological Psychology, 19,* 321-349.

Lee, D. N. (1980). The optical flow field: The foundation of vision. *Philosophical Transactions of the Royal Society B, 290,* 169-179.

Mizuno, R., Ito, K., & Okamoto, M. (2009). Analyses of user's action for perceiving shapes using an active perception device. In J. Wagman, & C. Pagano (Eds.), *Studies in Perception and Action X* (pp. 83-87). New York, NY: Psychology Press.

Visell, Y. (2009). Tactile sensory substitution. Models for enaction in HCI. *Interacting with Computers, 21,* 38-53.

Acknowledgements. This research was supported by projects FFI2009-13416-C02-02 of the Spanish Ministry of Science and Innovation and S2009/DPI-1559 of the Autonomous Region of Madrid.

Studies in Perception & Action X
E. Charles & L.J. Smart (Eds.)
© 2011 Taylor & Francis Group, LLC

Hypersets Analysis of Some Physical Systems and their Numerical Implementations

Dobromir G. Dotov[1], Nigel Stepp[1]

[1]Center for the Ecological Study of Perception and Action, University of Connecticut

Graphs of sets and hypersets – sets with impredicative loops – were used previously (Chemero & Turvey, 2007) to tease out what Rosen found to be the essence of complexity (Rosen, 1991). The guidelines provided there in the frame of analyzing autocatalysis in the Brusselator were applied to three systems used in the study of self-organization of action.

The first system in the list is the ramified charge transportation network (the *Arbotron*). It attracted attention recently for its potential to model certain aspects of self-organizing systems, namely, the fractal structure of transportation networks such as tree branches, the cardiovascular system, etc (Jun & Hübler, 2005). A numerical implementation inspired by it exhibited both qualitatively and quantitatively comparable behavior (Marani, Banavar, Caldarelli, Maritan, & Rinaldo, 1998). The two systems result in qualitatively different graphs, however, the former involving impredicative loops, while the latter not. A route for an explanation of this puzzle might be suggested by thinking about the graph of the Lorenz attractor.

Method

The analysis begins by representing every relevant variable as the set of things that produce it. In this way, the current I in the Arbotron is the set of resistance R and experimenter-provided voltage V. In the graph then arrows point towards each member of this set which is then referred to the set of things that produces it. R is the product of the source electrode SE, boundary electrode BE, conductivity of the bearing balls σ, and the electric force $\nabla^2\varphi$. Following along, we see that the electric force field is the product of the electric potential φ, which is a product of the the current I and the distribution of the charged balls $\mathbf{x}$. The latter is the product of the electric force $\nabla^2\varphi$ and the current I. Finally, the entropy dS/dt is taken to be the product of φ. One can see the resulting impredicative loops of the RCTN in Figure 1.

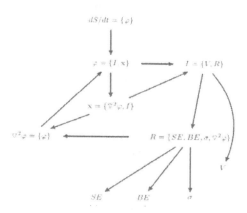

Figure 1. Hyperset graph of the ramified charge transportation network.

In the case of the numerical implementation all activity is already expressed in terms of equations, an advantage not present in the physical implementation. For this reason we refer to a different version of the hyperset analysis. Here we write the equations as mappings between pairs of inputs and outputs (see Chemero & Turvey, 2008). The algorithm used for an Arbotron simulation begins with solving (discrete) Poisson's equation $\nabla^2\varphi=\rho$ for the unknown φ with known boundary conditions φ_Γ and initially randomly distributed point-charges ρ. Next the gradient is calculated, $\nabla=<\varphi, \nabla\varphi>$, which allows one to move the point-charges around using a certain predetermined function, $f_\rho =<\{\nabla\varphi, \rho\}, \rho>$. Changes in the set of point-charges that are in contact with the boundary necessitate re-calculating the boundary condition, again using a predetermined mapping $f_\Gamma = <\rho, \varphi_\Gamma>$. Since at this point the algorithm starts over, there is nothing more to put in the graph and Figure 2 is complete. The same basic procedure was used for the Lorenz attractor $dx/dt = \sigma(y - x); \ dy/dt = x(\rho - z) - y; \ dz/dt = xy - \beta z$, see Figure 3.

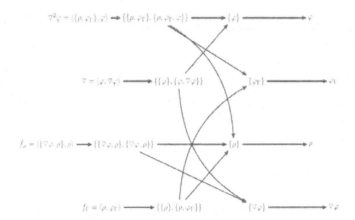

Figure 2. Hyperset graph of the numerical Arbotron.

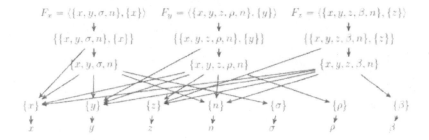

Figure 3. Hyperset graph of the Lorenz system.

Results and Discussion

The main finding in this study is that while the self-assembling Arbotron appears to have impredicative loops neither a numerical simulation which otherwise exhibits comparable behavior nor the Lorenz attractor which is often used as a paradigmatic example of self-organization are impredicative. In order to understand what is the source of this categorical distinction, it might prove fruitful thinking what is the essence of each system. The essence of the Lorenz system lies in its equations which are independent of anything that happens when they are being iterated; they were defined by Lorenz the modeller. On the other hand, the system could become impredicative were it capable of arriving at its equations of motion autonomously. It follows that while a scientist could have a good theory of some aspect of a self-organizing physical system which allows her to reproduce this aspect when the theory is being tested in a numerical experiment, this success does not guarantee that the autonomy of such a system is being captured.

References

Chemero, A. & Turvey, M. (2007). Complexity, hypersets, and the ecological perspective on perception-action. *Biological Theory, 2* (1), 23–36.

Chemero, A. & Turvey, M. (2008). Autonomy and hypersets. *BioSystems, 91* (2), 320–330.

Jun, J. & Hübler, A. (2005). Formation and structure of ramified charge transportation networks in an electromechanical system. *Proceedings of the National Academy of Sciences of the United States of America, 102* (3), 536.

Marani, M., Banavar, J., Caldarelli, G., Maritan, A., & Rinaldo, A. (1998). Stationary self-organized fractal structures in an open, dissipative electrical system. *Journal of Physics A: Mathematical and General, 31*, L337.

Rosen, R. (1991). *Life itself: A comprehensive inquiry into the nature, origin, and fabrication of life*. Columbia University Press.

Studies in Perception & Action X
E. Charles & L.J. Smart (Eds.)
© 2011 Taylor & Francis Group, LLC

Control of Speed in the Sensorimotor Area During a Visually Guided Joystick Movement: A High-density EEG Study

Øyvin Engan, Ruud van der Weel & Audrey van der Meer

Developmental Neuroscience Laboratory, Department of Psychology,
Norwegian University of Science and Technology, N-7491 Trondheim, Norway

The functional significance of the motor cortex has been related to both spatial encoding of motor output, which includes parameters such as position, direction and velocity, and to the direct control of muscles and force. Single cell recordings on monkeys have shown that neurons in the motor cortex display directional preferences in which the rate of firing increases when the animal is moving in the direction corresponding to the place field of the cell while it gradually decreases to movements in other directions (Schwarts, Kettner, Georgopoulos, 1988). However, the single cell does not discharge to specific movements only and therefore a large number of cells will be active in movements in any particular direction. Research on neuronal networks shows that the response of a larger cell population, in which the single cell makes a vectorial contribution according to its preferred direction, can determine the direction of the movement (Georgopoulos, Kettner & Schwartz, 1988). The attribution of the single cell in the network is not necessarily restricted to one kind of information as the same cell can respond to different parameters such as direction, velocity, position and acceleration (Ashe & Georgopoulos, 1994). Further the single cell responding to both velocity and direction during reaching, can be explained by velocity acting as a gain factor on the cells' directional tuning curve by affecting the firing rate of the individual cells, in which increased velocity results in increased firing rate of the cells with preferred direction close to the direction of the actual movement (Moran & Schwartz, 1999).

In the present study, high-density electroencephalography (EEG) recording was applied to examine the brain electrical activity accompanying a visually guided joystick movement intercepting with a target decelerating in one of three different approaches. The main focus of interest was how the speed of the stimulus affects the EEG activity in motor cortex. In our study the direction of the joystick movement was fixed while the speed of the stimulus varied. On the basis of speed acting as a gain factor while the direction of the movement remained constant, we expected higher brain electric activity accompanying increased speed.

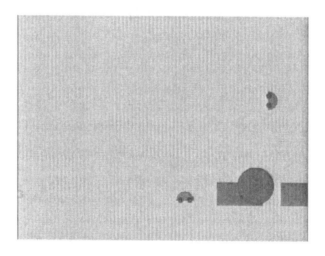

Figure 1. The stimulus car drove horizontally from left to right while the joystick car followed the vertical axis to the open gap between the two occluders on which the subjects were instructed to focus their eyesight. Gaze was recorded for back-up purposes with a Tobii x50 infra red eye camera and monitored on the experimenters screen as a ball.

Method

10 subjects (4 females), mean age 27.1 ± 4.8, with normal or corrected to normal eyesight were recruited among students and

lecturers at the Norwegian University of Science and Technology. The EEG activity was recorded with Geodesic Sensor Net (GSN 200). An array of 256 Ag/AgCl electrodes was evenly distributed across the head surface, where Cz acted as reference electrode. The joystick movements were executed with Current Designs`Fiber Optic Joystick.

The subjects visually tracked a stimulus car moving horizontally from left to right over a wide screen on which it was projected. The final approach of the stimulus car was occluded before it reappeared in a gap on the far right of the screen. In the starting point the speed of the stimulus car was 0.84 m/s, subsequently it decelerated in one of three ways: fast (10 % deceleration), medium (50 % deceleration and slow (90 % deceleration. By the means of a joystick the subjects controlled an identical car moving vertically between the starting point in the upper right corner and the touchdown area in the middle of the gap after the occlusion (Figure 1). The subjects were instructed to crash the joystick car into the stimulus-car in one continuous swift downward movement, not applying cognitive problem solving strategies. To avoid unnecessary cortical activation due to head or eye movements, the subjects were instructed to focus their eyes on the gap between the two occluders.

Only trials resulting in a successful crash and otherwise in concordance with the experimental instructions were analysed using the software program Brain Electrical Source Analysis (Besa) 5.3. None of the subjects included in the analysis had more than 10 % of the channels defined as bad. Individual averages were computed for the fast, medium and slow condition. The averages were then interpolated to 81 standard electrode positions and combined to generate a grand average in which the movement-related potentials (MRP) were identified. Next, the equivalent MRPs were selected in the individual averages and peak amplitude, mean amplitude and area for the selected regions was calculated.

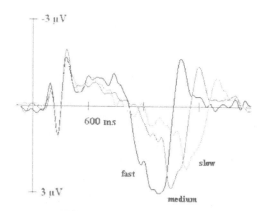

Figure 2. Grand average waveform display of channel Cz for fast, medium and slow condition. Trial onset is at x = 0. The amplitude of the positive potential starting at about 1000 ms is larger for the fast condition than medium and slow respectively and, as expected, the earliest peak amplitude is for fast followed by medium and slow.

Results and Discussion

The grand average waveform display shows that the beginning of the joystick movement was accompanied by a positive MRP in Cz starting at about 70 ms and ending at 600 ms after the joystick onset (Figure 2). According to the source analysis 93.4 % of the variance can be explained by two dipoles, one located in the medial frontal lobe (74.5 %) and another in the right occipital lobe (18.9 %)

Based on the individual files an average for peak amplitude, mean amplitude and area (μV*ms) were calculated for the MRPs in channel Cz. Peak amplitude was larger in the fast condition (4.3 μV, SD = 1.7) than in medium (3.6 μV, SD = 1.2) and slow (2.9 μV, SD = 1.2) respectively. A repeated measures ANOVA performed on peak amplitude with speed (fast, medium and slow) as within subject factor revealed a main effect of speed, $F (2, 9) = 10.336$. $p < .05$.

Mean amplitude for the MRP followed the same pattern and was larger for fast (2.4 µV, SD = 0.9), then medium (1.8 µV, SD = 0.8) and slow (1.3 µV, 0.6). A repeated measures ANOVA showed a main effect for speed, F (2, 9) = 39.455, p < .05.

In the final category area (µV * ms), the fast condition also generated the larger area (1123.4, SD = 440), followed by medium (939.8, SD = 408.2) and slow (779.1, SD = 363.5). The repeated measures ANOVA showed a main effect of speed, F(2, 9) = 25.375, p < .05 .

The concurrence of larger brain electrical activity with increased speed can reflect the involvement of a neuronal ensemble encoding for visual motion and the subsequent motor output, thereby providing visuomotor control when executing the movement. In our study, there was a significant effect of speed for peak amplitude, mean amplitude and area in channel Cz and the main part of that activity was according to the source model caused by one dipole located in M1-S1. The differentiated activity in M1-S1 can be explained by a neural network responding to increased speed by gradually increasing the discharge rate, however this doesn't necessarily imply a neuronal ensemble dedicated to speed only, as the neuronal population code may account for multiple parameters such as speed and direction.

References

Ashe, J., & Georgopoulos, A. P. (1994). Movement Parameters and Neural Activity in Motor Cortex and Area 5. *Cerebral Cortex, 6, 590-600.*

Georgopoulos, A. P., Kettner, R. E., & Schwartz, A. B. (1988). Primate Motor Cortex and Free Arm Movements to Visual Targets in Three-Dimensional Space. Ii. Coding of the Direction of Movement by a Neuronal Population.*The Journal of Neuroscience, 8(8), 2928-2937.*

Moran, D. W. & Schwartz, A. B. (1999). Motor Cortical Representation of Speed and Direction During Reaching. *Journal of Neurophysiology, 82(5), 2676-2692.*

Schwartz, A. B., Kettner, R. E. & Georgopoulos, A. P. (1988). Primate Motor Cortex and Free Arm Movements to Visual Targets in Three-Dimensional Space. I. Relations Between Single Cell Discharge and Direction of Movement. *The Journal of Neuroscience, 8(8), 2913-2927*

Studies in Perception & Action X
E. Charles & L.J. Smart (Eds.)
© 2011 Taylor & Francis Group, LLC

The Effect of Fractal Event Structure on Anxiety and Memory

Gordon, Jason M. [1], Blau, Julia J. C. [2], Carello, Claudia[2]

[1]Psychology Department, University of Connecticut, [2]Center for the Ecological Study of Perception and Action, Department of Psychology, University of Connecticut, 406 Babbidge Road, Storrs, CT 06269, USA

As we perceive and act in our environment, our experience is organized into events. Although events have been treated as sequential divisions of time (Zacks & Swallow, 2007), the complexity of events may be better represented by a nested structure (Gibson, 1979; Gibson & Lawrence, 1975). One means of measuring this nesting that takes advantage of modern techniques is fractal analysis.

Fractals are mathematical distributions with self-similar structure at all scales, and can be characterized using the Hurst exponent, H. Recent investigations (Blau, Petrusz, Gordon, & Carello, under revision) have successfully applied this to event perception. For segmentation of events "in the wild" (cf. Hutchins, 1995)—Blau et al., found that the temporal structure falls within a constrained range ($H = .57 - .67$). Decay of memory and presentation of information in the world have a similar, power-law structure (Anderson & Schooler, 1991), this raises the possibility that a change in the fractality of presentation might influence recall, what is unclear is how.

In film, different genres of movies have different levels of fractality (Cutting, DeLong, & Nothelfer, 2010) with action movies the highest and dramas the lowest. However, the category "action" is ill-defined. Indeed, many "action" movies have a low H_{edit} and many non-action films have a high H_{edit}. We re-conceptualize this difference with respect to anxiety, namely, movies that are anxiety-provoking have a high H_{edit}. It stands to reason that film editors utilize particular structures of presentation in order to elicit particular feelings, over and above the content of the film. Therefore, we chose to manipulate arousal independent of the structure of presentation, in an effort to disentangle the two.

Method

Images were drawn from a database that has been normed for arousal and valence (the International Affective Picture System, IAPS; Lang, Bradley, & Cuthbert, 2008). We selected 258 high-arousal and 258 low-arousal images (Figure 1), controlled for valance. Each set (Low and High) was randomized and presented in three slideshows distinguished by the temporal structure of presentation ($H_{presentation}$ = .50, .65, or .88).One participant at a time viewed one of the slides shows on a computer screen. In all, six participants viewed each of the six slideshows. After viewing the 258 pictures, participants were asked to rate, on a 10-point scale, how anxious they felt during the presentation. They then completed a memory test consisting of 40 images, half from the slideshow and half new pictures, chosen from the same database

Figure 1. Photographs similar to those taken from the IAPS data base. (top) Low arousal images included items such as mushrooms and rotary fans. (bottom) High arousal images included items such as puppies and explosions.

(matched for valence and arousal). For each picture in the memory test, participants simply indicated "yes" if they remembered seeing the image and "no" if they did not.

Results and Discussion

Memory

Hits and false alarms were used to calculate d′, which was entered in a 3 H × 2 Arousal analysis of variance (ANOVA). The main effect of arousal, $F(1, 38) = 5.97$, $p < .02$, indicates that the discriminability of high arousal images was better than the discriminability of low arousal images. Although the main effect of $H_{presentation}$ was not significant, $F(2, 38) = 2.27$, $p > .10$, its effect was seen in its interaction with arousal, $F(2, 38) = 3.88$, $p < .03$. As Figure 2 shows, the difference between high and low arousal images was limited to $H_{presentation} = .50$ and .88. The discriminability of high and low arousal images did not differ for $H_{presentation} = .65$, $t(13) = 1.23$, $p > .20$. An alternative description of this interaction is that $H_{presentation}$ was not significant for low arousal images, $F(2, 19) = 2.39$, $p > .10$, but was significant for $H_{presentation}$ high arousal images, $F(2, 19) = 3. 45$, $p = .05$. As is apparent from Figure 2 (left), $H_{presentation} = .65$ again stands out: Discriminability was lowest. Recall that $H = .65$ is the value that characterized natural event segmentation for ordinary settings (Blau et al., under review). It seems that pictures presented with a temporal structure that is, in some sense, mundane are less discriminable regardless of their arousal level. When the temporal structure departs from that, high arousal enhances discriminability. The less common or typical temporal structures may have served as an indicator to pay attention.

Anxiety

The anxiety ratings were entered in a 3 H × 2 Arousal ANOVA. Only the main effect of arousal was significant, $F(1, 39) = 54.47$, $p < .0001$. Unsurprisingly, people reported feeling more anxious after viewing a slideshow with high arousal images than low arousal images. Neither the main effect of $H_{presentation}$ nor its interaction with arousal was significant, both $Fs \approx 1$. As Figure 3

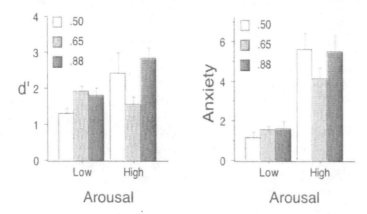

Figure 2. The discriminability index differed as a function of $H_{presentation}$ only for high arousal images (left). Self-ratings of anxiety were higher for high arousal images and unaffected by $H_{presentation}$ (right) .

shows, anxiety was greater for high arousal images at every level of $H_{presentation}$. Although the interaction was not significant, the topology of the anxiety ratings echoed that of d', namely, with a dip for high arousal images at $H_{presentation} = .65$.

The separation of content from structure provides insight into the importance of temporal structure, in general, and fractality, in particular, in understanding human perception. Namely, differences in temporal structure can have cognitive consequences over and above content. It is particularly noteworthy that the effect of $H_{presentation}$ was not monotonic; it is not simply that the higher the H the better the memory. Rather, what emerged was a pattern in which temporal structures that deviated from the commonplace, both enhanced discriminability—but only of high arousal images. At present, the anxiety ratings seem independent of temporal structure. And while the similar topology for high arousal images should not be oversold, it cannot be ignored and warrants further investigation. Of particular interest would be an anxiety measure that was less explicit. In addition, the valence dimension was not manipulated here (see Figure 1). The present results have potential application in clinical and cognitive (specifically memory) arenas.

References

Anderson J. R., & Schooler, L. J. (1991). Reflections of the environment in memory. *Psychological Science, Vol 2(6),* 396-408.

Blau, J. J. C., Petrusz, S. C., & Carello, C. (2010a) *Fractal Structure of Perceived Events in Film: Real Lessons from Real Events. (Under Review).*

Cutting, J. E., DeLong, J. E., and Nothelfer, C. E. (2010). Attention and the evolution of Hollywood film. *Psychological Science.*

Gibson, J. J. & Lawrence, J. T. F. N. (1975). Events are perceivable time is not. In *The study of time.* New-York: Springer-Verlag.

Gibson, J. J. (1979/1986). *The ecological approach to visual perception.* Hillsdale, NJ: Erlbaum.

Goldberger, A. L., Amaral, L. A. N., Hausdorff, J. M., Ivanov, P. Ch., Peng, C.-K., & Stanley, H.E. (2002) Fractal dynamics in physiology: Alterations with disease and aging. *PNAS, 99*(1), 2465-2471.

Hutchins, E. (1995). *Cognition in the wild.* Boston, MA: MIT Press.

Lang, P. J., Bradley, M. M., & Cuthbert, B. N. (2008). International affective picture system (IAPS): Affective ratings of pictures and instruction manual. Technical Report A-8. University of Florida, Gainesville, FL.

Zacks, J. M., & Swallow, K. M. (2007). Event segmentation. *Current Directions in Psychological Science, 16(2),* 80-84.

Acknowledgements. The authors acknowledge the support for this work by Defense Advanced Research Projects Agency (DARPA) Physical Intelligence (subcontract HRL 000708-DS). The views, opinions, and/or findings contained in this article are those of the authors and should not be interpreted as representing the official views or policies, either expressed or implied, of the DARPA or the Department of Defense.

Studies in Perception & Action X
E. Charles & L.J. Smart (Eds.)
© 2011 Taylor & Francis Group, LLC

Noise Patterns in 6- to 8-year-old Children's Eye Movements During Crowded Visual Search

Bianca Huurneman[1,2], Ralf F. A. Cox [1,2], & F. Nienke Boonstra [2]

[1]Behavioural Science Institute, Radboud University Nijmegen, The Netherlands,
[2]Bartiméus Institute for the Visually Impaired, Zeist, The Netherlands.

In vision science and ophthalmology, researchers often encounter that young children have more difficulty in deciphering small and closely spaced symbols (Atkinson et al., 1986). This phenomenon, called (foveal) crowding or masking, entails that object discrimination deteriorates when a target object is surrounded by distracters. The first quantitative study that aimed to investigate foveal crowding found the poorest acuity results when the adjacent contour is located 2 to 3 times the minimum angle of resolution (MAR; Flom et al., 1963). This study also presented three general reasons for decreased target discrimination in the presence of crowding bars, viz. lateral interactions (i.e. environment), cognitive factors (i.e. brain), eye movements (i.e. body), or a combination of these factors.

A considerable number of studies have tried to explain foveal crowding in children by referring to immature selective attentional mechanisms or inadequate control of selection, and/or to immature directional control of gaze (Bondarko & Semenov, 2005; Manny, Fern, & Loshin, 1987; Kothe & Regan, 1990). In children, therefore, a clear relation between crowding, attention, and eye movements has been hypothesized. However, to date, there are only two visual search studies which have examined the relation between crowding and eye movements, in adults (Vlaskamp & Hooge, 2006; Vlaskamp, Over, & Hooge, 2005). Conclusions that can be drawn from these studies are that (1), at inter symbol spacing (ISS) smaller than 1.5, search time per element increased with decreasing element spacing, and (2) that number of fixations and fixation duration increased and saccade amplitude decreased with increasing crowding.

Additionally, research on the dynamic organization of eye movements during visual search have provided empirical evidence for fractal scaling, power laws, and self-organized criticality (Aks, Zelinsky, & Sprott, 2002). These results have been interpreted in terms of dynamic 'memory' of the underlying system guiding the search process. More specifically, timeseries of fixations displayed short-range correlations or brown $(1/f^2)$ noise, which indicates short-term memory across eye movements. On the other hand, time series of fixation differences (a measure of displacement) showed long-range correlations or pink (1/f) noise, indicating long-term memory. These interesting and novel aspects of visual search, have not yet been studied in the context of crowding (or ISS), nor has their existence been demonstrated in children's eye movements.

In sum, it seems that the control of eye movements and the development of selective attention may play a big role in explaining why children experience more difficulty in discriminating closely spaced objects. In the present study we will use a visual search paradigm to study the effect of ISS on the dynamics of eye movements in children. In particular, the noise patterns of raw fixations and fixation differences will be examined for contingencies across timescales.

Method

A visual search task appropriate for children was designed. The symbols used in this test were the LH-optotypes (heart, circle, house, square; Hyvarinen, Näsänen & Laurinen, 1980). Six- to eight-year-old children were asked to search for the unique symbol in a square matrix, in which all four symbols were present (Figure 1). The dimensions of this matrix were 4 x 4 symbols. For each child, the symbols were presented at twice the size of the smallest symbol the child could recognize (a measure of their visual acuity).

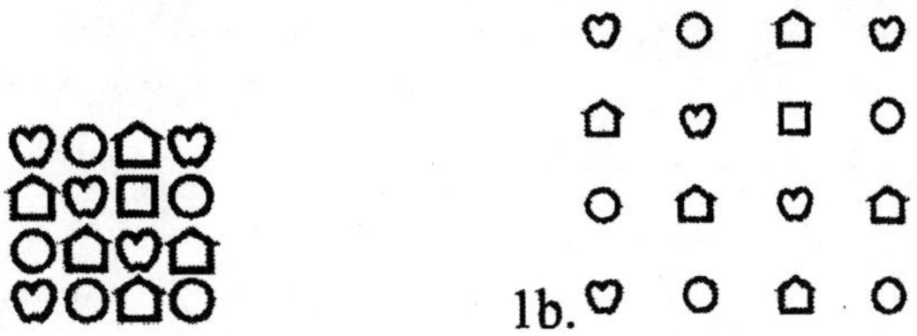

Figure 1. Two examples of stimuli: (a) matrix with small ISS, and (b) matrix with large ISS. Here, 'square' is the unique symbol.

The location and type of the unique symbol was varied, to make sure the child had to actively search for it. The influence of crowding was measured by applying 5 different ISS: 2, 4, 8, 16, and 32 arcmin. At each ISS 4 different matrices were presented making a total of 20 trials, presented in random order. The smallest symbol measured 2 x 2 mm^2, which at a fixed working distance of 60 cm entails a size of 0.20x 0.20°. Similarly, ISS increased linearly from 0.33mm^2 for 2 arcmin until the largest of 5.28 x 5.28 mm^2 for 32 arcmin.

Stimuli were presented on a Tobii T120 (1024 x 768 pixels; pixel size: 0.33 x 0.33 mm^2), providing timeseries of children's fixation at 60 Hz. All timeseries existed of 512 data points and were processed using spectral analysis (FFT). Spectral slopes were calculated from the log-log power spectra. Additionally, we measured the response time (RT) and response correctness (% Correct).

Results and Discussion

Table I presents the results of task performance. Mean RT increased with increasing spacing, $F (4, 52) = 2.790$, $p = .036$. There was no significant influence of ISS on percentage of correct responses, $F (4, 52) = 1.048, p = .392$.

Table I: Performance measures (mean (SD))

ISS (arcmin)	RT (sec)	% Correct	Spectral Slope	
			Fixations	Fixation Difference
2	14.6 (6.6)	76.0 (25.3)	-0.89 (.29)	-0.15 (.24)
4	14.7 (7.1)	75.7 (24.2)	-1.01 (.35)	-0.08 (.24)
8	16.5 (6.7)	76.3 (25.0)	-1.05 (.38)	-0.10 (.21)
16	16.1 (6.7)	81.9 (24.8)	-1.20 (.35)	-0.15 (.24)
32	16.7 (6.5)	75.9 (28.4)	-1.48 (.26)	-0.15 (.20)

A significant relation between the spectral slope of the raw fixations and ISS was found, $F (4, 25) = 50.372$, $p = .000$. Spectral slopes increased from just below the value indicative of pink noise (-1) for low ISS, towards the value indicative of Brown noise (-2) for high ISS. Brown noise was found for relatively large ISS in adult visual search (Aks et al., 2002).

The spectral slope of the fixation differences did not significantly differ with ISS. An interesting observation can be made when comparing these slopes to those reported earlier for adults (Aks et al., 2002): In children the values are all near those indicative of white noise (0), with no correlation between individual fixation differences, whereas for adults they are much higher (closer to -0.6; Aks et al., 2002), expressing long-range correlations.

These results show a relation between ISS and the temporal structure of fixation timeseries in a visual search task in children. This suggests qualitative changes in the search patterns depending on the amount of crowding, entailing the involvement of different forms of dynamic memory. Reasons for the differences with adult patterns might partly be task related, but might very well be developmental in nature, expressing a changing relationship between attention, gaze, and search processes.

References

Aks, D. J., Zelinsky, G., & Sprott, J. C. (2002). Memory across eye movements: 1/f dynamic in visual search. *Journal of Nonlinear Dynamics in Psychology & the Life Sciences, 6,* 1-25.

Atkinson, J., Primm-Smith, E., Evans, C., Harding, G., & Braddick, O. (1986). Visual crowding in young children. In: Jay B., ed. *Proceedings of the workshop on detection and measurement of visual impairment in preverbal children.* Boston: Nijoff, 1986.

Bondarko, V.M., & Semenov, L.A. (2005). Visual acuity and the crowding effect in 8- to 17 year old schoolchildren. *Human Physiology,   31(5),* 532-538.

Flom, M.C., Heath, G., & Takahaski, E. (1963). Contour interaction and visual resolution: contralateral effect. *Science, 142,* 979-980.

Hyvärinen, L., Näsänen, R. & Laurinen, P. (1980). New visual acuity test for pre-school children. *Acta ophthalmologica, 58 (4),* 507-511.

Kothe, A.C., & Regan, D. (1990). The component of gaze-selection/ control in the development of visual acuity in children. *Optometry and Vision Science, 67(10),* 770-778.

Manny, R.E., Fern,K.D., & Loshin, D.S. (1987). Contour interaction function in the preschool child. *American Journal of Optometry & Physiological optics, 64 (9),* 686-692.

Vlaskamp, B.N.S., & Hooge, I. Th.C. (2006). Crowding degrades saccadic search performance. *Vision Research, 46,* 417-425.

Vlaskamp, B.N.S., Over, E.A.B., & Hooge, I.Th.C. (2005). Saccadic search performance: the effect of element spacing. *Experimental Brain Research, 167,* 246-259.

Acknowledgements. This research was supported by ZonMW-Inzicht grant 60-00635-98-066 to the second and third authors.

Studies in Perception & Action X
E. Charles & L.J. Smart (Eds.)
© 2011 Taylor & Francis Group, LLC

Dots, Line, Contour & Surface Edge Trigger Centre-surround Pickup Mechanism

John M Kennedy, Marta Wnuczko, Marcelo Santos, Peter Coppin & Karan Singh

University of Toronto

We present here a theory about a pickup mechanism important for picture perception. That is, perception theory needs a description of what is available to vision, such as visible surfaces, a theory of the mechanism that picks up the information about what is available, and a way to extend this to depiction. In short, what do visual borders do in a visual system?

The general question being addressed here is what enables both dotted and continuous lines to depict surface edges. This is a key problem for ecological theory of pictures and for Gestalt theory of grouping. Line and contour pictures provide ecological information for surfaces, and the elements in the pictures can be dots, continuous lines and contours. What enables these elements to be effective in depicting surface edges?

Gestalt grouping factors influence grouping of elements, but offer no pickup mechanism. Kennedy (2009) argues dotted lines, continuous lines and surface edges trigger the same perceptual "filaments" but do not provide a pickup mechanism to achieve this end. Here we show centre-surround structures can do the job.

Pickup via centre-surround structures

The retina is composed of receptor cells. The cells fall in different areas of the retina, some being in a roughly circular field and some in a ring shape around the circle, as shown by the left rings in Figure 1.

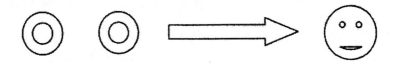

Figure 1. Pickup: Two centre-surround C- cells (left) trigger a C+ cell deeper in the visual system (arbitrary symbol on right)

The receptors in the central circle and the receptors in the surrounding ring (the centre and its surround) influence a cell deeper in the visual system. Call this a C- cell. The centre and the surround receptors influence the C- cell in opposing ways. If the amount of light on the centre and surround receptors is equal then the opposing influences balance each other. In this case, C- remains at its resting firing rate. So far as the rest of vision is concerned, the light on the centre and surround receptors is uniform. The optic array is deemed to be uniform. The ecological information specifies a uniform part of the environment.

If the light energy on the central receptors is more (or less) than that on the surround, the centre and surround influences are unbalanced. C- departs from resting firing rate. A dot in the centre of a central-surround field with uniform light in the rest of the field will result in different influences reaching C- from the centre and surround.

A pair of neighboring centre-surround fields and the associated C- cells could influence a cell deeper in vision: call this a C+ cell. The C+ cell requires two C- cells changing their resting rate before it will change its resting rate.

Of interest, besides a dot, a C- cell will also be triggered by a line covering most of a field's centre and comparatively little of its surround. Hence, a continuous line can trigger two C- cells, and a C+ cell.

Of further interest, a contour between regions of different luminance on a surface can lie on the periphery of the centre, and the centre and surround will receive unequal amounts of light. The

contour can stretch across to a second centre-surround field, and
thereby trigger two C- cells and a C+ cell.

Finally, a surface edge often results in different luminances on
either side of its optic array projection. Hence it could trigger two
C- cells and a C+ cell.

Results and Discussion

The result of the centre-surround, 2 C- cells and C+ cell pickup
mechanism is that optic arrays generated by dots, continuous lines,
luminance contours and surface edges would trigger one and the
same deep cells. This offers a pickup structure answering a
problem that has been finessed by Gestalt theory of grouping.
Gestalt theory said proximity and other spatial variables encourage
grouping but did say how grouping occurs in vision. The pickup
mechanism allows a single effect, such as a filament, to be
stimulated by different optic arrays. It shows how a dotted line can
have the same effect in vision as a continuous surface edge.
Therefore, this may be a basis of outline depiction.

While dots and continuous edges have the same effect, why
would the perceptual result of the mechanism be that a dotted line
depicts a continuous edge but a continuous edge does not depict a
dotted line? Why the asymmetry in the effect?

The ecological information for a continuous surface edge
includes a continuous luminance border in the optic array, and
units of texture along the border. The units of texture fit a
continuous function much like $y = ax + b$. There is no information
in a continuous border to specify a particular set of discontinuous
texture units. Evolutionary pressure surely favors pickup of
information for surface edges and information for continuous
functions. It could not encourage the use of what is not specific as
a basis for seeing something in particular.

We have described centre-surround cells as triggered by
imbalance. Let us be explicit. Strictly speaking, the centre can be
sending excitatory influences to the C- cell, and the surround
sending inhibition. Or the reverse. Likewise, dots can be dark or
light. In this vein, it is worth noting that C+ cells may increase

their activity above their resting rate, or decrease it. Evidently, there are many permutations to consider – including lines made of black and white dots alternating. Likely, all the combinations of black and white dots and inhibited or excited C- cells trigger C+ cells of some kind, excitatory or inhibitory, but there may be biases favoring some combinations over others. An example is a matrix of dots composed of black columns and white columns. Perception generally groups the dots as parallel black and white lines. It is less likely to group the dots as rows of dots alternating black and white.

Centre-surround fields are defined by luminance inputs to the retina. However, to generalize the present analysis the other visual borders must be entertained.

There are 8 ways to create visual borders given by combinations of luminance and spectral inputs, monocular and binocular effects, and static and purely kinetic divisions. The standard border is often taken to be monocular, luminance-defined and static. Dots defined in this way can operate as lines in outline drawings, that is, they can depict surface edges. It may the other 7 visual borders can define dots and have them operate as outline drawings. One reason for thinking this is that in principle all the visual borders can provide information about surfaces. Certainly binocular and kinetic inputs are highly effective bases for seeing planes that have well-defined continuous edges. The planes can be polarized, that is they can appear to be different in one direction than in another, a defining attribute of a surface. In particular they can appear to be facets of opaque solids, surrounded by transparent media.

The binocular and monocular inputs that define continuous borders in vision can be made of discrete elements, often resembling scattered moving texture or static wallpaper prints with objects separated by empty spaces. Vision sees continuous borders joining the texture and cutting across empty spaces. The inputs are surely based on ecological optic arrays that specify surface edges. Since in binocular and kinetic vision regions of texture units separated by spaces appear as surfaces with edges, a line of texture units such as dots could be taken by vision as indicating a continuous surface feature, in particular as depicting a continuous surface edge.

In principle, the centre-surround pickup theory can be applied to all the ways visual borders can define dots.

Three cautions are in order: One is that shape-from-shadow perception is not triggered by monocular luminance-defined outline displays, and we predict this inability will be present for contours and lines defined in kinetic and binocular displays. Shadow is specified by the shape of a luminance difference, not a contour shape. A second is that purely spectral inputs produce less well-defined borders than luminance borders. The third is that monocular texture borders between two texture fields per se do not suggest well-defined borders. To do so they need to be accompanied by luminance differences across the borders, or contours and ends of lines defining subjective contours. Indeed, texture units at the border of a texture field can be grouped and separated from the rest of the field, with the grouping standing alone, not as the border of the texture field. The implications of these cautions remain to be discovered.

References

Kennedy, J. M. (2009) Outline, mental states and drawings by a blind woman *Perception, 38,* 1481-1496.

Studies in Perception & Action X
E. Charles & L.J. Smart (Eds.)
© 2011 Taylor & Francis Group, LLC

Learning to Explore in Partial-Length Perception

Zsolt Palatinus & Claire Michaels

Center for the Ecological Study of Perception and Action, Univ. of Connecticut

Michaels and Isenhower (2011a,b) asked whether learning in dynamic touch could be understood in terms of changing exploration. In particular, they employed the partial-length paradigm, wherein perceivers are asked to report how far an unseen object extends to one or both sides of the hand. They adopted the concept of *information space* from direct learning (Jacobs & Michaels, 2007) and assumed that styles of exploration accessed particular regions of the space. To provide strict limits on the possible information space, they constrained rotation of the rod to a single axis, leaving gravitational torque and inertial torque as the only variables shaping the space.

Michaels and Isenhower (2011a, b) derived a continuous variable space ranging from (virtually) exclusive use of gravitational torque to (virtually) exclusive use of inertial torque. The usefulness of loci in the space of variables differed markedly, with the peak useful around a 50:1 weighting of moment of inertia, as illustrated in Figure 1. Michaels and Isenhower demonstrated that, at least for some experimental participants the weighting was achieved by accelerating the rod on the order of 50 rad/sec^2, which would require a torque specific to partial length. In other words, the judgment was said to reflect the torque needed to accelerate the rod to the chosen acceleration, and the acceleration identified the locus in the information space.

Only 2 of Michaels and Isen-hower's (2011) 5 participants showed reattunement, and, thus, a relation between reattunement and acceleration. Was it the case that other perceivers used some other strategy? Or, as suggested by a reviewer, was the lack of

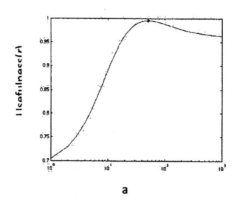

a

Figure 1. The usefulness function of the employed stimuli. The peak occurs at 53 rad/s^2.

learning due to the difficulty of making two judgments on each trial and getting feedback on both. In this paper, we ask participants to make only one judgment and again ask if there is evidence for the account of partial-length perception forwarded by Michaels and Isenhower: 1) improved performance accompanied by convergence toward optimal acceleration, 2) judgments well predicted by gravitational torque and moment of inertia, and 3) a high correlation between judgments and exerted muscle torque.

Method

Five right-handed students at the University of Connecticut participated in the experiment; one was naïve; four had been in whole-length dynamic touch experiments before. Wooden dowels 2.54 cm in diameter and 25, 36, 45, 53 and 62 cm in length were used in the stimulus set. Several 2 mm diameter drilled holes served as axes of rotation for wielding. The combination of object lengths and hole locations yielded 13 stimulus-objects. The there were six randomized blocks of 13 trials such that each stimulus was presented once per block.

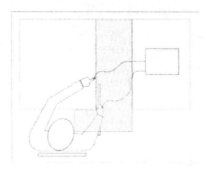

Figure 2. Schematic of the apparatus showing participant, rod, Polhemus, and occluding screen.

The experimental setup is schematized in Figure 2. The rod was mounted on a metal pin at approximately knee-height. The participant gripped the rod firmly such that the pin was between their middle and ring fingers. The pin constrained rod movement to a single axis in a sagittal plane. Participants made partial length judgments by moving their left index finger to the point on the table above the perceived the end of the rod. The orientations and location of both right hand and left index finger were sampled at 60 Hz using a magnetic tracking system (Polhemus Fastrak, Polhemus Corporation, Colchester, VT) and 6-D Research System software (Skill Technologies, Inc., Phoenix, AZ).

On each trial, participant was asked to grasp the horizontally oriented rod, and the marker was electronically aligned. Recording began, and the participant wielded the rod as long as desired before pointing to the end. On Blocks 2-5, feedback was given by the experimenter pointing to the actual end of the rod. Participants were encouraged to again wield the rod after the feedback had been given.

Results and Discussion

Performance as measured by a correlation coefficient between perceived and actual partial length is plotted in Figure 3A. Performance was good, but for most participants there was not much improvement. A one-within analysis of variance (ANOVA) showed that block was not significant, $p > .10$. Only Participant 1 shows dramatic improvement; the other participants performed well even on the first block. As to whether participants converged on the optimal acceleration (Prediction 1), Figure 3B presents the average peak accelerations during wielding for each participant on each plot. While an ANOVA revealed that average acceleration increased significantly, $F(5, 20) = 3.66$, $p = .016$, suggesting some retuning in the direction of the optimum, the individual participants did not march uniformly toward the optimum, as we had seen in other dynamic touch experiments (Michaels, Arzamarski, Isenhower, & Jacobs, 2008).

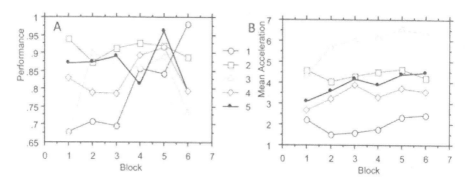

Figure 3. Panel A: Average performance by participants and blocks. Panel B: Average peak acceleration by participants and blocks.

As to Prediction 2, multiple regressions of judgment against gravitational torque (in the horizontal posture) and moment of inertia did indeed demonstrate that these variables predicted judgments well, $.653 < R < .973$, for all blocks of all participants. Prediction 3 was of high correlations between judgment and peak muscle torque (gravitational torque + peak acceleration • moment of inertia). These relations were indeed observed, as shown in Figure 4. Moreover, there appears to be a general increase over blocks, most noticeable in Participant 1, in dependence on muscle torque.

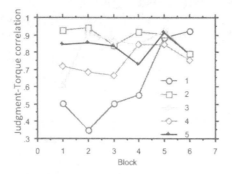

Figure 4. Correlation of peak muscle torque and judgment.

In sum, the major predictors support the general hypotheses that subjects modulate their acceleration to access a locus on the information line, change that acceleration with learning, and base their judgments on the torque needed to create that acceleration. However, Michaels and Isenhower (2011b) identified alternate strategies based on the same general principles: 1) Perceivers exert a constant muscle torque on all trials and the resulting *acceleration* specifies partial length, and 2) Perceivers exert an arbitrary and variable torque and the *ratio* of that torque to the resulting acceleration informs judgments. To test for the possible use of these strategies, we compared the correlations of judgments with each of the three predictors (torque, acceleration and their ratio). The results are presented by participant in Figure 5. The correlation of judgment and acceleration is always the worst, but it was by no means zero. That, together with the reliable superiority of the ratio, suggests that it, rather than torque is the operative variable in this partial length paradigm.

To conclude, Michaels and Isenhower proposed that muscle torque was the information for partial-length perception, and good informational loci are accessed by appropriate, vigorous acceleration. The current results suggest a broader interpretation: the ratio of torque to acceleration, rather than torque alone,matters, and again vigorous wielding accesses the best loci. As was the case with Michaels and Isenhower (2011b), we did not find not much learning—reattuning to a more informative locus in information

Palatinus & Michaels

space. For most participants, performance was very good on the first block, so there was little room for improvement or for reattunement through changed wielding.

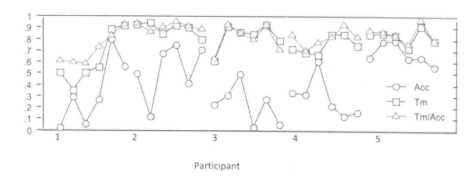

Participant

Figure 5. Correlations of candidate information variables and judgments.

References

Jacobs, D. M., & Michaels, C. F. (2007). Direct learning. *Ecological Psychology*, 19, 321-351.

Michaels, C. F., Arzamarski, R. Isenhower, R., & Jacobs, D. M. (2008). Direct learning in dynamic touch. *Journal of Experimental Psychology: Human Perception and Performance, 34(4)*, 944-957.

Michaels, C. F., & Isenhower, R. W. (2011a). An information space for partial length perception in dynamic touch. *Ecological Psychology*.

Michaels, C. F., & Isenhower, R W. (2011b). Information space is action space: Perceiving the partial lengths of rods rotated on an axle. *Attention, Perception & Psychophysics, 73*, 160-171

Acknowledgements. The research reported here was supported by the National Science Foundation under Grant BCS-0820154.

Studies in Perception & Action X
E. Charles & L.J. Smart (Eds.)
© 2011 Taylor & Francis Group, LLC

Sensitivity of Toe Clearance to Leg Joint Angles During Extensive Practice of Obstacle Crossing: Effects of Vision and Task Goal

Sérgio Tosi Rodrigues[1], Valéria Duarte Garcia[1,2], Arturo Forner-Cordero[3]

[1]Laboratório de Informação, Visão e Ação, Faculdade de Ciências, Universidade Estadual Paulista - Bauru, [2]Programa de Mestrado em Neurociências e Comportamento, Instituto de Psicologia, Universidade de São Paulo, [3]Laboratório de Biomecatrônica, Escola Politécnica, Universidade de São Paulo

During obstacle crossing, a minimal vertical distance between swing foot and obstacle top (toe clearance) has to be preserved to avoid tripping and falling (Patla, 1997). A methodology to determine the sensitivity of toe clearance to swing leg joint angles during gait has been proposed by Moosabhoy and Gard (2006). High sensitivity means that smaller joint angle changes would generate larger changes in the toe clearance. Thus, the sensitivity joint profiles should reflect the strategy to obtain a desired toe clearance, a critical aspect of locomotion control usually dependent on visual information, when available. The main purpose of the present study was to analyze the effects of unavailability of visual information and task goals on the sensitivity of toe clearance to leg joint angles during extensive practice of the obstacle crossing task. Goals of accuracy and velocity were explored to avoid variability possibly associated with the choice of step velocity

Method

Twenty-eight young adults with normal vision were equally divided in four groups: two blindfolded groups had task goals defined as accuracy (A) and velocity (V); the other two groups (AC and VC) were their respective controls, with vision available.

Participants walked with bare feet along a five meter flat pathway with an obstacle of 26 cm height located at 3 m from the starting point. Each participant performed 1,000 trials of the obstacle crossing task; the first trial and one every 50 trials were video recorded (60 Hz) for kinematical analysis. Motion data were filtered with fourth order Butterworth filter (cut-off frequency of 4 Hz) and used to obtain the dependent variables (Figure 1): critical time, toe peak time, toe-obstacle distance, obstacle-heel distance, toe clearance, toe clearance sensitivity to hip, knee, and ankle angles (TCS_H, TCS_K, and TCS_A, respectively), step velocity, and error. Data from each dependent variable were submitted to a group by trials ANOVA, with repeated measures in the last factor. The significance level adopted was 0.05.

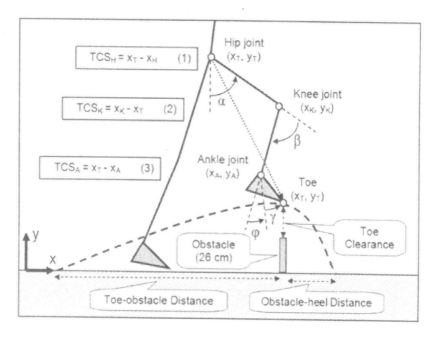

Figure 1. Swing leg model defining the coordinate system used for the sensitivity analysis during obstacle crossing. Boxes on the left side: equations 1, 2, and 3 calculate toe clearance sensitivity to hip (TCS_H), knee (TCS_K), and ankle (TCS_A) joint angles.

Results and Discussion

This study analyzed the effects of unavailability of visual information and task goals of accuracy and velocity on the sensitivity of toe clearance to leg joint angles during extensive practice of the obstacle crossing task. Unavailability of vision during the test was expected to change the locomotion pattern while motor experience increases via repetition. Additionally, the manipulation of task goals could clarify for obstacle crossing the effects of the well-known speed-accuracy trade-off as opposed to a self-selected gait speed situation. The sensitivity analysis was used to identify eventual joint angles strategies to accommodate motor adjustments related to practice and the absence of vision.

Unavailability of visual information resulted in larger toe clearance only in the first trials and disappeared as practice continued; during initial trials, vision availability increased toe-obstacle distance for both task goals. Higher number of crossing errors was observed for the experimental groups. Increased sensitivity values for hip and knee joints occurred at critical time; critical time was not affected by task goal or practice. Toe peak time occurred clearly earlier than critical time, but was modulated by both task goal and practice. Surprisingly, results demonstrated that an extensive amount of practice was not capable of altering the toe clearance and its sensitivity to swing leg joint angle and critical time during obstacle crossing. However, practice changed step velocity and the amount of errors.

This experiment presented evidence that there are strong regularities in the kinematical profiles of the swing leg during obstacle crossing that are not dependent of practice. One thousand trials of practice did not change consistently critical time, toe clearance, and toe clearance sensitivities to hip, knee, and ankle rotations. The order of relative importance of leg joint rotations (hip, knee, and ankle), the moment of peak of sensitivities close to critical time, and critical time itself were maintained throughout trials. Effects of group seemed to show that both the unavailability of vision and the increase of velocity have similar effect, reducing

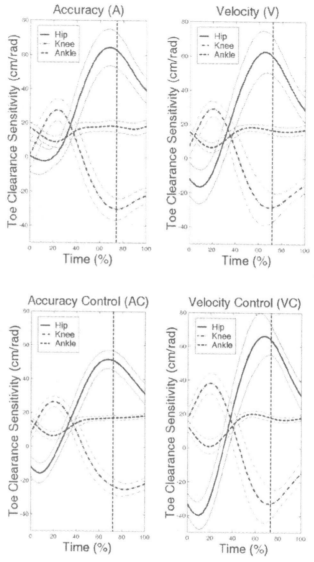

Figure 2. Mean (±*SD*) toe clearance sensitivity (cm/rad) to hip, knee, and ankle as a function of time (%) of accuracy (top left), velocity (top right), accuracy control (bottom left), and velocity control (bottom right) groups. The dashed vertical lines indicate the critical time.

the magnitude of the sensitivity of hip and knee to toe clearance at critical time. The results are in agreement with the notion of trade between safety and efficiency in locomotor control (Sparrow & Newell, 1994; Sparrow et al., 1996). The situations of higher risk such as crossing an obstacle without vision available or in a faster manner require a strategy in which toe clearance is more sensitive to the motion of more proximal leg joints (hip and knee), generating rotations with larger modifications of foot positions and possibly avoiding tripping and falling (Forner Cordero, Koopman & van der Helm, 2003); such interpretation needs further investigation.

References

Forner Cordero, A., Koopman, H. F. J. M., & van der Helm, F. C. T. (2003). Multiple-step strategies to recover from stumbling perturbations. *Gait & Posture, 18*(1), 47-59.

Moosabhoy, M. A., & Gard, S. A. (2006). Methodology for determining the sensitivity of swing leg Toe Clearance and leg length to swing leg joint angles during gait. *Gait & Posture, 24*, 493-501.

Patla, A. E. (1997). Understanding the roles of vision in the control of human locomotion. *Gait & Posture, 5*, 54-69.

Sparrow, W.A., & Newell, K. M. (1994). The coordination and control of human creeping with increases in speed. *Behavioural Brain Research, 63*, 151-158.

Sparrow, W.A., Shinkfield, A. J., Chow, S., & Begg, R. K. (1996). Characteristics of gait in stepping over obstacles. *Human Movement Science, 15, 605-622.*

Acknowledgements. This study was supported by scholarship to Valéria Duarte Garcia (Fundação de Amparo à Pesquisa do Estado de São Paulo, Brazil – Process # 2006/06452-7).

Studies in Perception & Action X
E. Charles & L.J. Smart (Eds.)
© 2011 Taylor & Francis Group, LLC

Longitudinal Development of Looming: How Optical Variables may Become Information

Ruud van der Weel & Audrey van der Meer

Developmental Neuroscience Laboratory, Department of Psychology,
Norwegian University of Science and Technology,
N-7491 Trondheim, Norway (http://www.svt.ntnu.no/psy/nulab/Home.html)

If direct perception is the detection of higher-order variables that specify significant properties of the environment and constrain action, then evolutionary theory has to account for how species become sensitive to those invariants, and developmental learning theory must account for how an infant perceiver becomes more attentive to them. Already at EWEP3 in Germany, Michaels and Beek (1995) proposed three alternatives as to how the pick-up of higher-order perceptual variables may come about: (a) *sensitivity* Assuming that adult perceivers of some species are indeed sensitive to certain optical variables at birth, how could it be developed? Psychologists usually use this term to refer to the ability to detect certain energy types, so that one could not develop sensitivity; (b) *attentiveness* This implies that one could detect the higher-order variable all along but did not have perceptions or actions constrained by it; and (c) *smart perceptual devices* (Runeson, 1977).

Devices that register higher-order variables can be developed. It does not seem likely that perceivers come equipped to register any and all levels of complex variables of stimulation, perform at random until they stumble onto the proper complex, and thereafter 'directly perceive'. Rather, lower level, merely correlated variables might be exploited initially and perhaps guide the search for or come to be selected as integral parts of a higher-order informational complex, or both.

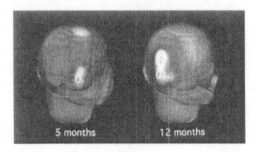

Figure 1. Looming related brain activity in the same infant at 5 and 12 months of age. Note the change in localisation of electrical activity in response to the looms (in white). Related to this shift is an underlying change of the use of the lower-order variable velocity to the higher-order variable time-to-collision. This might indicate the development of a "smart perceptual device".

A recent study published by Van der Weel and Van der Meer (2009) investigated the ability in infants to see whether an object is approaching on a direct collision course and, if so, when it will collide. Using high-density electroencephalography in 5- to 11-month-old infants and a looming stimulus approaching under three different accelerations, it was investigated how the young human nervous system picks up information for impending collision. The results showed that infants' looming related brain activity was characterised by theta oscillations (3.5-7.5Hz). Brain source analyses revealed clear localised activity in the visual cortex. Analysing the temporal dynamics of the source waveform, we provided evidence that the temporal structure of different looming stimuli was sustained during processing in the more mature infant brain, providing infants with increasingly veridical time-to-collision information about looming danger as they grow older and become more mobile. In the present study we investigate the use of different perceptual variables and how these are processed in the infant brain.

Method

Using a longitudinal design, 10 infants (6 boys) were tested at 5 and 12 months of age. Methods used are described in Van der Weel   and   Van   der   Meer   (2009)   at http://www.springerlink.com/content/82p0423421026p33/.

Results and Discussion

The results showed differences in occurrence of peak Visual Evoked Potential (VEP$_{peak}$) with age. At 5 months, infants displayed VEP$_{peak}$ earlier in the looming sequence, $F(1, 9) = 6.072$, $P < 0.05$, with a longer duration than at 12 months, $F(1, 9) = 6.913$, $P < 0.05$. We also found that with age VEP$_{peak}$ propagated from the right O_2 (occipital) area at 5 months to the more left O_1 - P_3 (parietal) area at 12 months (see *Figure 1*).

We also investigated which timing variable the infants used at VEP$_{peak}$. An analysis based on the index of dispersion showed that with age, four infants shifted from using the lower-order variable involving the loom's velocity at 5 months to a higher-order variable involving the loom's time-to-collision at 12 months. Interestingly, the infants that started out using time-to-collision already at 5 months became more extreme time-variable users when tested again at the age of 12 months.

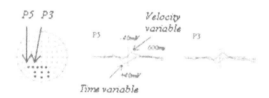

Figure 2. VEP activity at electrode sites P5 and P3. Note that infants using the lower- order variable velocity show a negative VEP$_{peak}$, whereas infants using the higher-order variable time-to-collision show a positive VEP$_{peak}$.

Finally, visual inspection of grand average VEP_{peak} of infants using different variables (see Figure 2) at 5 months revealed differences in VEP morphology where infants using velocity showed a negative VEP_{peak} whereas infants using time-to-collision showed a positive VEP_{peak}, $t(8) = -3.5$, $P< 0.005$.

There is a clear developmental trend in our data. We interpret this trend to include the development of a smart perceptual mechanism (Runeson, 1977), allowing older infants to judge time-to-collision more effectively using the higher-order perceptual variable of time-to-collision as certain parietal brain regions higher up the dorsal stream get more specifically tuned to this type of information. Especially the marked difference in VEP morphology (see *Figure 2*) between infants using velocity and time-to-collision is interpreted as a sign in this direction. Further analyses on VEP morphology will be carried out to investigate the underlying temporal dynamics of the changing VEP signal.

References

Michaels, C. & Beek, P.J. (1995). The state of ecological psychology. *Ecological Psychology, 7(4)*, 259-278.

Runeson, S. (1977). On the possibility of "smart" perceptual mechanisms. *Scandinavian Journal of Psychology,18*, 172-179.

Van der Weel, F.R. & Van der Meer, A.L.H. (2009). Seeing it coming: Infants' brain responses to looming danger. *Naturwissenschaften, 96*, 1385-1391

Studies in Perception & Action X
E. Charles & L.J. Smart (Eds.)
© 2011 Taylor & Francis Group, LLC

Chapter 2:

Coordination and Action

Studies in Perception & Action X
E. Charles & L.J. Smart (Eds.)
© 2011 Taylor & Francis Group, LLC

Bimanual Coordination: The impact of Choosing the Focus of Attention

Bruno Nascimento Alleoni[1,2], Ana Maria Pellegrini[1]

[1]Sao Paulo State University, Brazil
[2]Escola Superior de Tecnologia e Educação de Rio Claro, São Paulo, Brasil

Visual attention is directed to the spatial and temporal characteristics of the two hands displacements when they are close to each other as in the work of a watchmaker. The amplitude of the displacement of the two hands with a duration between 190 and 260 msec. allows for a better precision in the performance based on visual feedback (Keele & Posner, 1968). When the two hands are farther way from each other, the performer follows the displacement of only one of the hands in order to identify the relevant body and task components for a precise execution of the task. Thus, if the performer prioritizes information from one of the hands, than the choice to which hand to attend may have a strong influence on the level of performance. The results of the performance when attending to the preferred hand in simple tasks showed to be more stable than to the non-preferred hand (Amazeen et al, 1997) however, focusing attention to the non-preferred hand showed to be the best strategy for a better synchronization (relative phase close to zero) in children dual task performance (Pellegrini et al, 2004). In addition, Baudalf & Deubel, (2008) showed that when performing a bimanual reaching movement and a letter discrimination task, the alternation of the focus of attention between hands led to better results in the motor task. In summary, in dual task performance, there are evidences of interactions between the hand preference (internal factor) and the visual focus of attention (external factor). The aim of the present study was to verify the impact of the choice of the hand to attend in bimanual tasks as a function of hand preference.

Method

Eight right-handed (RH) and seven left-handed (LH) adult volunteers based on the Index of Laterality (Oldfield, 1971) participated in the present study. The task consisted of touching alternately the endpoint of a pen in two targets pre-set under a transparent screen of a digitizing table (Tablet). The Tablet with two independent input channels was built specifically for bimanual studies by CenPRA. The touching on the Tablet surface took place after displacements from one target to the other according to the experimental condition. The targets were squares of 2 cm of side and were 2 cm apart from each other. Although the size of the targets were the same in all experimental conditions, the number of targets to be touched in same direction by each hand varied from 1 to 3 according to the experimental condition (1:1, 2:1, 3:1 and 3:2). In each condition the left number indicates the number of targets to be touched by the preferred hand (see example in Figure 1).

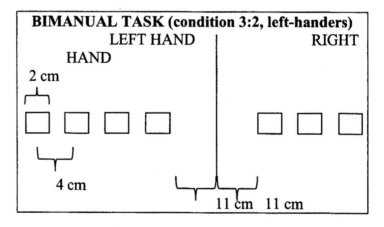

Figure 1. Schematic representation of the bimanual task in condition 3:2 for left-handers.

In the first session, Condition 1:1 was performed in three temporal intervals (300, 600, 900 msec.) followed by conditions 2:1 (300 msec. for the preferred hand and 600 msec. for the non-preferred hand), 3:1 (300 msec. for the preferred hand and 900 msec. for the non-preferred hand), and 3:2 (600 msec. for the preferred hand and 900 msec. for the non-preferred hand) without information regard to which hand to focus, therefore with the focus of attention of the subject choice. There were 15 trials in condition one, five of them to each temporal interval and five trials for each of the other conditions. Trial duration was 20 seconds and controlled by a digital metronome.

In the second session, participants performed five trials in condition 1:1 with 300 msec. interval with attention directed to the preferred hand and five trials to the non-preferred hand. In the sequence, they perform 10 trials in each of the other three conditions as in the first session, with five trials to the preferred and five to the non-preferred hand. The visual focus of attention was monitored by the experimenter through a video camera which transmitted the eyes displacement in real time. The images were analysed for identification of the amount of changing in the direction of the eyes in each trial. For the purposes of this poster, only the following measures were analyzed: spatial error (pixels) and eye displacement.

ANOVAs for unequal-n were performed for the variables spatial error (pixels) and eye displacement. For identification of differences between main factors as well as interactions, Tukey HSD post hoc Tests were employed.

Results and Discussion

A repeated-measures analysis of variance (ANOVA) on the spatial error with the factors hand (2) X attention (3) indicates that the interaction of hand and attention reached level of significance ($F_{2,32} = 63.,358$, p<.05) showing that independent of hand preference and condition the spatial error for the attended hand was smaller than that of the non-attended hand. Similar results were reported by Treffner and Turvey (1995) but they differ from those

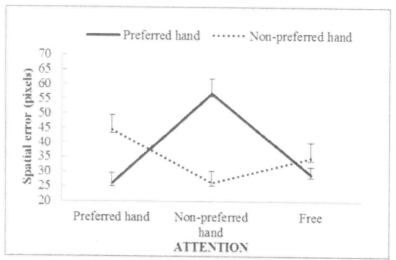

Figure 2. Mean and standard deviation of the spatial error (pixels) for each hand as a function of the focus of attention.

studies that used relative phase as the dependent variable (Amazeen et al., 1997; Pellegrini et al., 2004).

When the focus of attention was of the participant choice, they showed to prefer to move their eyes from one hand to the other, monitoring the two hands during task performance. Right-handed subjects showed a larger number of eye movements then the left ones. The right-handed participants changed the focus of vision 10.91 times in average, while the left-handed 12.83 in the 20 seconds trial. When subjects maintained the focus of attention to the same hand, this fact occurred only at the preferred hand as already observed in Swinnen et al (1996) and Treffner and Turvey (1995) studies. Therefore, we can conclude that, independently of hand preference, the option to choose the hand to attend allow the subject the best control of her action.

References

Amazeen, E. L., Amazeen, P. G., Treffner, P. J., & Turvey, M. T. (1997). Attention and handedness in bimanual coordination dynamics. *Journal of*

Experimental Psychology: Human Perception and Performance, 23 (5), 1522-1560.

Baldauf, D., & Deubel, H. (2008) Visual attention during the preparation of bimanual movements. *Vision Research, 48,* 549-563.

Fitts, P. M. (1954) The information capacity of the human motor system in controlling the amplitude of movement. *Journal of Experimental Psychology, 47* (6), 381-391.

Hoffmann, E. R., Chang, W. Y., & Yim, K. Y. (1997) Computer mouse operation: is the left-handed user disadvantaged? *Applied Ergonomics, 28* (4), 245-248.

Keele, S. W. & Posner, M. I. (1968) Processing of visual feedback in rapid movements. *Journal of Experimental Psychology, 77,* 55-158.

Oldfield, R. C. (1971) The assessment and analysis of handedness: the Edinburgh inventory. *Neuropsychologia, 9,* 97-113.

Pellegrini, A. M., Andrade, E. C., & Teixeira, L. A. (2004) Attending to the non-preferred hand improves bimanual coordination in children. *Human Movement Science, 23,* 447-460.

Swinnen, S. P., Jardim, K., & Meulenbroek, R. (1996) Between-limbs asynchronies during bimanual coordination. *Neuropsychologia, 34* (12), 1203-1213.

Treffner, P. J., & Turvey, M. T. (1995) Handedness and the asymmetric dynamics of bimanual rhythmic coordination. *Journal of Experimental Psychology: Human Perception and Performance,21* (2), 318-333.

Acknowledgements.

To: CenPRA, Centro de Pesquisa Renato Archer, MCT, Campinas for providing the TABLET hardware and software used in this study.

CNPQ, for the graduate assistantship, #134087/2006.

Studies in Perception & Action X
E. Charles & L.J. Smart (Eds.)
© 2011 Taylor & Francis Group, LLC

Intentions, Context and Constraint in Isometric Single-Digit Force Production Dynamics

Dilip N. Athreya & Michael A. Riley

Center for Cognition, Action & Perception, Department of Psychology,
University of Cincinnati

Context plays an important role in human voluntary control. In particular, context might act as an exogenous constraint that restricts the degrees of freedom of perception-action systems. Recently, Holden et al. (2010) found that subtle changes in context (i.e., in experimental conditions that imposed different degrees of exogenous constraints) changed the $1/f$ fractal dynamics of cognitive performance. In general, any exogenous constraints seem to introduce more randomness into the dynamics of the behavior. For example, Chen et al. (2001) reported scaling exponents for inter-tap intervals that were closer to white noise when tapping a finger to in sync with a metronome (an exogenous constraint) compared to tapping based on a remembered beat pattern, which was closer to pink noise. Similarly, Kuznetsov and Wallot (2011) found that time estimation based on memory produced scaling exponents close to pink noise while temporal estimations with accuracy feedback (another type of exogenous constraint) moved the exponents towards the direction of white noise.

Intentions are also crucial in voluntary control of action. Intentions must be appropriate to steer the relevant muscles in order to achieve the desired goal. Differences in one's intention usually lead to differences in performance. For example, in human behavioral research different instructions are used to induce different intentions in order to elicit different behaviors. But, what is the nature of such intentions? Kloos and Van Orden (2010), while addressing the origins of intentions in voluntary behavior, proposed to treat intentions as constraints that self-organize into temporary dynamical structures (Juarrero, 1999) while restricting degrees of freedom in human behavior. Further, they claim that human performance variation could be modulated by the relative degrees of involuntary and voluntary control, where involuntary control is restricted by exogenous constraints (e.g., feedback or available affordances) and voluntary control is restricted by endogenous constraints (e.g., intentions). Accordingly, any introduction of exogenous constraints would increase the uncontrolled degrees of freedom and in consequence increase the randomness in the behavior.

In the current study, we investigated these claims in a voluntary, isometric, single-digit force production task by manipulating feedback about the amount of force produced, thereby changing the degree of exogenous constraints.

Method

Forty-two University of Cincinnati undergraduates participated for course credit. All participants had normal or corrected-to-normal vision. A force transducer (Bertec Corporation, Columbus, OH) with a 100 Hz sampling rate was used to obtain isometric finger force production data. A computer monitor was used to display feedback (rendered in *Matlab*) of participants' finger force production in the feedback conditions.

In two experiments, participants were randomly assigned to either a no-feedback or a feedback group (Experiment 1: $N = 12$ per group; Experiment 2: $N = 8$ per group). Participants in both experiments were asked to produce a self-selected comfortable amount of force with the index finger of their preferred hand, and to maintain the same level of force at which they started for the duration of each trial. In Experiment 1, one minute of constant force production constituted a trial, and there were a total of 5 trials with breaks in between the trials. In Experiment 2, participants were asked to maintain force continuously for 5 minutes without any break (only one trial per participant). In both experiments, participants in the feedback group watched a white screen with a blue line that changed its trace in real time according to the force produced by the participant. In the no-feedback condition, the screen was white and the force trace was absent.

Results and Discussion

Data from both experiments were first truncated by eliminating the first 5 s (500 data points) and then de-trended using a quadratic fit. Outliers from the data (any data point beyond 3 standard deviations) were removed. Data were submitted to spectral analysis to obtain spectral slopes. Spectral slopes from both experiments indicated that isometric, single-digit force production dynamics exhibited fractional Brownian noise, fBm (see Figure 1).

In order to compare and contrast the results of Experiments 1 and 2, data from Experiment 2 (i.e., 5 minute trials) were parsed into 5 one-minute segments. For each experiment, a 2 (condition) × 5 (trial) analysis of variance (ANOVA) on the spectral slopes revealed a significant difference in the dynamics with respect to the presence or absence of feedback (Experiment 1: $F(1, 22) = 4.47$, $p < .05$; Experiment 2, $F(1, 14) = 7.71$, $p < .05$). A spectral slope equal to -2 is considered a boundary between persistent and anti-persistent fBm behavior. With feedback the force dynamics exhibited anti-persistent behavior (slope > -2) but exhibited persistent behavior (slope < -2) without feedback (see Figure 2). In Experiment 1, there was a significant interaction between condition (feedback or no feedback) and trials, $F(1, 4) = 2.53$, $p < .05$. A simple-effects one-way ANOVA for the feedback condition showed a significant trial effect, $F(4, 11) = 2.67$, $p < .05$), but post-hoc comparisons revealed no significant differences between any trial pair. The trial simple effect was not significant for the no-feedback condition ($p > .05$).

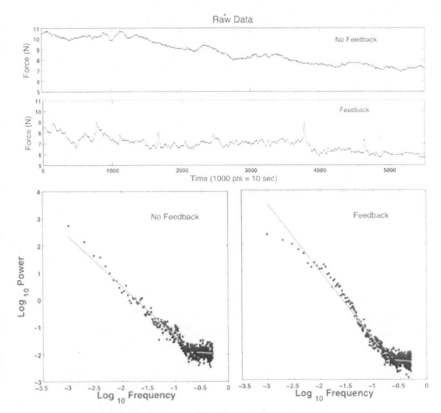

Figure 1. The top panel shows raw force data from Experiment 1. The bottom panel shows respective spectral plots along with their linear fits.

A *t*-test on intact 5 minute trials from Experiment 2 indicated similar differences across feedback conditions as in Experiment 1, $t(14) = -2.44$, $p < .05$. Also, as in Experiment 1, the feedback condition exhibited anti-persistent fBm while the no-feedback condition exhibited persistent fBm.

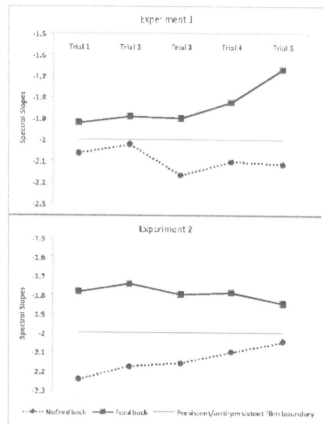

Figure 2. Spectral slope values from the feedback and no-feedback conditions in Experiment 1 (top) and Experiment 2 (bottom).

In both experiments, the $1/f$ scaling exponents exhibited a loss of correlation structure (spectral slopes had a smaller absolute value) when an exogenous constraint (feedback) was introduced into the behavioural context. Our results are consistent with previous empirical evidence by Kuznetsov and Wallot (2011) and Chen et al. (2001), and support the hypothesis by Kloos and Van Orden (2010) that the presence of exogenous constraints introduces uncontrolled degrees of freedom that result in behavioral fluctuations that are more random.

References

Chen Y., Ding M., & Kelso, J.A.S. (2001): Origins of timing errors in human sensorimotor coordination. *Journal of Motor Behavior, 33*, 3-8.

Holden, J. G., Choi, I., Amazeen, P. G., & Van Orden, G. (2010). Fractal $1/f$ dynamics suggest entanglement of measurement and human performance. *Journal of Experimental Psychology: Human Perception and Performance.*

Juarrero, A. (1999). *Dynamics in Action: Intentional behavior as a complex system.* MIT Press, Cambridge: MA

Kloos, H. & Van Orden, G. (2010). Voluntary behavior in cognition and motor tasks. *Mind & Matter, 8*, 19-43.

Kuznetsov, N., & Wallot, S. (2011). Accuracy feedback in continuous temporal estimation. *Unpublished manuscript.*

Acknowledgements. Supported by NSF grants BCS 0926662 and BCS 0728743. We thank Guy Van Orden, Jay Holden, and Nikita Kuznetsov for their contributions.

Studies in Perception & Action X
E. Charles & L.J. Smart (Eds.)
© 2011 Taylor & Francis Group, LLC

A TMS Approach to the Problem of Motor Coordination

Alain Boyadjian[1,2], François Tyč [1,2], et Brasil-Neto Joaquim[3].

[1] CNRS UMR 6196, marseilles. [2] Université du Littoral.
[3] Universidade de Brasilia. Laboratôrio de neurociências e comportamento.

Bersntein claimed that the major concern in motor control is to cope with the redundant motor system (i.e. muscles and joints) that have to be coordinated in a smart way to realize goal directed actions. The control of this redundant system was called degrees of freedom problem (d.o.f.). It leads us to question how neural system and particularly the motor cortex (M1) are organized. How M1 may participate actively in the emergence of non-linear neural output for synergies and linear movement? In this way, transcranial magnetic stimulation (TMS) offers a non-invasive way to test the excitability neural motor pathways involved in coordination.

We want to compare different neural output observed in different multijoint tasks with patient suffering from diseases affecting coordination (the Parsonage-Turner Syndrome, PTS; and the focal hand dystonia like writer's cramp, WC). We compare these results with other groups trained in multijoint tasks like volley ball, throwing dart learning.

The PTS is a shoulder girdle amyotrophy, neuralgic, with relative good clinical prognosis after 1 to 2 years. WC occurs with over use history in writing. These two diseases impair the coordination between upper or lower joint of the upper limb.

Method:

Stimulation protocol. In all experiments, the subject wear a snugly fitting cap positioned over the subject's head. A grid was drawn with stimulus sites spaced 1.5 cm from the vertex using the nasion-inion line and the inter-aural line as references. TMS was delivered using a MagStim 200 electromagnetic stimulator with a figure-of-8-coil. In PTS, the target muscles were Anterior Deltoid (AD) and the Extensor Carpi Radialis (ECR). In the WC study, the target muscles were the MD, ECR and First Dorsal Interosseus (FDI). See complete method in Tyč et Boyadjian (2011).

Tasks Subjects realized the static pointing in 2 conditions. In task 1 the subject had to let elbow on an arm rest and then the shoulder girdle muscles were at rest. In task 2, pointing was achieved using the whole arm, and then shoulder muscles were co-active at the same time than the distal ones.

Subjects: The PTS (33years) suffered the syndrome 7 years before the study in the left arm. In the , dystonic group (DGroup), the patients (53years±15) were diagnosed at least 10 years before the study. Results were compared with those of a control group (CGroup) (56 years± 7).

Data analysis A contour plot was drawn with coordinate system to measure the area of each muscle representation. The external borderline of the contour plot corresponded to the minimal discernable MEP. For excitability curves (I/O curves), we fit with sigmoïdal function (Devanne et al., 2002).

Results

In the PTS, the mapping showed a decrease in the left AD cortical representation. The excitability of AD was lower too as smaller MEP were elicited in left AD. The I/O curves showed that in both arm, the MEPs in distal ECR were higher when the AD were co-active (Fig. 1). Further analyses were done in order to show that smaller MEP and representation could not be relied on motor neuron death (not shown here). In dystonics, the study of excitability properties showed that distal ECR was facilitated in whole arm task condition like in the control group. In FDI, the excitability was higher in Dgroup and higher MEPs were elicited in the T2 condition than T1 contrarily to CGroup (cf. fig2). The task effect did not exist in the control group.

Boyadjian, Tyc, & Joaquim

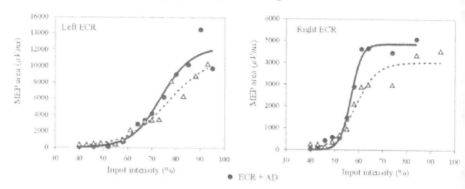

Figure 1. On the left and right panel the excitability of the ECR is higher when it was co-active with proximal AD muscle.

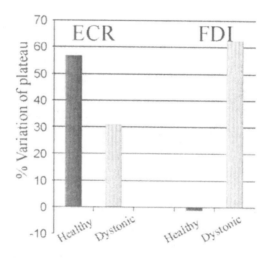

Figure 2. ratio based on the plateau of the excitability curve (cf method fig1). Ratio = plateau T2/ plateau T1. Contrarily to control group, WC subjects have higher motor output when MD and FDI were co-active.

In Mapping, MD areas were not different between groups, but for FDI and ECR, the cortical representations were bigger in the DGroup than in CGroup. The distance between CoGs of the MD and FDI and MD and ECR were smaller in the DGroup. The overlapping and ratios of overlapping between proximal MD and the distal ECR and FDI muscles were found to be higher in the DGroup.

Discussion

In all situations, we have shown that the M1 cortex is modified under training (Tyč et Boyadjian; 2005, 2011) or diseases. Classically, TMS studies using experimental task with discrete motor sequence of contraction of the target muscles. In these tasks change of properties in M1 are transient. At the beginning of the training sessions, the representation of the muscles increased, but at the end of the learning of the motor sequence, these representations returned to initial sizes. In coordination, like spike in volley-ball or throwing darts, on-line control constraints the neural system to conserve those plastic modifications. Interestingly, in the long-term motor learning tasks we proposed (Tyč et Boyadjian, 2011), the facilitation provoked by the co-activation of proximal muscle was interpreted as the emergence of the effectiveness of an integrated neural pathway (Devanne et al. 2002) reflecting the concept of coordinative structure proposed by Bernstein at the origin. In the present studies, we showed that after a disease the organization of M1 could be deeply altered. The observation in PTS was the same than in strokes, smaller representation and excitability accompanied with shift of the hot spot (location of the higher MEP elicited when applying TMS). Nevertheless, it is interesting to note that the neural pathways linking distal and the altered proximal muscle are still functional. We could speculate this is the reason why the subject returned to normal motor coordination. In the WC, with respect to coordination constraints, in our knowledge, no other experiment have shown such facilitation of muscle excitability when muscles of proximal joints like shoulder interact with such a distant joint (metacarpal joint) moved by the FDI. In the case of the pathology, the over facilitation of an integrated pathway could cause motor overflow. Even if the overflow is not mainly due to neural link between MD and FDI, one might speculate once again that cortical plasticity mechanisms useful in normal conditions provoke an inappropriate output of existing integrated pathway. It is a kind of collateral damage of mechanisms useful for synergy. So, coordination and M1 are coupled in a non-linear dynamic system where interaction between them is responsible of the change of each of them. M1 organization participates actively to the emergence of synergy motor patterns.

References.

Devanne H, Cohen LG, Kouchtir-Devanne N, Capaday C. (2002). Integrated motor cortical control of task-related muscles during pointing in humans. J Neurophysiol; 87:3006-17.

Tyč F, Boyadjian A. (2011). Plasticity of motor cortex induced by coordination and training.Clin Neurophysiol.;122(1):153-62

Tyč F, Boyadjian A, Devanne H. (2005) Motor cortex plasticity induced by extensive training revealed by transcranial magnetic stimulation in human. Eur J Neurosci;21:259-66.

Studies in Perception & Action X
E. Charles & L.J. Smart (Eds.)
© 2011 Taylor & Francis Group, LLC

Fitts' Law: A Joint-Action Approach

Justin Fine[1] and Eric L. Amazeen[1]

[1]Arizona State University, USA

Many situations require an *individual* to produce coordinated movements such as, walking, gymnastics, or playing the piano. Coordinated behavior is not restricted to the individual, though; many situations require *dyads* or *groups* to produce coordinated interpersonal movements such as, passing a soccer ball or dancing. The organization of a person's limbs is often considered to be the responsibility of the central nervous system. The observation that pairs of individuals can spontaneously synchronize movements suggests, to the contrary, that there are other non-centralized — perhaps dynamical — processes underpinning coordination (Schmidt, Carello, & Turvey, 1990).

We examined intra- and interpersonal coordination in a bimanual rhythmic Fitts' Law tapping task. Many investigators have demonstrated that during aimed movements such as pointing or tapping, speed is traded for accuracy as the difficulty of targets increase; this trade-off is known as Fitts' Law (Fitts, 1954). However, during bimanual tapping at targets of unequal difficulty Fitts' Law is violated — the hands are temporally synchronized (Kelso, Southard, & Goodman, 1979). These findings suggest that coordination emerges from non-centralized synergies, which constrain effectors to perform as a functional unit. Similar conclusions have been offered for interpersonal coordination, in which visually perceiving the movement of another individual's limbs is sufficient to support coordinated actions of *dyad* (Schmidt & O'Brien, 1997). No centralized controller is needed to dictate specific commands to individual limbs, especially when such a controller doesn't exist between people. We predict, then, that if dynamical processes govern coordination in general, then violations of Fitts' Law similar to Kelso et al. (1979) should be evident during interpersonal tapping.

Method

Intra- and interpersonal coordination was investigated by asking participants to tap rhythmically between pairs of square targets. The widths and distances of targets in a pair were manipulated independently for each hand. Using Fitts's Index of Difficulty (ID = $\log_2$ (2Amplitude/Width)), a target's difficulty was classified as either easy (width = 60mm; amplitude = 80mm; ID = 1.6) or hard (width = 20mm; amplitude = 240mm; ID = 4.6). The target ID associated with each hand was manipulated separately, creating four conditions defined by the difficulty associated with the Left Hand (easy or hard) and the difficulty associated with the Right Hand (easy or hard). For the purpose of analyzing both limbs, the combined IDs for these conditions were 3.17 for two easy targets, 6.17 for easy-hard/hard-easy pairings, and 9.17 for two hard targets. Participants' tapping was performed simultaneously with two hands (intrapersonal conditions), and one hand (dominant) together with another participant (interpersonal). An Optotrak motion-capture system recorded movement position (100 Hz) from infrared diodes attached to individuals' index fingers. Participants chose a comfortable tapping frequency, but were asked to tap as quickly and accurately possible for 60s. Participants were not explicitly instructed to coordinate movements.

Results and Discussion

Mean movement time (MT) for intra- and interpersonal conditions (Fig. 1a and Fig. 1b, respectively) were analyzed with a 2 (Coordination: intra- and interpersonal) × 2 (Index of Difficulty: easy, hard) × 2 (Other Hand: easy, hard) repeated-measures ANOVA. The variable Other Hand refers to the task being performed by the other hand. This analysis revealed a significant effect of Index of Difficulty, where mean MT increased from 276 ms for the easy task to 332 ms for the hard task, $F_{(1,15)} = 33.04, p < .05$. There was also a significant main effect of Other Hand, where mean MT increased from 281 ms when the other hand was performing an easy task to 328 ms when the other hand was performing a hard task, $F_{(1,15)} = 98.03, p < .05$. Fitts' Law was similarly violated for intra- and interpersonal conditions with mixed target IDs: the hand moving to an easy target slowed down to match the timing of the hand moving to a hard target. These results extend the findings by Kelso et al. (1979) to an interpersonal coordination task. Fitts' Law's failure in both the intra- and interpersonal cases suggests that the brain does not program motor units individually — a necessary assumption for applying Fitts' Law. Furthermore, the observation of an interpersonal violation of Fitts' Law indicates that violations of Fitts' Law, in general, are not the product of programming interference, as has been proposed. Instead, we argue (following Kelso et al., 1979) that such intra- and interpersonal coordination emerges from the soft-assembly of functionally grouped muscles and effectors.

The cross-spectral coherence for each time series was calculated to identify the degree of coordination (0 = no phase-locking to 1 = fixed phase-locking). These data (Fig. 2) were analyzed with a 2 (Coordination: intra- and interpersonal) × 3 (Index of Difficulty: easy-easy = 3.17, mixed = 6.17, and hard-hard = 9.17) repeated-measures ANOVA. There was a significant main effect of Coordination, $F_{(1,7)} = 55.51, p < .05$, indicating a greater level of coordination (mean coherence = .41) in the intrapersonal condition than in the interpersonal condition (mean coherence = .25). The main effect of Index of Difficulty was also significant, $F_{(2,14)} = 38.10, p < .05$, where the mean coherence was .25 for easy-easy trials, .31 for mixed targets (easy-hard & hard-easy), and .43 for hard-hard pairs. This main effect suggests that as Index of Difficulty increased the degree of coordination also increased. Despite the mean differences between intra- and interpersonal coordination — possibly reflecting differences in coupling strength (either anatomical or visual) — both tasks

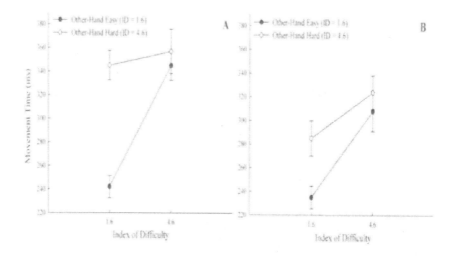

Figure 1: (A) Mean movement times for intrapersonal conditions. (B) Mean movement times for interpersonal conditions.

showed similar increases in coordination strength according to changes in ID. Specifically, harder tasks were associated with stronger coordination between hands. This is counterintuitive to Fitts' Law and its emphasis on executive computation; such an approach might predict weaker coordination strength as ID increases due to increased attentional and processing demands. Because *dyads* lacked a shared centralized controller, and intention in this case, these increases in coordination strength don't implicate a role for an executive cognitive planner.

Taken together, the present results extend and support the conclusion (Schmidt et al., 1990) that coordination emerges from an informational coupling (i.e., anatomical or visual) of limbs. These findings also suggest that similar dynamical processes provide a functional background of emergent behavior for both intra- and interpersonal coordination. Emergent coordination — for both *individuals* and *dyads* — may reflect the natural tendencies of coupled oscillators to become entrained to one another's rhythms. Cognition plays an important role in constraining this coupling, as evidenced by the effects of ID on

mean coherence, but its role is not the one predicted by Fitts' Law
— centralized computation.

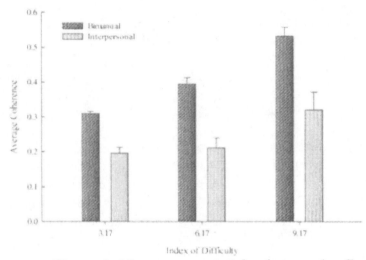

Figure 2: Mean cross-spectral coherence by Coordination
condition and ID.

References

Fitts, P. M. (1954). The Information Capacity of the Human Motor System in
   Controlling the Amplitude of Movement. Journal of Experimental
   Psychology, 47(6), 381-391.
Kelso, J. A. S., Southard, D. L., & Goodman, D. (1979). Coordination of 2-
   Handed Movements. Journal of Experimental Psychology-Human
   Perception and Performance, 5(2), 229-238.
Schmidt, R. C., Carello, C., & Turvey, M. T. (1990). Phase-Transitions and
   Critical Fluctuations in the Visual Coordination of Rhythmic Movements
   between People. Journal of Experimental Psychology-Human Perception
   and Performance, 16(2), 227-247.
Schmidt, R. C., & O'Brien, B. (1997). Evaluating the dynamics of unintended
   interpersonal coordination. Ecological Psychology, 9(3), 189-206.

Studies in Perception & Action X
E. Charles & L.J. Smart (Eds.)
© 2011 Taylor & Francis Group, LLC

Effect of Learning Racewalking on the Metabolic Aspects and Speed of the Walk-to-Run Transition

L. Majed, A-M. Heugas, I.A.Siegler

Univ Paris-Sud, Laboratoire C.I.A.M.S (UPRES EA 4532), Orsay, France

Walking and running are the two primary gaits used by humans during terrestrial locomotion. As speed of locomotion increases during walking or decreases during running, a critical speed is reached at which a gait transition naturally takes place. Why do human shift from walking to running at a particular speed? What are the factors that trigger the transition? Many explanations have been discussed in the literature [Ziv & Rotstein, 2009]. Some authors proposed that gait transitions occur in order to minimize total metabolic cost, known as "metabolic trigger". This energetic optimization theory [Sparrow, 1983] contends that the gait transition is made in response to metabolic efficiency determinants. However, Hreljac (1993) studied the energetically optimal transition speed and found it to be statistically higher than the preferred transition speed (PTS). From this perspective, the weight of "mechanical triggers" such as force attenuation limits, bone strain or anthropometrical variables was put forward. A third type of explanation proposed by Diedrich & Warren (1995) agrees on the complexity of the locomotive system and considers the transition as a nonequilibrium phase transition between attractors. In this case, the interaction of many variables can account for a possible candidate. The authors considered the total energy expenditure as a reliable data for the study of the dynamic landscape and the transition speed, thus not the proximal cause of transition. More recently, Heugas & Deschamps (2006) showed that expert racewalkers switch to racewalking before running, and that their PTS was significantly higher than non racewalkers. They concluded that expertise in racewalking could have modulated the dynamic landscape of human gaits. Our study tries to understand the effect of learning racewalking on PTS and its metabolic aspects for both ascending and descending speed conditions.

Method

Thirteen novice participants (25.15 ± 6.34 years) with a good aerobic fitness level ($VO_{2max} = 57.67 \pm 6.32$ $mlO_2.kg^{-1}.min^{-1}$) performed the experiment on a motorized treadmill. The experiment comprised two tests of PTS determination, one preceding and one following 7 sessions of a racewalking learning protocol. The tests consisted of transition trials in which treadmill velocity was varied, increasing from 5.5 $km.h^{-1}$ for the walk-to-run transition test (W-R) and decreasing from 11 $km.h^{-1}$ for the run-to-walk transition test (R-W). The positive or negative increment of velocity was 0.5 $km.h^{-1}$ per minute. Before learning sessions, participants were informed of the regulations and specific technique of racewalking. The intensity of velocity used for learning sessions was relative to each participant's PTS value. The learning protocol was conceived so that participants would possibly racewalk with a velocity of 10 $km.h^{-1}$.

Kinematic data (60 Hz) were recorded with a 6-camera infrared motion analysis system (VICON370, Oxford Metrics, UK) to assess the exact moment of transition between gaits that coincide with a sudden jump in the peak value of knee flexion during stance phase.

Breath-by-breath oxygen uptake (VO_2) and carbon dioxide (VCO_2) production were measured continuously using a telemetric air analyzer with dedicated hardware (Cortex MetaMax 3B, Germany) and software (MetaSoft). The net VO_2 per distance travelled was calculated [(steady state VO_2 – rest VO_2) ÷ velocity] to obtain the metabolic cost of transport (MCT) in $mlO_2.kg^{-1}.km^{-1}$ (di Prampero, 1986).

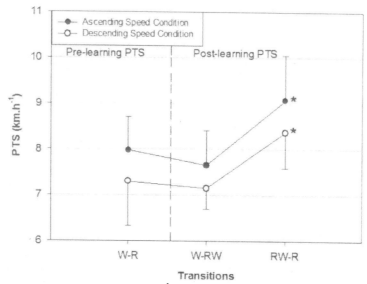

Figure 1. PTS (km.h⁻¹) of pre- and post-learning transition tests (separated by a dashed line) for both the ascending condition (filled circles) and the descending one (open circles). Walk-Run, Walk-Racewalk and Racewalk-Run represent the three types of transition.

Results and Discussion

Results showed a mean PTS for the pre-learning test of 7.64 ± 0.91 km.h⁻¹ (PTS_{W-R}: 7.97 ± 0.98 km.h⁻¹; PTS_{R-W}: 7.30 ± 0.71 km.h⁻¹, see Figure 1), which is in agreement with the literature [Ziv & Rotstein, 2009]. 10 participants (out of 13) used racewalking between walking and running during the post-learning transition test. ANOVA on PTS values with repeated measures on transition (Walk-Run, Walk-Racewalk and Racewalk-Run) and condition (ascending vs. descending) showed a main effect of condition [$F_{(1, 9)}$=17.2, $p<0.05$] and transition [$F_{(2, 18)}$=37.4, $p<0.05$]. Indeed higher PTS values were found in the ascending condition than in the descending reflecting an hysteresis. Post-hoc analysis indicates that transitions towards and from running were shifted to a significantly higher velocity after learning, whereas the PTS towards and from walking remained unchanged. It seems that the racewalking pattern became an attractive state of the locomotion dynamics in between the already existing stable gaits of walking and running. Moreover, racewalking comes in competition with the running attractor at the slowest running velocities (between 7.4 and 8.7 $km.h^{-1}$ approx.) and not with walking.

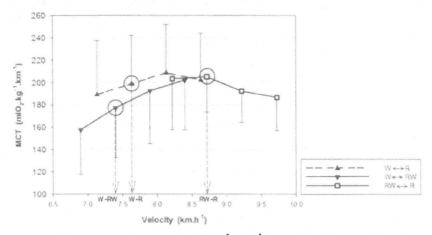

Figure 2. MCT ($mlO_2.kg^{-1}.km^{-1}$) for each transition as a function of velocity ($km.h^{-1}$). The circled symbols represent the transition level for the Walk-Run (triangle up), Walk-Racewalk (triangle down) and Racewalk-Run (open squares) transitions. One velocity level prior and two velocity levels following each transition are represented.

MCT values were submitted to an ANOVA with repeated measures on velocity (4 levels), transition (Walk-Run, Walk-Racewalk and Racewalk-Run) and condition (ascending vs. descending). Since no significant main effect of condition was found, the data were pooled together. The second ANOVA on MCT with 4 velocities × 3 transitions (Figure 2) revealed a significant interaction between the two factors [$F(6, 114)=9.7$, $p<0.05$]. When comparing MCT at PTS before and after learning, post-hoc analysis indicates a lower MCT for the walk-racewalk transition compared to walk-run transition. Whereas similar MCT values were found between the racewalk-run transition and the walk-run transition.

In sum, in the post-learning test, participants shifted from or towards walking at the same critical velocity than in pre-learning test, but at a lower MCT. In contrast the switch from or towards running seems to occur at the same critical value of MCT but at a higher velocity. Therefore, mechanical and metabolic constraints both seem to participate in the transition between gaits, but differently depending on the coordination considered. However, this first assessment will have to be supported by further analysis of the kinematic data.

References

Diedrich, F. J., & Warren, W. H. (1995). Why change gaits? Dynamics of the walk-run transition. *Journal of Experimental Psychology : Human Perception and Performance, 21,* 183-202.

Heugas, A. M., & Deschamps, T. (2006). Dynamics of competitive race walkers gaits: hypothesis of concomitant energetic cost. *World congress of Sport Medecine,* Beijing, China.

Hreljac, A. (1993). Preferred and energetically optimal gait transition speeds in human locomotion. *Medecine and Science in Sport and Exercice, 25,* 1158-1162.

Sparrow, W. A. (1983). The efficiency of skilled performance. *Journal of Motor Behavior, 15,* 237-261.

Ziv, G., & Rotstein, A. (2009). Physiological characteristics of the preferred transition speed in racewalkers. *Medecine and Science in Sport and Exercice, 41,* 797-804.

Studies in Perception & Action X
E. Charles & L.J. Smart (Eds.)

Coupling Gaze Data with EEG Recordings for a New Method in Studying Behavior Related Brain Activity

Magnus Holth, Audrey van der Meer & Ruud van der Weel

Developmental Neuroscience Laboratory,
Department of Psychology,
Norwegian University of Science and Technology,
N-7491 Trondheim, Norway
(http://www.svt.ntnu.no/psy/nulab/Home.html)

Multiple brain pathways based on the perceptual information of visual motion are involved in the control of eye movements. Tracking with the head and eyes a moving object that temporarily disappears behind an occluder requires perception of object permanence (Kaufman, Csibra & Johnson, 2003; Shuwairi, Curtis & Johnson, 2007) and the ability to estimate and predict the trajectory of the moving object (Rosander & von Hofsten, 2004, van der Meer, van der Weel & Lee, 1994). This, in turn, requires prospective control of eye movements, even in the case of relatively rapid saccades (Grealy, Craig & Lee, 1999).

The present study investigated in detail the control of prospective eye movements in young adults using both gaze and electroencephalography (EEG) recordings. The task comprised of several events requiring prospective control. First, participants needed to latch on with their eyes to a fast-moving object travelling under three different decelerations. The temporary occlusion of the car provoked the second prospective eye jump to the reappearance point, and finally participants pushed the response pad to stop the car at the reappearance point. All these events were used in an unconventional method for time-locking EEG data to a behaviorally defined onset for analyzing brain activity related to the control of prospective eye movements.

Method

Sixteen young adults (eight males) were included in the analyses, mean age was 24.6 years (SD = 5.1).

The participants visually tracked a horizontally fast-moving car that was projected onto a large screen. The car's final approach was temporary occluded, and a target area was defined where the participants were to stop the car by pressing a button.

The car started on the left-hand side at high speed (1.7 m/s) and moved under three different constant decelerations, "Low" (10% deceleration), "Medium" (50% deceleration) and "High" (90% deceleration). Depending on the deceleration condition, the occlusion period was between 65 and 141 ms.

EEG activity was recorded with the Geodesic Sensor Net 200 (GSN). An array of 256 Ag/AgCl sponge sensors was evenly distributed across the head surface, where Cz acted as reference electrode.

To control for where the participants were looking, eye movements were recorded with Tobii X50 infra-red eye camera and processed with the accompanying software Clear View on a HP computer.

Data acquisition was performed in one block. The participants were instructed to follow the car with the eyes and to stop the car in the designated area by pressing the response pad. A total of 210 trials (70 on each speed condition in a randomized order) were completed by each participant.

During the trial, three behaviorally defined events were selected for further analysis. The participants started the eye tracking movement with a saccade so as to catch up with the target motion (see first marker in Figure 1). The second event was the initiation of a prospective eye jump to the target area (see second marker in Figure 1). Data from the response pad marked the third event and defined when the participants stopped the car.

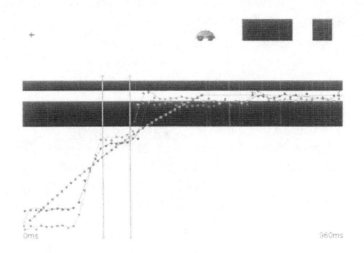

Figure 1. Eye data (↑ position and → time) from a typical trial with car travelling at "Medium" deceleration. The black areas represent the occluders. The first vertical marker represents the "Catch up" and the second vertical marker represents the "Eye jump". Squares represent the moving car, and dots represent the left and right eye.

These three behaviorally defined events were then used in an unconventional method to time-lock the continuous EEG recordings.

All EEG data analyses were carried out in the software program Brain Electrical Source Analysis (BESA) version 5.3. Bad channels were discarded by visual inspection. None of the participants included in the analyses had more than 10% of the channels defined as bad. The intervals for epochs of averaged EEG data were set to map the same period of brain activity. Because the behavioral events occurred at different latencies, these averaged EEG epochs have different intervals with the time-locking event at 0 ms. The interval was [-100; 900] ms for stimulus onset "Begin", [-600; 400] ms for both catch up event "Catch up" and eye jump event "Eye jump", and [-700; 300] ms for when the participants pushed the response pad "Response".

Due to the nature of the visual tracking task, and the impact of horizontal ocular artifacts, additional artifact correction was carried out for the EEG data.

Results and Discussion

Gaze data showed that the "Catch up" event occurred around 300ms after stimulus onset for the three deceleration conditions. The "Eye jump" event occurred about 170 ms later. Neither of these events differed significantly over the deceleration conditions, whereas the "Response" occurred at 569 ms (SD: 39.5), 648 ms (SD: 43) and 696 ms (SD: 74) for low, medium and high deceleration respectively. These data indicated that our participants started to take into account the car's deceleration after the "Eye jump", while the car was occluded, and before pressing the button to stop the car in the designated area.

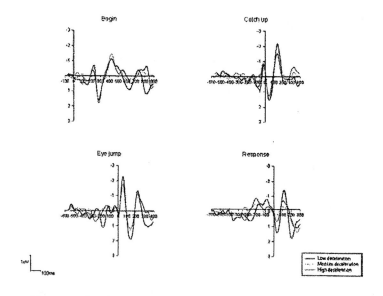

Figure 2. Averaged EEG data in Pz with the three deceleration conditions time-locked to the four events "Begin", "Catch up", "Eye jump" and "Response".

The averaged EEG data showed a negative peak for channel Pz in the same time window as where the participants started accounting for deceleration between "Eye jump" and "Response" (see Figure 2). These waveforms seemed to be clearest when time-locked to the "Eye jump" event, as evidenced by the lower variance of the negative peak latency. This was interpreted that the activity was related to the prospective "Eye jump", rather than any of the other events.

Our model of using behaviorally defined onsets in EEG analysis allowed for a direct comparison between participants independent of when the event happened, and can be considered a further step towards studying the visual brain in action (Milner & Goodale, 1995).

References

Grealy, M. A., Craig, C. M., & Lee, D. N. (1999). Evidence for on-line visual guidance during saccadic gaze shifts. *Proceedings of the Royal Society of London B, 266*, 1799-1804.

Kaufman, J., Csibra, G., Johnson, M. H. (2003). Representing occluded objects in the human infant brain. *Proceedings of the Royal Society of London B, 270*/S2, 140-143.

Milner, A. D., & Goodale, M. A. (1995). *The visual brain in action*. New York: Oxford University Press.

Rosander, K., & von Hofsten, C. (2004). Infants' emerging ability to represent occluded object motion. *Cognition, 91*, 1-22.

Shuwairi, S. M., Curtis, C. E., & Johnson, S. P. (2007). Neural substrates of dynamic object occlusion. *Journal of Cognitive Neuroscience, 19*(8), 1275-1285.

van der Meer, A. L. H., van der Weel, F. R., & Lee, D. N. (1994). Prospective control in catching by infants. *Perception, 23*, 287-302.

Studies in Perception & Action X
E. Charles & L.J. Smart (Eds.)
© 2011 Taylor & Francis Group, LLC

Fractional Derivatives and Prospective Information in Cart-Pole Balancing

David M. Jacobs[1], Daniela Vaz[2,3], & Claire F. Michaels[2]

[1]Facultad de Psicología, Universidad Autónoma de Madrid
[2]Center for the Ecological Study of Perception and Action, University of Connecticut
[3]Department of Physical Therapy, Universidade Federal de Minas Gerais

Many perceptual-motor tasks require online couplings of information and action. For example, maintaining postural balance entails continuous actions countering deviations from upright. Perceptual-motor delays are crucial to such actions. One might argue that, given a perceptual-motor delay of d ms, a perceptual-motor system can at best counter deviations that occur d ms before the corrective action. This jeopardizes successful control if the delay is large with respect to the time-scale of the action, in which case deviations might have changed substantially at the time of the corrective action.

One way to deal with perceptual-motor delays is with prospective information. Prospective information is information that specifies a future state of a system (Kim & Turvey, 1998). Notwithstanding a delay of d ms, actions are appropriately timed if based on information that specifies the state of the system d ms into the future. Our suggestion is that biological systems make use of prospective information and that one of the ways to describe this information is with the increasingly popular mathematical construct of fractional derivatives (Podlubny, 1999).

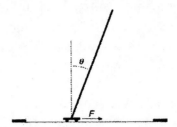

Figure 1: Schematic representation of the cart-pole task. A pole is attached to a cart with a hinge. Participants move the cart in the horizontal dimension with their dominant hand with the goal of keeping the pole from falling. *F*=Force applied by participant; *θ*=angle between pole and vertical.

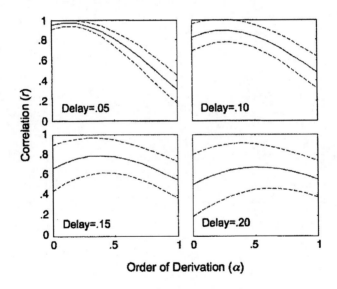

Figure 2: Average predictive value of fractional derivatives of different orders (α) with respect to recorded time-series of *θ* for delays of .05, .10, .15, and .20 s. The continuous curves give the correlations averaged over all valid experimental trials. The dashed curves give the averages plus and minus one standard deviation.

We illustrate this use of fractional derivatives with a recently performed experiment (Jacobs, Vaz, & Michaels, 2011) in which participants balanced a pole on a cart (Figure 1). Keeping the pole upright means keeping the angular deviation θ small. Without perceptual-motor delay, control described by the equation $F(t)=k\theta(t)$ leads to relatively successful balancing for a substantial range of initial conditions and k values. In this equation, $F(t)$ refers to the horizontal force applied to the cart at time t and k is a calibration parameter. The time-delayed control equation $F(t)=k\theta(t-d)$ is typically unstable (the pole falls down).

For some values of k and α, the time-delayed control system regains stability if the variable $\theta(t-d)$ is replaced by the prospective variable $\theta^{(\alpha)}(t-d)$, which is the fractional derivative of (possibly

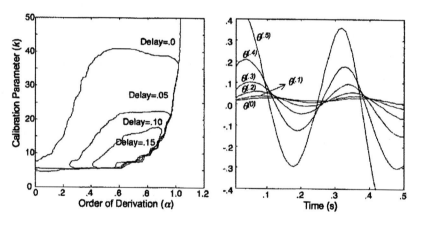

Figure 3: Left. Contour plots indicating the regions that allow successful balancing, for different delays, in a space coordinated by the fractional order of derivation, α, and the calibration constant, k. Right. Example of recorded time-series of θ and associated fractional derivatives with α ranging from 0 to 0.5 in steps of 0.1. The derivative of order 0 is θ. The other curves are the longer the more similar to the regular first order derivative of θ, which would be $\theta^{(1)}$. In our analyses the fractional derivatives were normalized so as to have similar amplitudes.

non-integer) order α of $\theta(t)$. This is so because fractional derivatives of non-integer order of a signal are often better predictors of the signal a short time-interval into the future than the signal itself. In our case, for some values of α, $\theta(t)$ is better predicted by the fractional derivative $\theta^{(\alpha)}(t\text{-}d)$ than by $\theta(t\text{-}d)$. This is shown in Figure 2 for the time-series recorded in the here-considered experiment. The figure shows the correlations of pole angle with fractional derivatives of orders between 0 and 1 (horizontal axis), for several perceptual-motor delays. To compute the correlations, a pole angle at time $t=t_0$ was related to a fractional derivative at time $t=t_0\text{-}d$. Figure 2 shows that the longer the delay, the higher the order of the derivatives of θ that best predict θ. This means that the longer the perceptual-motor delay of a system, the higher the order of the derivatives that are useful to the system.

To further illustrate this we computed a series of simulations based on the control equation $F(t)=k\theta^{(\alpha)}(t\text{-}d)$. The simulations assumed that the force exerted by participants was as described by that equation and calculated the resulting movement of the pole using the equations of motion of the system (Anderson, 1989). We ran simulations with delays of 0, .05, .10, and .15 s. The simulations were run for a maximum of 5 s, using initial conditions as recorded for one of the experimental trials. We computed the contours of the regions in the two-dimensional space coordinated by k and α within which the pole was maintained upright for more than 4 s. These contours are shown in Figure 3 (left panel). The longer a delay, the further to the right in the space one has to go to find the more useful loci. This means that a system with a longer perceptual-motor delay needs to rely on higher order derivatives, which, as shown in Figure 2, are more prospective than lower order derivatives. The right panel of Figure 3 gives an example of a recorded time-series of θ together with several fractional derivatives of this time-series.

Our experimental data indicate that the forces applied to the cart by human learners correlate reasonably well with fractional derivatives and that, after a short practice phase, the best-predicting fractional derivatives lie around $\alpha=.6$ (Jacobs et al., 2011). Hence, in the case of pole balancing, one can portray successful performance as a continuous coupling of an action (i.e., $F[t]$) to information that is sufficiently prospective with regard to the perceptual-motor delay (i.e., $\theta^{(\alpha)}[t\text{-}d]$). We find it interesting to speculate that this observation might hold more generally: Biological systems might deal with perceptual-motor delays by detecting appropriately prospective variables, which can be described with fractional derivatives.

References

Anderson, C. W. (1989). Learning to control an inverted pendulum using neural networks. *IEEE Control Systems Magazine, 9*, 31-37.

Jacobs, D. M., Vaz, D. V., & Michaels, C. F. (2011). *The learning of visually-guided action: an information-space analysis of pole balancing*. Manuscript in preparation.

Kim, N-G., & Turvey, M. T. (1998). Optical flow fields and Bernstein's "modeling of the future." In M. Latash (Ed.), *Bernstein's traditions in motor control*. Hillsdale, NJ: Erlbaum.

Podlubny, I. (1999). *Fractional differential equations: An introduction to fractional derivatives, fractional differential equations, to methods of their solution and some of their applications*. San Diego: Academic Press.

Acknowledgements. The research reported here was supported by project FFI2009-13416-C02-02 of the Spanish Ministry of Science and Innovation and by the National Science Foundation under Grant BCS-0820154.

Studies in Perception & Action X
E. Charles & L.J. Smart (Eds.)
© 2011 Taylor & Francis Group, LLC

Do Robot-child Interactions Affect Interpersonal Coordination?

Kinga Palatinus[1,3], Timothy Gifford[1,3,4], James Dixon[1,3], Anjana Bhat[2,3,4]

[1]Department of Psychology, University of Connecticut
[2]Department of Kinesiology, University of Connecticut
[3]Center for Ecological Study of Perception and Action, University of Connecticut
[4]Center for Health Intervention and Prevention, University of Connecticut

The ability to coordinate one's actions with those of another person is a crucial skill for social interactions and language acquisition, as well as learning about the world. For example children coordinate their gaze with that of their mothers to solve ambiguities in word learning. Similarly, turn taking helps to facilitate communication, understand others' intentions, and develop good interpersonal skills. Moreover, being in synchrony with another person increases one's feeling of 'connectedness' (Marsh et al., 2009).

Children with Autistic Spectrum Disorder (ASD) are characterized by a triad of behavioral deficits: social interaction, language/communication, and restricted and repetitive behaviors (DSM-IV). However, it is also known that motor impairments are common in children with ASD and they perform less synchronous movements than typically developing children in interpersonal synchrony tasks (Isenhower et al., 2009).

The current project is part of a larger study that seeks to develop a multisystem intervention based on theoretical links between motor and social behavior in ASD. The central hypothesis is that proper coordination and perception will allow children to connect socially (Leary and Hill, 1996, Grensbacher, 2008). We used robots as a tool for interacting with children with ASD for several reasons: robots are predictable, children love them, and they can have control over the interactions. It was also important for us that they can encourage whole-body interactions. The goal of the study is to investigate the effects of robot-child interactions on social and motor coordination of children with ASD.

Here we investigate the effect of robot-child interactions on interpersonal and intrapersonal coordination in typically developing children. We propose that the interactions with the robot and experimenter should improve the interpersonal coordination, but will have no impact on the intrapersonal coordination.

Method

Fourteen typically developing children participated in the experiment, forming two age groups (5 years old and 7 years old, 7 in each age group).

Training: Using a commercially available humanoid robot (iSobot), a four-week intervention protocol was developed for training. Children participated in the 'robot imitation game', which included various karate and dance movements for 8 sessions in total. Over these sessions the interactions were systematically increased in complexity.

Testing: Before and after the training, children were asked to perform some simple actions on their own: clapping with cymbals, marching, and shaking maracas. Then children were asked to play a copying game with a leader, which contained the same tasks they performed alone. The leader was following a metronome beat (85 and 95 bpm) through earphones.

Motion data was recorded during the pre- and post-test with a Polhemus motion tracking system at 240 Hz. Markers were affixed to the back of the hands and feet.

Results and Discussion

To investigate the synchrony between the leader and the child, we used cross-recurrence quantification analysis (CRQA) (Webber and Zbilut, 1994). CRQA quantifies important aspects of the coordination between two time series. By using delayed copies of the single time series, we can reconstruct the phase space, all the possible states of the system. In CRQA, both time series are embedded in one phase space that allows us to evaluate when a region is shared by the two systems (Shockley, 2005). When the trajectories are within a given radius, it qualifies as recurrence. Repeated recurrences allow us to measure the length of time in a shared region (Fig.1, grey tube). To allow for the possibility of changes in the recurrence measures over time, we applied an *epoching* procedure: instead of quantifying the whole time series, we divided it into smaller time windows (Webber and Zbilut, 2005). The length of recorded time series was 4800 data points, each window consisted of 1000, overlapped by 20%.

In order to compare coordination in the pretest and posttest, we performed growth curve analysis on the meanline variable. Predictors were pre-post, type of coordination (intra-inter), age and

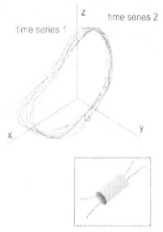

Figure 1. Phase space reconstruction

epoch. Seven-year-olds showed a significant improvement for interpersonal, but not intrapersonal, coordination (pre-post x coordination type = 7.99, z = 3.52). 5-year-olds did not show this effect coordination (pre-post x coordination type = 3.79, z = 1.49).

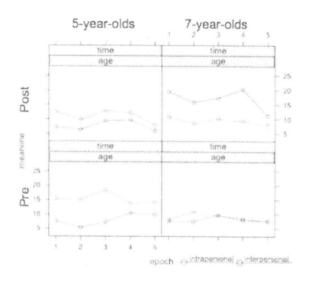

Figure 2. Meanline differences in the two age groups

Our results show a specific effect of the robot training: robot-child interactions improved the motor coordination of the older children in the social context. However, the younger children showed no improvement. This may indicate a developmental difference in ability to coordinate with an adult. The robot training did not have an effect on the intrapersonal coordination for either age group.

The improvement in the older age group is promising for the future development of intervention protocols for children with ASD.

References

Gernsbacher, M. A., Stevenson, J. L., Khandakar, S., & Goldsmith, H. H. (2008). Why does joint attention look atypical in autism? *Child Development Perspectives, 2, 38-45.*

Isenhower, R. W., **Marsh,** K. L., Silva, P., Richardson, M. J., Schmidt, R. C. (2009). Inter- and intra-personal coordination in autistic and typically-developing children. In: J. B. Wagman & C. C. Pagano (Eds.). *Studies in Perception and Action X.* New York, NY: Psychology Press. P40-43.

Leary, M. R., & Hill, D. A. (1996). Moving on: Autism and movement disturbance. *Mental Retardation, 34,* 39–53.

Marsh, K. L., Richardson, M. J., & Schmidt, R. C. (2009). Social connection through joint action and interpersonal coordination. *Topics in Cognitive Science,* 1(2), 320-339

Marwan, N., Romano, M. C., Thiel, M., Kurths J.(2007): Recurrence plots for the analysis of Complex Systems. *Physics Reports,* 438(5-6), 237-329

Shockley, K. D. (2005). Cross recurrence quantification of interpersonal postural activity.In M. A. Riley, & G. C. Van Orden (Eds.), Tutorials in contemporary nonlinear methods for the behavioral sciences (pp. 26-94). http://www.nsf.gov/sbe/bcs/pac/nmbs/nmbs.pdf

Webber, C. L., & Zbilut, J. P. (1994). Dynamical assessment of physiological states and systems using recurrence plot strategies. *Journal of Applied Physiology, 76,* 965-973.

Acknowledgements: This work was supported by National Institutes of Health grant R21MH089441 to Anjana Bhat (PI)"

Studies in Perception & Action X
E. Charles & L.J. Smart (Eds.)
© 2011 Taylor & Francis Group, LLC

"Do What I Say, Not What I Do"
Increased Motor Resonance with Real than Artificial Agent During Non-instructed Coordination Task

R.N. Salesse[1], M. Ntolopoulou[1], R.C. Schmidt[2],
J. Lagarde[1], T. Chaminade[3] & L. Marin[1]

[1]Movement to Health (M2H), EuroMov, Montpellier-1 University, FRANCE
[2]College of the Holy Cross, MA, USA
[3]Mediterranean Institute for Cognitive Neuroscience (INCM),
Aix- Marseille University – CNRS, Marseille, France

Action perception may involve a mirror-matching system, such that viewing an action directly activates neural networks involved in the execution of this action (Capa et al., 2010; Jeannerod, 2001; Rizzolatti & Craighero, 2004). Empirical evidence of mirror activity (or perception–action coupling) comes from studies of automatic imitation, i.e., the tendency for people to mimic others' behavior (Chartrand & Bargh, 1999). Kilner et al. (2003) asked participants to perform vertical or horizontal movement with the arm while watching a human or an industrial robot performing the same congruent or orthogonal incongruent movement. They have demonstrated that motor interference (increased variability of arm movements in the orthogonal direction of the movement performed) occurs when an actor intentionally coordinates with spatially incongruent arm movements of another person but not with the robot, suggesting that this effect is specific to interacting with other humans. However, using the same paradigm but with a humanoid robot, Oztop et al. (2005) showed an interference effect for both the human and the humanoid agents, suggesting that observing the action of humanoid robots and human agents may rely on similar mechanisms.

Explicit instruction to coordinate is a common feature of all the above experiments. But little is known about the human-robot interactions when participants are not instructed to do so. If coordinating with the action of robots and human agents relies on similar mechanisms, instructing or not to synchronize will affect similarly both situations similarly. Moreover, it was proposed that instructions significantly affect motor resonance in human-robot interactions (see Chaminade & Cheng, 2009 for a review). The following experiment was set out to compare human-human and human-artificial agent coordination when participants are not asked explicitly to synchronize with the confederate (typical situation for automatic, unconscious mimicry). We measured the impact of the agent on participants' behavior (movement variability) and on the coordination of the participant to the stimulus (Relative phase). The participants' task was to perform horizontal or vertical arm movement at their preferred frequency (with no instruction to coordinate) while watching a video displaying a human or a robot-like avatar performing vertical movements at different frequencies.

Method

Twelve self-declared right-handed students of the University of Montpellier 1 (10 males, 2 females, M= 21 years old, SD= 1.2) volunteered to participate in the experiment. Participants were randomly assigned to two experimental groups prior to the experiment (*Group effect*: Congruent/Incongruent).

Participants stood 1.5m away from the projection screen. In all conditions, participants watched 30s video sequences of an actor or a robot-like avatar (*Agent effect*: Avatar/Human) making right arm movements in the sagittal plane. The actor was extensively trained to make vertical sinusoidal movements of the right arm and was paced by a metronome at 0.4 Hz, 0.7 Hz or 1.0 Hz (*Frequency effect*). The same characteristics (frequency, amplitude, size) were applied to the movements of a geometric form roughly human-like. This avatar was made of 3D primitives (spheres, parallelepiped and cylinders). All video sequences were projected onto a 240×190 cm (see Figure 1A). Three small $1 \times 1 \times 1.5$ cm sensors were respectively fixed to the top of the right hand, to the top of the right shoulder and on the right hip (Figure 1) of all participants. Movements of the participants were recorded using magnetic motion tracking system at 240 Hz.

Participants of the Congruent group were asked to perform vertical movements with the same amplitude as the actor but at their preferred frequency (the natural one which allows maintaining the movement for hours) whatever the conditions. Participants of the Incongruent group performed horizontal movement with the same amplitude as the Congruent group. Participants in each group performed their movements watching an actor or a robot-like avatar at three different frequencies, eight times, for a total of 48 fully randomized trials lasting 30s each.

Orthogonal variance, the variance in movement trajectory in the error plane of instructed movement (i.e. the sagittal plane in congruent condition and the transversal plane in incongruent condition), was calculated to evaluate spatial interference. Frequency of the movement, an indicator of the entrainment tendency toward the observed frequency, was computed as the inverse of the averaged period of movement. Finally, we used the absolute value of the mean Relative phase to measure the coordination accuracy. Such value close to 0° indicates more coordination (more effective entrainment toward the stimulus). Because participants were not necessarily moving at the same frequency as the confederate, the slope of the relative phase was not equal to zero, so we first computed the relative phase between the participant and the confederate, and then we linearly detrended it. We finally calculated the absolute value of the circular mean of this relative phase.

Results and Discussion

2 Group (*Congruent/Incongruent*) × 2 Agent (*Avatar/Human*) × 3 Frequency (*0.4Hz/0.7Hz/1.0Hz*) ANOVAs were conducted on the Orthogonal variance of the movement performed, its Frequency, and the Absolute error of the relative phase between the participant and the confederate.

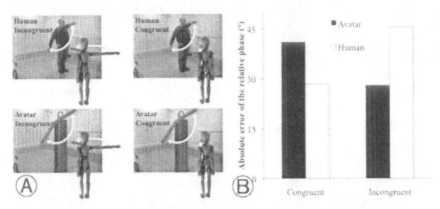

Figure 1. Panel A: Experimental apparatus, Panel B: Effect of Agency and Congruency on Absolute error of relative phase.

The Orthogonal variance variable failed to reveal any significant effect. There was a main Frequency effect ($F(2,20)=4.90$, $p<.05$, $\eta_p^2=.31$) on the frequency of the movement. Newman-Keuls decomposition of this effect shows that participants frequency evolved as a function of the stimulus frequency (respectively 0.66Hz in the 0.4Hz condition ; 0.70Hz for 0.7Hz ; and 0.76Hz for 1.0Hz), the former being significantly lower than the lastest frequency. This result suggests an entrainment of the movement frequency toward the confederate frequency. However, this entrainment is neither influenced by Agency nor by Congruency. The analysis of the Relative phase revealed a significant Group × Agent interaction ($F(1,10)=6.55$, $p<.05$, $\eta_p^2=.40$). Posthoc decomposition of this effect indicates that in the Incongruent group, participants are closer to being synchronized with the Avatar compared to the Human stimuli, while in the Congruent group, participants are closer to being synchronized with the Human than the Avatar stimuli (Figure 1B).

Motor resonance main claim is that observing a movement directly activates neural networks responsible for the execution of this movement. Furthermore motor resonance postulates that observing a movement facilitates execution of a similar movement, or instead hinders the execution of a different movement. Our results show both facilitation (decrease of absolute Relative phase for the Congruent group) and hindering (increase of absolute Relative phase for the Incongruent group) when expected, for humans compared to avatars. These findings both argue in favor of an increased effect of humans over avatar (Chaminade & Cheng, 2009). In congruent (facilitation) condition, relative phase for human is closer to 0° compared to avatar; in Incongruent (hindering) condition, relative phase for humans is further from 0° compared to avatar. Both groups point to a larger motor resonance (effect of observed action on the execution of movement) when observing humans than robots in the absence of explicit instruction to coordinate. These findings corroborate the proposal that anthropomorphism influences motor resonance.

References

Capa R.L., Marshall P.J., Shipley, T.F., Salesse R.N., & Bouquet C.A. (2010). Does Motor Interference Arise from Mirror System Activation ? The Effect of Prior Visuo-Motor Practice on Automatic Imitation. *Psychological Research*.

Chaminade, T. and Cheng, G. (2009). Social cognitive neuroscience and humanoid robotics. *Journal of Physiology Paris*, 103(3-5): 286.

Chartrand, T.L., & Bargh, J.A. (1999). The chameleon effect: The perception-behavior link and social interaction. *Journal of Personality and Social Psychology*, 76, 893-910.

Jeannerod, M. (2001). Neural simulation of action: A unifying mechanism for motor cognition. *Neuroimage*, 14, S103–S109.

Kilner, J.M., Paulignan, Y., & Blakemore, S.J. (2003). An interference effect of observed biological movement on action. *Current Biology*, 13, 522–525.

Kovacs, A.J., Buchanan, J.J., & Shea, C.H. (2010). Impossible is nothing: 5:3 and 4:3 multi-frequency bimanual coordination. *Experimental Brain Research*, 201, 249-259.

Oztop E, Franklin DW, Chaminade T, Cheng G (2005) Human-Humanoid Interaction: Is a Humanoid Robot Perceived as a Human? *International Journal of Humanoid Robotics* 2:(4) 537-559.

Rizzolatti, G., & Craighero, L. (2004). The mirror-neuron system. *Annual Review of Neuroscience*, 27, 169–192.

Acknowledgements. This experiment was supported by a grant from the Agence Nationale de la Recherche (Project SCAD # ANR-09-BLAN-0405-01) and the Integrated Project SKILLS IP (IST # 035005) from the European Commission.

Studies in Perception & Action X
E. Charles & L.J. Smart (Eds.)
© 2011 Taylor & Francis Group, LLC

To Know or Not to Know: Adaptations to Expected and Unexpected Visual Occlusions in Interceptive Actions

Pieter Tijtgat[1], Simon J. Bennett[2], Geert J.P. Savelsbergh[3], Dirk De Clercq[1] and Matthieu Lenoir[1]

[1]Dept of Movement and Sports Sciences, Ghent University,
[2]Research Inst for Sport and Exercise Sciences, Liverpool JM University,
[3]Inst for Biomedical Research into Human Movement and Health, Manchester M University, and Research Inst MOVE, Faculty of Human Movement Sciences, VU University Amsterdam

The human perceptuo-motor system has been shown to adapt to visual occlusions by altering movement preparation and processing. (Carlton, 1981; Mazyn, Savelsbergh, Montagne, & Lenoir, 2007). However, these occlusion trials were received in blocked order, and hence there was a clear expectation regarding the availability of upcoming sensory information (Zelaznik, Hawkins, & Kisselburgh, 1983). Predicated on the suggestion that the visuomotor system is cognitively impenetrable (Song & Nakayama, 2007; Whitwell, Lambert, & Goodale, 2008), differences between block and random reaching and grasping have been explained as trial-by-trial adaptations For catching, Dessing, Wijdenes, Peper, & Beek (2009) showed that early occlusion (i.e., vision occluded for approximately initial third of flight time) only had an effect when trials were presented in random order. The lack of effect on movement kinematics when trials were presented in blocked order, was suggested to result from trial-by-trial adaptations in the visuomotor gain. In other words, the ball velocity of both the previous and current trial were taken into account, and when in agreement there was an appropriate adaptation of visuomotor gain. Such adaptation is thought to occur within the neural structures controlling the motor apparatus and hence is not an influence of advance knowledge. While not intending to refute the possibility of trial-by-trial adaptations in the aforementioned work, it is important to consider that trials performed in blocked order also permit the expression of implicit advance knowledge regarding the upcoming availability of information. Accordingly, the effect of these two factors has yet to be disentangled. To this end, the present study used a design in which trials were only received in a random situation, either with or without explicit advance knowledge (see Button, Davids, Bennett & Savelsbergh, 2002, for a comparable design). Providing explicit advance knowledge was expected to enable participants to prepare an optimised response to the availability of visual information. On the contrary, the absence of explicit advance knowledge was hypothesized to result in an initial default control strategy under visual occlusion.

Method

Yellow, mid-pressured tennis balls were launched at a distance of 10 m from the participant's frontal plane by a ball-projection machine with an average ball speed of 10.62 m/s. Discrete visual occlusions of 400 ms were randomly interspersed between no occlusion trials with a pair of PLATO liquid-crystal occlusion goggles. In one condition the presence and type of occlusion was announced a priori (expected), whereas in another condition no such information was provided (unexpected). The catching movement with the right arm was tracked with a 3D motion analysis system (Qualisys, Gothenburg, Sweden) operating at 240Hz. Kinematics of 20 good ball catchers were calculated and submitted to separate 2 expectancy (expected, unexpected) x 3 occlusion (no, early, late) ANOVA with repeated measures on both factors.

Results and Discussion

Throughout the preparation and the unfolding of the catching movement, significant differences between the expected and unexpected condition were evident, and thus indicated an influence of explicit advance knowledge on the adaptive behavior in the face of visual occlusion. Contrary to our prediction of a shorter latency when an occlusion was expected, it was found that movement was initiated earlier in the unexpected (291 ms) than in the expected (307 ms) condition ($F_{1,19}=8.394$, $p<0.01$). It seems that when participants were given advance knowledge of an impending occlusion, they could adapt with different aspects of their subsequent motor response (see below, see also Tijtgat, Bennett, Savelsbergh, De Clercq, & Lenoir, 2010), rather than simply initiating the movement earlier in response to the appearance of the ball. Conversely, when participants did not know in advance that there would be an occlusion, they started to move earlier in order to locate the catching hand in the vicinity of the approaching ball, irrespective of whether an occlusion occurred or not. In the one-handed catching task, we suggest that the earlier onset is evidence of preparing for the worst case scenario (Daum, Huber, & Krist, 2007). This mode of control provided the participants with a longer temporal window (movement time was 15 ms longer in the unexpected condition, $F_{1,19}=7.930$, $p<0.05$) to negotiate an unexpected visual occlusion. Expectancy was also found to mediate the gross orientation of the catching hand ($F_{2,38}=8.061$, $p<0.01$). When there was a possibility that there might be a late occlusion (i.e. unexpected no, expected late or unexpected late occlusion trials), there was an increased forward displacement of the wrist in anticipation of having to catch without vision (goggles could be occluded from 600 ms after release until the final catch). Conversely, when it was expected that there would not be an occlusion (expected no occlusion trials) no such adaptation was evident. There were also interactions between expectancy and occlusion for PHA ($F_{2,38}=3.547$, $p<0.05$) and GT ($F_{2,38}=6.812$, $p<0.005$), which showed that expectancy influenced the final grasping phase of the catching action (Fig. 1). When late occlusion trials were expected, peak hand aperture did not increase as much as when early occlusion trials were expected, although grasping time was equal. This presumably occurred because participants expected to complete the grasp without access to vision. For late

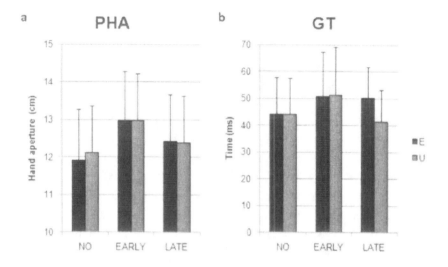

Figure 1. a Peak of hand aperture (PHA, X-axis starts at 10 cm) and *b* Grasping time (GT) as a function of occlusion (NO-EARLY-LATE) and expectancy (E = expected, U = unexpected).

occlusion trials that could not be anticipated, specific adaptations to the timing of the grasp were lacking and therefore peak hand aperture occurred later. Nevertheless, a different situation-based solution was adopted (i.e. a higher peak of hand opening velocity and a later peak of hand closing velocity) in order to prevent failure in catching performance.

Taken together, the observed differences between expected and unexpected occlusion trials suggest an influence of explicit advance knowledge on movement preparation and execution. This interpretation contrasts the exclusive notion of trial-by-trial adaptations as has been put forward in previous experiments (Song & Nakayama, 2007; Whitwell et al. 2008; Dessing et al., 2009). Notwithstanding the undeniable adaptive process based on previous trials, it is our belief that explicit (i.e. conscious or declarative) knowledge is available to the human perceptuo-motor system. Indeed, while a common neural network has been identified for procedural and declarative learning, additional brain regions (e.g. posterior parietal, superior parietal and dorsal prefrontal cortex) were activated when declarative knowledge was provided in sequence learning (Willingham, Salidis, & Gabrieli, 2002). Therefore, the current results confirm the importance of considering expectancy as an 'important constraint on movement systems' (Davids & Button 2000, p. 515). In this way, a goal keepers' fast reaction will be affected by the advance knowledge of the opponents preferred shooting direction, just like someone's walking pattern will change when a slippery floor is announced before. As such, expectancy should not be disregarded in future experimental methodologies.

References

Button, C., Davids, K., Bennett, S.J., & Savelsbergh, G.J.P. (2002) Anticipatory responses to perturbation of co-ordination in one-handed catching. *Acta Psychologica, 109,* 75-93

Carlton, L. G. (1981). Processing Visual Feedback Information for Movement Control. *Journal of Experimental Psychology-Human Perception and Performance, 7,* 1019-1030.

Daum, M. M., Huber, S., & Krist, H. (2007). Controlling reaching movements with predictable and unpredictable target motion in 10-year-old children and adults. *Experimental Brain Research, 177,* 483-492.

Davids, K. & Button, C. (2000). The cognition-dynamics interface and performance in sport. *International Journal of Sport Psychology, 31,* 515-521.

Dessing, J. C., Wijdenes, L. O., Peper, C. E., & Beek, P. J. (2009). Adaptations of lateral hand movements to early and late visual occlusion in catching. *Experimental Brain Research, 192,* 669-682.

Mazyn, L. I. N., Savelsbergh, G. J. P., Montagne, G., & Lenoir, M. (2007). Planning and on-line control of catching as a function of perceptual-motor constraints. *Acta Psychologica, 126,* 59-78.

Song, J. H. & Nakayama, K. (2007). Automatic adjustment of visuomotor readiness. *Journal of Vision, 7,* 1-9

Tijtgat, P., Bennett, S. J., Savelsbergh, G. J. P., De Clercq, D., & Lenoir, M. (2010). Advance knowledge effects on kinematics of one-handed catching. *Experimental Brain Research, 201,* 875-884.

Whitwell, R. L., Lambert, L. M., & Goodale, M. A. (2008). Grasping future events: explicit knowledge of the availability of visual feedback fails to reliably influence prehension. *Experimental Brain Research, 188,* 603-611.

Willingham, D. B., Salidis, J., & Gabrieli, J. D. E. (2002). Direct comparison of neural systems mediating conscious and unconscious skill learning. *Journal of Neurophysiology, 88,* 1451-1460.

Zelaznik, H. N., Hawkins, B., & Kisselburgh, L. (1983). Rapid Visual Feedback Processing in Single-Aiming Movements. *Journal of Motor Behavior, 15,* 217-236.

Studies in Perception & Action X
E. Charles & L.J. Smart (Eds.)
© 2011 Taylor & Francis Group, LLC

Sensorimotor Synchronization with Discrete or Continuous Slow Stimulus.

Manuel Varlet[1], Ludovic Marin[1], Johann Issartel[2], R. C. Schmidt[3], Benoît G. Bardy[1]

[1] Movement to Health, EuroMov, Montpellier-1 University, Montpellier, France, [2] Dublin City University, Dublin, Ireland, [3] Department of Psychology, College of the Holy Cross, Worcester, MA, USA.

We often move in synchrony with auditory rhythms such as while listening music, applauding or dancing with other people. The control of such coordination is one of the main issues in experimental psychology and several studies have investigated the processes underling the synchrony of our movements with a metronome (Repp, 2005). It has been demonstrated that the processes underlying the synchronization depend on whether the movement is continuous or discontinuous. More specifically, synchronized continuous and discontinuous movements present differences at the level of cycle-to-cycle dynamics. An event-based timing has been revealed in synchronization of discontinuous movements and an emergent timing in synchronization of continuous movements, which are characterized respectively by a negative or non-negative lag 1 autocorrelation of the series of movement's periods (Torre & Delignières, 2008). Continuous and discontinuous movements also present differences at the level of within-cycle dynamics. The limit cycle (velocity vs. position) of synchronized discontinuous movements has an important nonlinearity and asymmetry whereas the limit cycle of continuous movements is nearly circular with a slight asymmetry at the point where the metronome occurs (Torre & Balasubramaniam, 2009). It has been demonstrated that cycle-to-cycle and within-cycle dynamics are not independent and that the specific movement trajectories observed for continuous or discontinuous movements contribute to the achievement of emergent and event-based timings, respectively.

The continuity of the trajectory depends on the kind of rhythmic movement performed (e.g., tapping or oscillation), however, previous research has also demonstrated a significant influence of the movement frequency. The continuity of the movement decreases for lower frequencies and increases for higher frequencies (Huys, Studenka, Rheaume, Zelaznik, & Jirsa, 2008; Mottet & Bootsma, 1999). Consequently questions can be raised about whether changes in movement continuity due to stimulus frequencies may result in a switch from an emergent to an event-based timing. In addition, although clear differences between discontinuous and continuous movements have been demonstrated, it has been never investigated whether the continuous or discontinuous nature of the stimulus could influence as well the synchronization. In daily environment, auditory rhythms can be discrete such as the sound of a metronome but can be also continuous such as the sound of a violin or a trumpet. Accordingly, we investigated in the current study whether the frequency and the discrete or continuous nature of auditory stimuli may influence the between and within cycle dynamics of sensorimotor synchronization.

Method

Seated in a chair and wearing headphones, fifteen participants were instructed to synchronize for 60 s the oscillations of a wrist pendulum with a discrete or continuous auditory stimulus. We used three stimulus frequencies (0.5, 0.75 and 1.0 Hz) that ranged around the eigenfrequency of the pendulum. The discrete stimuli consisted of a tone of 80 ms at a frequency of 800 Hz and the continuous stimuli consisted of continuous sinusoidal modulation (at 0.5, 0.75 or 1.0 Hz) between 400 Hz and 800 Hz.

We discarded the first 5 s of each trial to eliminate transient behavior. The displacements of participants were centered around zero and low-pass filtered using a 10 Hz Butterworth filter. The inflexions points of the signal were extracted to compute the periods of movement. To investigate cycle-to-cycle dynamics, we computed then the autocorrelation functions and tested for the difference to zero of the lag 1 autocorrelation with single mean t-tests (e.g., Torre & Balasubramaniam, 2009). To examine within-cycle dynamics, we computed the average normalized limit-cycles over all participants. Each cycle was normalized using 60 points equidistant in time and the cycles were averaged point by point (e.g., Mottet & Bootsma, 1999).

Results and Discussion

In line with previous findings for synchronized oscillations, the lag 1 autocorrelation did not significantly differ from zero for the stimulus frequencies of 0.75 and 1.0 Hz (all $p > .05$) suggesting the involvement of an emergent timing (Torre & Delignières, 2008). However, our results demonstrated a significant negative lag 1 autocorrelation at 0.5 Hz for both discrete ($t(14) = -7.39$, $p < .05$) and continuous ($t(14) = -2.48$, $p < .05$) stimuli revealing an event-based timing, which was not expected for the synchronized oscillations of a pendulum (see Figure 1). Such results demonstrated that participants switch to an event-based timing with lower frequencies.

As depicted in the Figure 2, graphical analysis of average limit cycles demonstrated also an effect of the stimulus frequency on within-cycle dynamic in accordance with previous research (Huys et al., 2008). As indicated by limit cycles, which were more circular, the continuity of participants' movements increased with higher frequencies for both discrete and continuous stimuli. The discontinuity observed in limit cycles at 0.5 Hz for both discrete and continuous stimuli can be linked to the event-based timing revealed by the autocorrelation functions analysis. With clear effect on both between and within cycle dynamics, our results extend previous research showing that the timing changes as a function of the movement frequency (Huys et al., 2008) and

Varlet, et al.

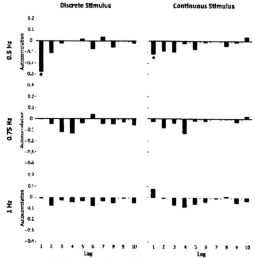

Figure 1. Mean autocorrelation functions of periods produced by participants as a function of the frequency and the discrete or continuous nature of the stimulus.

provided further evidence of close relationships between these two dynamics (Torre & Balasubramaniam, 2009).

Average limit cycles analysis also revealed an increase of the continuity of participants' movements with continuous stimuli. For all stimulus frequencies, that the average limit cycles were more circular for the continuous compared to the discrete stimulus is easily noticeable for 0.5 Hz. Although in general the limit cycles were close to a circle for both discrete and continuous stimuli for 0.75 and 1.0 Hz, the slight asymmetry toward the point where the metronome occurred was only observed for discrete stimuli (Torre & Balasubramaniam, 2009). Contrary to the frequency effect, however, the specific properties revealed for the limit cycles due to the discrete or continuous nature of the stimulus cannot be clearly linked in the current study to changes in cycle-to-cycle dynamics and we consider this issue an important research direction.

More generally, this study encourages further explorations on whether the frequency and (dis)continuous nature of auditory rhythms influence the synchronization of our movements.

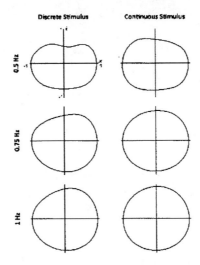

Figure 2. Mean limit cycles produced by participants as a function of the frequency and the discrete or continuous nature of the stimulus.

References

Huys, R., Studenka, B. E., Rheaume, N. L., Zelaznik, H. N., & Jirsa, V. K. (2008). Distinct timing mechanisms produce discrete and continuous movements. *Plos Computational Biology, 4.*

Mottet, D., & Bootsma, R. J. (1999). The dynamics of goal-directed rhythmical aiming. *Biological Cybernetics, 80,* 235-245.

Repp, B. H. (2005). Sensorimotor synchronization: a review of the tapping literature. *Psychonomic Bulletin & Review, 12,* 969-992.

Torre, K., & Balasubramaniam, R. (2009). Two different processes for sensorimotor synchronization in continuous and discontinuous rhythmic movements. *Experimental Brain Research, 199,* 157-166.

Torre, K., & Delignieres, D. (2008). Distinct ways of timing movements in bimanual coordination tasks: contribution of serial correlation analysis and implications for modeling. *Acta Psychologica, 129,* 284-296.

Acknowledgements. This research was supported by SKILLS, an Integrated Project (FP6-IST contract #035005) of the Commission of the European Community and by a grant from the Agence Nationale de la Recherche (Project SCAD # ANR-09-BLAN-0405-01).

Studies in Perception & Action X
E. Charles & L.J. Smart (Eds.)
© 2011 Taylor & Francis Group, LLC

Whole Body Decision Methodology

Daniela V. Vaz[1,2], Miguel Moreno[3,4], Nigel Stepp[5], Mohammad Abdolvahab[2,4], & M. T. Turvey[2,4]

[1]Universidade Federal de Minas Gerais, [2]CESPA-University of Connecticut, [3]Texas A & M University, Corpus Christi, [4]Haskins Laboratories, [5]HRL laboratories.

The elegance of the method developed by Donders to quantify what he called the "Speed of Mental Processes" has had a pervasive influence on the study of human cognitive processes. He proposed that an estimate of the duration of a determined mental operation could be obtained by comparing the time taken to complete two tasks differing only by the addition of the target mental operation (Abrams & Balota 1991). The availability of this methodology laid the foundations for mental chronometry. The vast majority of studies within this research effort have relied on reaction time (RT) techniques (Balota and Abrams 1995). Fisher and Zwaan (2008) argue that in studies of human cognition performed according to this experimental paradigm, actions have been considered as less important attachments to the apparently more sophisticated mental operations underlying cognition such as object identification, language comprehension, or decision-making. Therefore motor actions in these studies have been reduced to simple button presses under the assumption that such procedure would isolate, as much as possible, the cognitive processes of interest.

However, experiments relying primarily on button presses measures are limited, they provide a measure of the temporal requirements of various types of decision-execution processes, but can only indicate a single point in the flow of perception-action. Other events taking place throughout the decision-execution stream may be equally or perhaps even more revealing of the cognitive processes that are taking place (Balota & Abrams, 1995). Here we propose a methodology that can be useful for uncovering the continuous dynamics of processes converging to a particular response. The method was inspired in the dissatisfaction with traditional views of cognition that resulted in a "neglect of motor control in the science of mental life" (Rosenbaum, 2005), and is consonant with the notion that cognition is grounded in, and essentially inseparable from, perception and action. The method was thus named Whole Body Decision (WBD) methodology (Moreno et al., 2011). We describe the application of the method in the investigation of lexical decision.

In the visual lexical decision task a letter string is presented and the participant has to respond as quickly as possible whether the letter string is a word or not. Typically the participant is seated and the response is a key press, one hand is used to press a *Yes* key and the other hand to press a *No* key. The standard finding is that the RT to correctly decide *Yes* is shorter than the RT to correctly decide *No* (Balota & Abrams, 1995)

In order to have a larger window to look into the temporal aspects of the response, the typical lexical decision task was modified to include more significant consequences for postural stability and thus engage the whole body more evidently. The version of the task used in this study involved raising the right or left arm rapidly while standing to indicate whether the presented string was a word or not. Since Belenki et al (1967) it has been known that several postural adjustments anticipate the focal movement, perhaps for the purpose of offsetting perturbations of posture and balance. Specifically, arm movement powered by the *deltoid* muscle (shoulder) is preceded by activation of the contralateral *erector spinae* muscle (lower back) as well as activation of the ipsilateral *biceps femoris* muscle (thigh). The ispsilateral *soleus* (lower leg) which is constantly active due to its postural role in standing, demonstrates a brief period of suppression followed by increased activation before arm movement (Bouisset & Zattara, 1981). In our experiments we asked whether lexical decision, evident in the focal movement response, would also be evident in non-intentional bodily adjustments. Of significance was the question of whether the standard reaction time difference for *Yes* and *No* responses would be evident in the activity of postural muscles before the beginning of voluntary arm movement response.

Method

Surface electromyography was used to monitor the resolution of the lexical decision task at the level of focal and postural muscles. Continuous measures from the presentation of the stimuli throughout the execution of the response were employed. Two experiments were performed. In the first experiment the activity of the *deltoids, erector spinae* and *biceps femoris* was monitored bilaterally. Arm movement was monitored with an electrogoniometer. In the second experiment the *soleus* was monitored bilaterally instead of the *deltoid*.

Each experiment involved 10 native speakers of English. Four of them participated in both Experiments 1 and 2. All participants had normal or corrected to normal vision and reported no muscular disorders or abnormalities in reading competence. Standard skin preparation and electrode placement were followed by instructions to respond to stimulation as soon as possible by quickly raising the appropriate arm to indicate a response. Participants stood approximately 1 m in front of a computer screen set 1.75 m above the floor. The examiner determined trial start. Each trial consisted of a blank screen (500 ms), a fixation stimulus (white circle, 100ms), another blank screen (400 to 3400 ms) and the letter string (1000 ms). Ten practice trials (5 words and 5 non-words) were followed by 134 test trials (half words, all with similar frequency in the English language, and half non-words, displayed in random order). To avoid confounding effects of laterality, half of the participants raised the dominant arm for a *Yes* response and half raised the non-dominant arm.

Ensemble averages of electromyography activity were used to determine reaction times at the level of each muscle. A routine in MATLAB was used to precisely identify beginning of arm movement, the onset of activation for the *deltoid, erector spinae* and *biceps femoris*, as well as the onset of suppression of the *soleus*.

Results and Discussion

Results for both experiments replicated the standard *Yes-No* difference in reaction times. A paired *t*-test revealed that the RT to correctly indicate *Yes* with arm movement was significantly shorter then the RT to indicate *No*. On average, participants took 650 ms to respond *Yes* and 720 ms to respond *No* in the first experiment ($p < 0.001$) In Experiment 2, probably because four of the participants were performing the task for the second time, the average RT was shorter, at 525ms for *Yes* and 601ms for *No* ($p < 0.001$)

In addition, the electromyography of the postural muscles confirmed the specificity of postural adjustments. Analyses of Variance (ANOVA) revealed that the patterns of activity were clearly distinct for raising the right and left arms ($p < 0.001$ and $p < 0.01$ for the first and second studies, respectively). The specificity of these patterns indicated that postural adjustments could be reliably used as indices of the lexical decision.

ANOVA of muscle activity revealed that the *Yes-No* difference in RT was present not only in the arm response, but in all muscles tested ($p < 0.01$ in both experiments). Onsets of muscle activity for *Yes* responses were approximately 60 to 70ms shorter than onsets for *No* responses, in both experiments. A significant decrease in RT was found across muscles, again in both experiments ($p < 0.001$ and $p < 0.01$). For instance in Experiment 2 the *biceps femoris* anticipated the *Yes* arm response by approximately 128 ms and the *No* response by approximately 118 ms (Figure 1 and 2).

This first pass in the application of the WBD methodology focused on RT measures and showed that the execution of a lexical decision response starts taking place much more quickly than traditional paradigms suggest. Nevertheless the strength of the WBD methodology lies in the richness of measures it can offer. In addition to RT estimations, the method provides scope for measures consistent with Balota and Abrams (1995) claims that

Vaz, et al.

behaviour subsequent to response initiation can inform about cognitive processes. Further studies will investigate the temporal structure of EMG signals across measurement sites can reveal any continuity of processes throughout the stimulus presentation, decision, and execution. More specifically, further studies will tackle the question of whether decision and execution comprise a seamless continuous process.

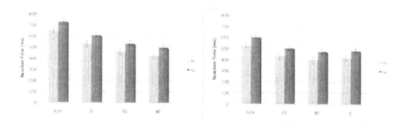

Figure 1. Reaction times across measurement sites for experiments 1 (left panel) and 2 (right panel). D: *deltoid*, ES: *erector spinae*, BF: *biceps femoris*, S: *soleus*.

References

Abrams, R. A. & Balota, D. A. (1991) Mental chronometry: beyond reaction time *Psychological Science,* 2: 153-15.

Balota, D.A. & Abrams, R.A. (1995). Mental chronometry: beyond onset latencies in the lexical decision task. *J Exp Psychol Learn Mem Cogn,* 21(5): 1289-302.

Belenkii, Y. Y., Gurfinkel, V., & Paltsev, Y. I. (1967). Elements of control of voluntary movements. *Biofizika,* 12: 135–141.

Bouisset, S. & Zattara, M. (1981) A sequence of postural movements precedes voluntary movement. *Neuroscience Letters,* 22: 263-270.

Fischer, M. H. & Zwaan, R. A. (2008). Embodied language: A review of the role of the motor system in language comprehension. *The Quarterly Journal of Experimental Psychology,* 61(6): 825-850.

Moreno, M. A., Stepp, N. & Turvey, M. T. (2011, in press). Whole body lexical decision. *Neuroscience Letters.*

Rosenbaum, D. A. (2005). The Cinderella of psychology: The neglect of motor control in the science of mental life and behavior. *American Psychologist,* 60: 308-317.

Acknowledgements: National Institute of Child Health and Human Development Grant HD-01994 to the Haskins Laboratories. Partial support was provided by a scholarship from National Council for Scientific and Technological Development (CNPq-Brazil) and a fellowship from the University of Connecticut to Daniela V. Vaz.

Studies in Perception & Action X
E. Charles & L.J. Smart (Eds.)

Nested Timescales of Motor Control: a Trade-Off Study

M. L.Wijnants[1], A. M. T. Bosman[1], R. F. A. Cox[1], F. Hasselman[1], & G. Van Orden[2]

[1]Behavioural Science Institute, Radboud University Nijmegen, the Netherlands,
[2]CAP Center for Cognition, Perception, and Action, University of Cincinnati

Near the limits of coordination trade-off phenomena emerge. In the study of motor control especially speed-accuracy trade-off has played an historic role (Fitts, 1954). In this study, we employ a Fitts task in which participants drew lines back and forth two targets with a stylus, as fast and accurately as possible, for a prolonged time. We adopt the framework of control hierarchy theory (Pattee, 1973) to describe motor control in terms of nested sources of interacting constraints, acting across multiple timescales.

Specifically, we analyzed performance measures across three different timescales. The finest timescale yields a measurement of the movement trajectories themselves (*within-trial*). This description of performance is not implied by aggregate *single-trial* outcomes (speed and accuracy) which, in turn, are not implied by *supra-trial* measures ($1/f$ noise, explained below). Control hierarchy theory predicts vertical coupling among such nested performance measures (Van Orden, Moreno, & Holden, 2003).

The canonical model of speed-accuracy trade-off in goal directed movement is Fitts' law, which linearly relates movement time and movement amplitude in accurate aiming movements (Fitts, 1954). The implied trade-off between speed and amplitude constitutes a *horizontal coupling*: both measurements describe performance at the aggregate level of single trials. Consequently, Fitts' original model made no predictions about movement trajectories, unlike later reformulations. For instance, Meyer's optimal control model (1988) captured movement variability as a function of movement velocity, and thus established a *vertical coupling* among timescales of performance.

In a recent study we provided another example of vertical coupling (Wijnants et al., 2009). In a challenging Fitts task, extensive practice led to faster movements, and more 1/*f* noise in movement time series. 1/*f* noise is a scaling relation between the different frequencies and amplitudes of a data signal. High-frequent changes in response are typically small, and embedded in overarching (lower-frequent) changes of higher amplitude. This statistically self-similar, fractal, nesting has the same proportional relationship across scales (Figure 1c-d), as opposed to a Gaussian white noise time series (Figure 1a-b).

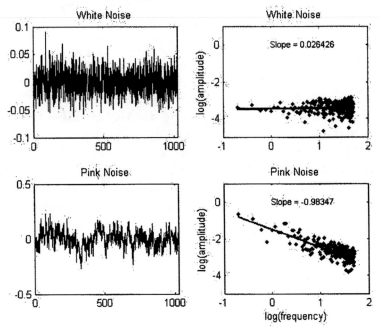

Figure 1a-d. Typical examples of white noise (a) and 1/*f* noise (c), and their respective power spectra (b and d).

The observation of vertical couplings challenges the conception of control as a causal chain of independent components, each entailing their own dominant timescale of control. Control appears to be distributed more widely. Changes in local parameters affect other local parameters, but also global parameters. In reaction, complex systems accounts conceive control as the emergent self-organization of action driven by the interaction of multiple hierarchical constraints (Juarerro, 1999). Here we pursue that suggestion empirically.

A corroboration of control hierarchy theory would imply interacting constraints across timescales in a Fitts task. These constraints include kinematic properties of the skeleto-muscular system, speed and accuracy, and $1/f$ noise in movement time and movement amplitude series. To investigate the predicted couplings, 15 participants performed a very difficult Fitts task, in which task constraints were in conflict and thus induced speed-accuracy trade-off. 15 different participants performed a very easy Fitts task, in which task constraints were compatible.

Method

Thirty undergraduate students were randomly assigned to one of the two difficulty conditions. In each case, 1100 trials were performed as fast and as accurately as possible. In the easy condition targets were 2cm larger and 8cm apart, in the difficult condition targets were 0.4cm large and 24cm apart.

Within-trial (kinematics). Our finest timescale performance measure pertains to the movement trajectories themselves. The squirt of energy inserted in each half-cycle after deceleration (Kugler & Turvey, 1987) was measured by analyzing acceleration profiles near movement reversals. To quantify the dissipation of mechanical energy we computed an index of harmonicity. Higher values (closer to 1) indicate simple harmonious arm oscillations, lower values (closer to 0) indicate extensive energy dissipation at movement reversals.

Single trial aggregates. We measured movement time (speed) and the percentage of hits (accuracy) for each participant.

Supra-trial dynamics. The presence of $1/f$ noise was measured in the movement time and movement amplitude series produced by each participant. In addition to spectral analysis (Figure 1b and d) we applied Standardized Dispersion Analysis and Detrended Fluctuation Analysis. The resulting estimates were transformed into an average fractal-dimension-statistic (*FD*) that provided our measure of supra-trial dynamics. A value of 1.5 indicates white noise, a value near 1.2 indicates 1/*f* noise.

Results and Discussion

We exploited the inter-individual variability in our experiment to correlate each of the performance measures, as shown in Table 1. The upper triangle represents the difficult task condition, the lower triangle represents the easy condition.

	Harmonicity	MT	Accuracy	FD MT	FD MA
Harmonicity		-.83**	-.91**	-.53*	.47*
MT	-.32		.76**	.45*	-.41°
Accuracy	.16	.04		.67**	-.45*
FD MT	-.17	-.04	.07		-.65**
FD MA	-.51*	.40°	.25	**.61****	

Table 1. Spearman Correlations among Measures of Harmonicity, Movement Time (MT), Accuracy, and Fractal Dimensions of Movement Time (MT) and Movement Amplitude (MA). Note: ** $p < 0.01$, * $p < 0.05$, ° $p < 0.07$

In the difficult condition, we replicated the well-established couplings among kinematic performance and speed/accuracy (vertical), and among speed and accuracy (horizontal). Also the supra-trial 1/*f* dynamics are horizontally coupled: the *FD's* of movement time and movement amplitude trade-off. In addition, 1/*f* noise is vertically coupled to harmonicity (within-trial) and speed and accuracy (single trial). In sum, slower, more accurate movements dissipate more kinetic energy, and show less 1/*f* noise in movement time series, but more 1/*f* noise in movement amplitude series. Faster, less accurate movements recycle more kinetic energy, and show more $1/f$ noise in movement time, but less $1/f$ noise in movement amplitude.

In the easy condition constraints were not in conflict. *FD*'s of movement time and amplitude were *positively* correlated, and no trade-offs were observed at the faster timescales of performance. This allowed for an efficient recycling of kinetic energy, and both fast and accurate performance. The pattern of correlations presented fully corroborates the predictions of control hierarchy theory, and confirms the role of $1/f$ noise in the coordination of perception and action.

References

Fitts, P. M. (1954). The information capacity of the human motor system in controlling the amplitude of movement. *Journal of Experimental Psychology: General, 47,* 381–391.

Juarrero, A. (1999). *Dynamics in action.* Cambridge, MA: MIT Press.

Kugler, P. N., & Turvey, M. T. (1987). *Information, natural law, and the self-assembly of rhythmic movement.* Hillsdale, NJ: LEA.

Meyer, D. E., Abrams, R., Kornblum, S., Wright, C. E., & Smith, J. E. K. (1988). Optimality in human motor performance: ideal control of rapid aimed movements. *Psychological Review, 95,* 340-370.

Pattee, H. H. (1973). The physical basis and origin of hierarchical control theory. In H. Pattee (Ed.), *The challenge of complex systems* (pp. 73–108). New York: Braziller.

Van Orden, G., Moreno, M. A., & Holden, J. (2003). A proper metaphysics for cognitive performance. *Nonlinear Dynamics, Psychology, and Life Sciences, 7, 49-60.*

Wijnants, M. L., Bosman, A. M. T., Hasselman, F., Cox, R. F. A., & Van Orden, G. (2009). 1/f scaling in movement time changes with practice in precision aiming. *Nonlinear Dynamics, Psychology, and Life Sciences, 13,* 75-94.

Studies in Perception & Action X
E. Charles & L.J. Smart (Eds.)
© 2011 Taylor & Francis Group, LLC

The Dominance and Compatibility Between Multi-modal Perceptions: Presenting Optic Flow and Acoustic Flow by Moving Room

Chih-Mei Yang, Chia-Chun Huang, and Ding-Liang Kuo

Department of Physical Education, National Taiwan Normal University

Characteristics of different substances have been metricized for comparison under the same units. For example, "°C" in temperature, "db" in sound, and "c.p." in light. But the resulting measures did not necessarily reflect what animals sense and perceive. All properties of the environment must refer to animals; properties of the environment can induce proper action in animals.

In studying perception and action coupling mechanisms based on his ecological psychology, Gibson (1979) figured out that optic energy could convey the action possibility afforded by the environment. Optic flow caused by moving animals or changing environments can provide information about the relative relationship between the animal and environment, which can cause action. Organisms can perceive these relationships directly, without knowing their character or identifying them in advance.

Similarly, acoustic flow can help animals' actions. Multi-modal perceptions help organisms to act and meet their goals. Repp and Penel (2002) asserted that auditory dominance could be observed in temporal perception in human beings. This means that audition provides more temporal information then vision. In contrast, visual dominance appears in spatial perception (Slutsky & Recanzone, 2001; Stratton, 1897; Vroomen, Bertelson, & de Gelder, 2001). In an information-rich environment, different perceptual modalities can be perceived consciously and unconsciously, but the question about how these perceptions work together is waiting for answers.

This study was aimed at manipulating different perceptual modalities to see how body sway is affected by participants' immediate surroundings and to investigate the interaction between animals and their environment. The research questions for this study are: 1) Is optic or acoustic flow dominant in perception when stand balance and posture control are required? 2) Are these two perceptual modalities compatible or conflicting?

Method

There were 12 young adults (age 20-40) who participated in this experiment. They were healthy, had normal vision, and reported no vestibular or balance-related disease. A Polhemus LIBERTY system and a MotionMonitor motion capture system were used for collecting body sway data. The experimental set-up included a moving room that can present optic and acoustic flow caused by the synchronous and asynchronous room motion, see Figure 1.

Figure 1. Experimental setup.

The participants were required to stand naturally for 40 seconds under 12 experimental conditions, each of which repeated twice. The experimental conditions were based on the levels of three factors: 1) information present in optic array only, acoustic array only, optic and acoustic synchronously, or optic and acoustic asynchronously by ½ cycle lag; 2) room stationary or room in motion; 3) participants' action requirements of following or non-following, but the conditions of following action required in room stationary were excluded.

There were 7200 points of body and room positions recorded at 240 Hz during the middle 30 seconds in each trial. Standard deviations (SDs) for each trial were calculated for body sway, and cross-correlations between participants and room motion were computed. Then both of them were statistically analysed by one-way repeated design ANOVAs for verifying the roles of the optic and acoustic flow in perception mechanisms.

Results and Discussion

1. Body sways
   1.1. Non-following standing:
   Body sways differed in the eight experimental conditions ($F(7,217) = 2.089$, $p < .05$, $\eta^2 = .05$). The post hoc comparison shows that the body sways in "acoustic information only" are larger than others, but the difference between optic and acoustic flows could not be observed.
   1.2. Following standing:
   There were differences in body sways while participants were required to follow the room motion based on optic information, acoustic information, or both ($F(5,155) = 45.654$, $p < .05$, $\eta^2 = .43$). The post hoc comparison shows that body sway in optic following was larger than in acoustic following. This result was different from non-following standing. It means that the optic modality can provide more information to help following movements. In addition, the presence of optic information decreased body sways during acoustic following. It means the optic information would interfere with acoustic perception.

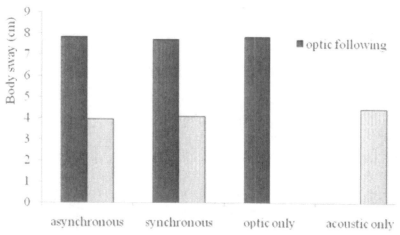

Figure 2. Body sway in conditions of following standing.

2. Cross correlation

There were differences in cross correlation coefficients among different conditions ($F(9,270) = 107.034$, $p < .05$, $\eta^2 = .21$). The post hoc comparison shows that the correlation is stronger while following optic information, than while following acoustic information, and the correlation during non-following is weakest.

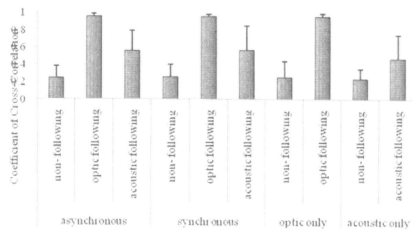

Figure 3. Coefficients of cross correlation among conditions of room motion.

This result confirms the aforementioned body sways comparison. It also demonstrates that the perception of optical information can help animals act properly.

Based on the data from the experimental manipulations, we concluded that 1) Optic flow is dominant in perception when stand balance and posture control are required. 2) Acoustic perception can interfered with optic information, but reverse effect will not happen.

References

Gibson, J. J. (1979). *The ecological approach to visual perception.* Hillsdale, NJ: Lawrence Erlbaum.

Repp, B. H., & Penel, A. (2002). Auditory dominance in temporal processing: New evidence from synchronization with simultaneous visual and auditory sequences. *Journal of Experimental Psychology: Human Perception and Performance, 28,* 1085-1099.

Slutsky, D. A., & Recanzone, G. H. (2001). Temporal and spatial dependency of the ventriloquism effect. *Neuroreport, 12,* 7-10.

Stratton, G. M. (1897). Vision without inversion of the retinal image. *Psychological Review, 4,* 341-360 and 463-481.

Vroomen, J., Bertelson, P., & de Gelder, B. (2001). The ventriloquist effect does not depend on the direction of automatic visual attention. *Perception & Psychophysics, 63,* 651-659.

Studies in Perception & Action X
E. Charles & L.J. Smart (Eds.)

Chapter 3:

Affordances

Studies in Perception & Action X
E. Charles & L.J. Smart (Eds.)
© 2011 Taylor & Francis Group, LLC

The Effects of Movement/Perceptual Experiences and Walking Speed on Perceiving Affordances for Aperture Passage

Chih-Hui Chang & Ming-Young Tang

National Kaohsiung Normal University, Kaohsiung, Taiwan

Affordances are properties of the animal-environment system that describe the relationship between the animal and the environment (Gibson, 1986; Stoffregen, 2003). Providing movement/perceptual experiences has positive effects on perceiving object lengths (Riley, Wagman, Santana, Carello, & Turvey, 2002), perceiving affordances for catching fly balls (Oudejans, Michaels, Bakker, & Dolne, 1996) and perceiving affordances for going under passages (Stoffregen, Yang, Giveans, Flanagan, & Bardy, 2009). We investigated the influence of movement/perceptual experiences during the perception of affordances for aperture passage. We were interested in whether the compatibilities of the movement/perceptual experiences of walking, i.e. floor walking versus treadmill walking would affect the perception of affordances differently.

When walking through an aperture, the minimum aperture width that a person can walk through is distinct for different walking speeds (Warren & Whang, 1987), and the perception of whether an object can be carried through an aperture is different for walking and running (Wagman & Malek, 2007). We were interested in whether individuals would be able to perceive their pass-abilities at the slowest and fastest daily-life walking speeds. Moreover, previous studies (Adolph & Avolio, 2000; Mark, 1987; Wagman & Taylor, 2005) have shown that individuals were able to perceive affordances when their action capabilities were altered due to changes in body dimensions. We also investigated the effects of altered body dimensions on perceiving affordances for aperture passage.

Method

Thirty-six healthy adults volunteered to participate and were randomly assigned to either a floor walking group (n = 18, age = 20.85 ± 3.15 yrs., shoulder width = 40.98 ± 2.28 cm) or a treadmill walking group (n = 18, age = 20.13 ± 1.57 yrs., shoulder width = 41.05 ± 3.32 cm). The shoulder widths of the participants in the two groups were not significantly different, $F(1, 34) = 0.004$, $p > .05$. All were healthy, active, had no history of motor disorders and had normal or corrected normal vision. Consent was obtained from participants prior to the study. The experimental procedure was approved by the Institute Review Board (IRB) of National Kaohsiung Normal University.

The experiment was conducted in a 38 m long, 3.2 m wide and 3 m high corridor. A 1.77 m wide and 2.14 m high doorframe was located 5 m from the end of the corridor. Two pieces of 0.88 m wide and 2.14 m high heavy black curtain were hung on the doorframe alone a curtain track to form an aperture. The aperture could be moved manually by the experimenters.

There were two Movement/Perceptual conditions (M/P condition), a floor walking and a treadmill walking conditions. In the floor walking condition, participants were required to stand 14.5 m away from the aperture and walk toward it. They were then required to make judgments in a judgment zone, which was 3.5 m away from the aperture and 1.8 m long. In the treadmill walking condition, participants were required to make judgments when they were walking on the treadmill, which was 3.5 m away from the aperture. In both M/P conditions, the judgment was regarding whether they could walk through the aperture with a specific walking speed, and without rotating their shoulders. Participants were required to walk at both the fastest and the slowest walking speeds. In the fastest and slowest walking conditions, participants walked at the fastest and the slowest speeds, respectively, that they would walk in their daily lives. We measured the actual walking speeds of the two groups. A pair of T-shaped shoulder pads, which artificially added 16 cm to their shoulder widths, were put on the participants' shoulders.

Methods of limits (Goldstein, 2007) were used to determine the absolute threshold of the minimum passable width. The process included two stages: in the first stage, the aperture width could be moved in either ascending or descending order from 35 cm to 107 cm in 12 cm increments. Once the absolute threshold of the first stage was determined, the absolute threshold and ±2, ±4, and ±6 were used in the second stage in either ascending or descending order. The absolute threshold of the second stage was the participants' perceived minimum aperture width.

Results and Discussion

Arbitrary units
    Perceived minimum aperture width in cm was the dependent variable. A 2(M/P condition) × 2 (Walking speed) × 2 (Shoulder pad) mixed design 3-way ANOVA with the last two factors as repeated measures showed a significant Shoulder pad effect, $F(1, 34) = 229.87$, $p < .05$, partial $\eta^2 = .87$. When wearing shoulder pads (60.67 ± 10.50 cm), the perceived minimum aperture width of the participants was larger than when not wearing shoulder pads (44.42 ± 9.66 cm). The Walking speed effect was significant, $F(1, 34) = 11.02$, $p < .05$, partial $\eta^2 = .25$. The perceived minimum aperture width in arbitrary units was larger when participants walked at the fastest speed (53.34 ± 13.43 cm) as compared to when they walked at the slowest speed (51.75 ± 12.48 cm). The M/P condition effect and the interaction effects were not significant, each $p > .05$ (see Figure 1a).

Body-scaled units
    The ratio of the perceived minimum aperture width to the perceiver's shoulder widths, π, was the dependent variable. A 2(M/P condition) × 2 (Walking speed) × 2 (Shoulder pad) mixed design 3-way ANOVA with the last two factors as repeated

measures showed a significant Walking speed effect, $F(1, 34) =$ 11.08, $p < .05$, partial $\eta^2 = .25$. The perceived minimum aperture width in body-scaled units was larger when participants walked at the fastest speed (1.09 ± 0.22) as compared to when they walked at the slowest speed (1.06 ± 0.19). The Shoulder pad effect was not significant when the body-scaled information was taken into consideration, $F(1, 34) = 0.41$, $p > .05$. The M/P condition effect and the interaction effects were not significant, each $p > .05$ (see Figure 1b).

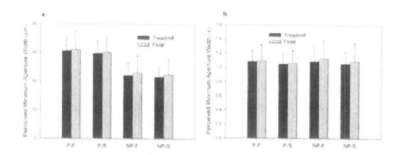

Figure 1. Perceived minimum aperture width in arbitrary units (a) and in body-scaled units (b) with the different walking speed conditions, shoulder pad conditions, and perceptual conditions. P-F = Pad-the Fastest walking, P-S = Pad-the Slowest walking, NP-F = No Pad- the Fastest walking, NP-S = No Pad- the Slowest walking.

Walking on a treadmill or walking on the floor did not influence the perception of affordances for walking through passages. As in previous studies (Adolph & Avolio, 2000; Mark, 1987; Wagman & Taylor, 2005), individuals learned their altered action capabilities in a brief amount of time of walking on the floor and/or treadmill and perceived the distinct affordances. Individuals perceived their pass-abilities when their body dimensions were changed due to added shouldered pads. Moreover, individuals perceived affordances for different action magnitudes; they perceived their pass-abilities for different walking speeds in both the floor walking and the treadmill walking conditions.

References

Adolph, K. E., & Avolio, A. M. (2000). Walking infants adapt locomotion to changing body dimensions. *Journal of Experimental Psychology: Human Perception and Performance, 26*, 1148-1166.

Gibson, J. J. (1986). *The ecological approach to visual perception.* Hillsdale, NJ: Lawrence Erlbaum. (originally published in 1979).

Goldstein, E. B. (2007). *Sensation and perception* (7th ed.). Belmont, CA: Thomson Wadsworth.

Mark, L. S. (1987). Eyeheight-scaled information about affordances: a study of sitting and stair climbing. *Journal of Experimental Psychology: Human Perception and Performance, 13*, 361-370.

Oudejans, R. R. D., Michaels, C. F., Bakker, F. C., & Dolne, M. A. (1996). The relevance of action in perceiving affordances: perception of catchableness of flyballs. *Journal of Experimental Psychology: Human Perception and Performance, 22*, 879-891.

Riley, M. A., Wagman, J. B., Santana, M.-V., Carello, C., & Turvey, M. T. (2002). Perceptual behavior: Recurrence analysis of a haptic exploratory procedure *Perception, 31*, 481-510. .

Stoffregen, T. A. (2003). Affordances as properties of the animal-environment system. *Ecological Psychology, 15*, 115-134.

Stoffregen, T. A., Yang, C.-M., Giveans, M. R., Flanagan, M., & Bardy, B. G. (2009). Movement in the perception of an affordance for wheelchair locomotion. *Ecological Psychology, 21*, 1-36.

Wagman, J. B., & Malek, E. A. (2007). Perception of whether an object can be carried through an aperture depends on anticipated speed. *Experimental Psychology, 54*, 54-61.

Wagman, J. B., & Taylor, K. R. (2005). Perceiving affordances for aperture crossing for the person-plus-object system. *Ecological Psychology, 17*(2), 105-130.

Warren, W. H., Jr., & Whang, S. (1987). Visual guidance of walking through apertures: body-scaled information for affordances. *Journal of Experimental Psychology: Human Perception and Performance, 13*, 371-383.

Acknowledgements. This research was supported by Taiwan National Science Council grant # NSC 96-2413-H-017-008. We thank Ting-Yu Lin and Suu-Yin Chen, who helped with data collection.

Studies in Perception & Action X
E. Charles & L.J. Smart (Eds.)
© 2011 Taylor & Francis Group, LLC

Affordance Compatibility Effects on the Initiation of Action Selection

Tehran J. Davis & Michael A. Riley

Department of Psychology, Center for Cognition, Action, & Perception,
University of Cincinnati

To perceive an affordance is to perceive an action-relevant relationship that holds within an animal-environment system. Given that many behaviors are planned in advance of their execution, the ability to perceive affordances prospectively is invaluable for controlling goal-directed actions (Hirose & Nishio, 2001; Turvey, 1992). Action selection is often constrained by the existence of and the perception of some particular affordance. In many cases, whether one action or another is afforded will result in qualitatively different behavior (Fajen & Turvey, 2003). For example, if an opening affords safe passage to a desired location, an individual may elect to pass through it. If it does not, the individual may need to find another route. This example highlights another aspect of affordances and goal directed actions—that the perception and exploitation of affordances is often not an end into itself, but is often nested within a larger occasion. For instance, getting a cup of coffee from the break room may require one to perceive and act on the pass-through-ability of several different doorways that lie between one's cubicle and the location of the coffee pot. At any given point, the route traveled may be influenced by both the immediate affordances of the environment, as well as the long-term goals of the individual. Determining how an action unfolds on-line with respect to the layout of affordances and location of the final goal was the aim of the current study.

As the first step in a larger project, we studied the effects of affordance layout on the time required to select a means of completing a goal-directed task. For dual-choice tasks, initiation times (IT) serve as an index of decision uncertainty. Previous reports have suggested that IT decreases as a function of ease of affordance perception (Stins & Michaels, 1997, 2000) and increases with the amount of uncertainty of action selection (Smith & Pepping, 2010). We used IT to assess the effects of uncertainty on action selection by asking individuals to choose one of two openings to pass through in order to safely arrive at a goal location. Individuals responded by either moving an object to the goal (via a mouse) or by pressing a key to select one aperture or the other.

Method

Sixteen participants took part in this study for course credit. Each participant sat at a table, approximately 1 m across from a computer monitor. A computer-generated environment containing an oval object, a barrier wall with two openings, and a designated goal area was projected on the monitor. Participants were assigned the task of safely moving (or imagining that they were moving) the object from the starting point at the bottom of the screen to the goal location either at the top left or top right of the screen. In order to complete this task, the object needed to pass through one of two openings in the barrier (Figure 1). The openings had five possible sizes, scaled to the width of the object: 0.85, 1.00, 1.15, 1.30, and 1.45. The two openings present on a given trial differed in size by a *small* (0.15) or *large* (0.30) amount. At least one of the two openings always afforded passage of the object. If the wider of the two apertures was on the same side as the goal, the pairing was deemed *compatible*. This arrangement yielded four compatibility conditions: *small-compatible*, *large-compatible*, *small-incompatible*, and *large-incompatible*.

Choice IT was measured in two response conditions. In the *mouse* condition, participants used a computer mouse to move the object through one of the openings and to the goal without making

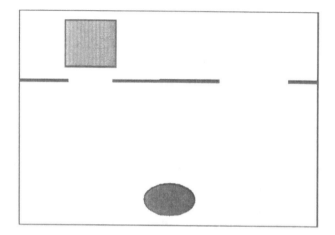

Figure 1. Layout of the virtual environment. The square at the top left is the goal location. In this example, the aperture that afforded passage (on the right) is incompatible with the location of the goal.

contact with the barrier. Once participants moved the object to the goal, the screen was cleared and the object was returned to its starting position for the next trial. In the *key press* condition, the object remained fixed at the starting position for the duration of trial, and participants selected the aperture through which they would take the object by pressing a corresponding button (left button for left opening, right button for right). Choice IT was taken as the time that it took for participants to initiate an action. In the *key press* condition, IT was measured as the amount of time from stimulus presentation until a button was pressed. In mouse movement trials IT was taken as the amount of time from stimulus presentation until the object had been vertically displaced from the starting point at least 1.25cm.

Results and Discussion

IT data were submitted to a 2 (response type) × 2 (size) × 2 (compatibility) ANOVA. A main effect was found for *response type*, $F(1,15) = 12.15$, $p < .01$, $\eta_p^2 = .44$, such that mean IT was faster in the mouse movement condition (despite the conservative criterion) than in the key press condition (Figure 2). The *response type × size* [$F(1,15) = 8.62, p < .05, \eta_p^2 = .36$] and *response type × compatibility* [$F(1,15) = 19.35, p < .01, \eta_p^2 = .57$] interactions were also significant. Simple-effects ANOVA for *key press* IT revealed main effects of *size* $F(1,15) = 23.18, p < .01, \eta_p^2 = .61$, with IT in the small condition ($M = 928 \pm 227$ ms) being greater than in the large condition ($M = 873 \pm 192$ ms), and *compatibility, $F(1,15) = 31.50, p < .01, \eta_p^2 = .68$,* such that IT in *compatible* ($M = 844 \pm 201$ ms) conditions was faster than *incompatible* ($M = 957 \pm 219$ ms) conditions. Simple-effects ANOVA for *mouse movement* IT revealed a similar *compatibility* effect, $F(1,15) = 5.34, p < .05, \eta_p^2 = .26$, such that IT in *compatible* ($M = 714 \pm 142$ ms) was faster than *incompatible* ($M = 740 \pm 148$ ms) conditions. No *size* effect was observed for the *mouse movement* condition.

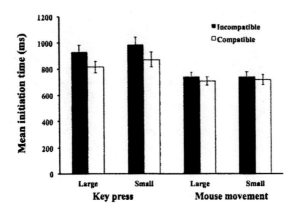

Figure 2. Mean *key press* and *mouse movement* IT as a function of compatibility and size conditions.

The effect of *size* was only present in the *key press* condition, while the effects of *compatibly* was greater in the *key press* condition than in the *mouse movement* condition. Taken together, these results suggest that each of these effects on choice IT was attenuated when having participants perform the functional action of moving towards a goal versus mapping that action to an arbitrary response (a key press).

References

Fajen, B. R., & Turvey, M. T. (2003). Perception, categories, and possibilities for action. *Adaptive Behavior, 11*, 276-278.
Hirose, N., & Nishio, A. (2001). The process of adaptation to perceiving new action capabilities. *Ecological Psychology, 13*, 49-69.
Stins, J. F., & Michaels, C. F. (1997). Stimulus-response compatibility is information-action compatibility. *Ecological Psychology, 9*, 25-45.
Stins, J. F., & Michaels, C. F. (2000). Stimulus-response compatibility for absolute and relative spatial correspondence in reaching and in button pressing. *The Quarterly Journal of Experimental Psychology, 53A*, 569-589.
Turvey, M. T. (1992). Affordances and prospective control: An outline of the ontology. *Ecological Psychology, 4*, 173-187.

Acknowledgements. Supported by NSF grants BCS 0926662 and BCS 0728743.

Studies in Perception & Action X
E. Charles & L.J. Smart (Eds.)
© 2011 Taylor & Francis Group, LLC

Perceiving Affordances for Gap Crossing: Accuracy, Prediction, and Age Effect

Chia-Pin Huang[1], Hank Jwo[1], Chung-Yu Chen[2], and Chih-Mei (Melvin) Yang[1]

[1]National Taiwan Normal University, [2]National Taiwan College of Physical Education

The ecological approach (Gibson, 1979) has been widely applied to the study of motor behavior, especially the relationship between individuals' actions and their surroundings. Environmental information is an important influence on individuals' action. They have to perceive what the environment affords and act appropriately. This linking of behavior and information has been described as perception-action coupling.

Perceptual ability is affected by brain development in early age (Gallahue & Ozmun, 2006). As infants grow up, they gain more movement experiences and depend on more environmental information; as a result, their body-scaled ratio becomes a critical relevant reference. Besides body-scaled ratio, the range of motion in hip and leg-strength, which decreases with age after 30 years old, can affect lower-limb movements of older adults (Konczak, Meeuwsen, & Cress, 1992). Thus, several critical factors concerning the lower-limb can influence individuals' actions in their environment (e.g. stepping on stages, gap crossing, obstacle crossing etc.). From developmental perspective, children primarily estimate their environment through walking and climbing experience. After 12 years old, both perceptual and movement systems mature, and individuals can perceive their environment more precisely. Body-scaled ratios play a more important role in perception-action coupling.

Previous research has focused on visual deprivation in favor of haptic information (generated with sticks) when exploring the ability to cross gaps. There are no cross-sectional studies examining different aged individuals, and the main factors that might affect their ability to cross are still unknown. Therefore, the purpose of this study is to examine perception-action coupling and the main factors in gap crossing across different age groups.

Method

Twenty-two children in late childhood ($M = 12.1 \pm 0.3$ yrs), eighteen adults ($M = 25.1 \pm 6.8$ yrs) and nineteen older adults ($M = 71.6 \pm 5.0$ yrs) were recruited in this experiment. All participants were females. Participants' height, eye-height, leg length, leg strength, and range of motion in hip were measured. The first three body segment parameters were measured by Martin-type anthropolometer (T. K. 11242, Takei Scientific Instruments.). Height was measured with participants standing on ground bare foot, and looking ahead. Eye-height was defined as the distance from the pupil of the eye to ground where the participants stood. Leg length was calculated by standing height minus seated-height from the ground.

Leg strength was measured by Back-leg lift dynamometer (T. K. K. 5710C, Takei Scientific Instruments.). Participants stood on dynamometer with parallel feet, and bent their knees about 110°. To get more precise numbers, grips were adjusted to let participants extend their arms straight and pull upward. They kept upper body upright and stepped on dynamometer forcefully. Every participant executed the trial twice. To measure the angle of hip joint, protractor was used. In the beginning, participants were requested to keep prone posture and lifted their legs with straight knees. This is the way maximum extension angle was measured. To measure maximum bent angle, participants were asked to lie down and lift their thigh with bent knees. They brought their knees as close to the front of their chests as possible. The maximum extension angle and maximum bent angle were combined as the maximum hip joint angle.

Two tasks were performed by each participant. First, they judged the crossability of gaps. Second, they had to actually cross the gaps. The gap was constructed by two plastic cushions. One cushion is 6m long and 2m wide, and the other is a 2m × 2m square (see Figure 1). Camera was placed in the middle of the gap to record the movement pattern of crossing. Participants stood at 6m from the gap, and they were sheltered by a black curtain, which totally obstructed the visual information when experimenters adjusting the gap. In the judgment situation, the curtain was removed for 3 sec and then covered back again. During the actual crossing trails, participants walked toward the gap with normal walking speed and then crossed the gap. In judging or actual crossing, the gap widths showed up from 50 cm to 130 cm, and 5 cm were added each time. All participants had to conduct 17 trails in each condition.

A 3 (age) × 2 (crossing) mixed design two-way ANOVA with crossing as repeated measure, was used to analyze the interaction between ages and crossing conditions. Stepwise regression was used to find out the correlation among height, eye-height, leg-length, leg strength, range of motion in hip and judged versus actual crossing conditions. Principal component analysis was used to examine whether the same qualities could be categorized.

Results and Discussion

The differences between judging and actual crossing in children and older adults were higher then adults. Gallahue and Ozmun (2006) indicated that lack of movement experience caused errors in visual-motor coordination. In contrast, infants with more experience exhibited better movement patterns. Moreover, infants detected more relevant information from environment.

However, the disparity between perception and action decreased as age increases. Children below 12 years old had less confidence and movement ability. As they grew older, they gained more movement experience. This allowed them to achieve more accurate couplings between perception and action. For older adults, fitness might be a major factor of disparity among perception and

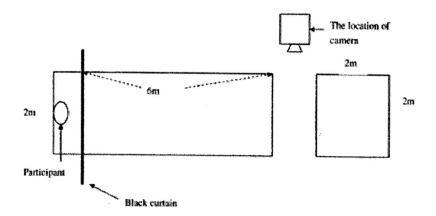

Figure 1. A schematic top view of the gap and camera position

action. With aging, human beings lost their muscular fibers and subsequently their muscle strength. Relatedly, the skeletal system lost joint flexibility as people got older.

The range of motion in hip was found the best predictor of actual gap crossing across these three ages groups. Eye height and leg length were also positively correlated with older adults' judged gap crossing; perceptual judgment and leg strength were also positively correlated to actual gap crossing (see Table 1). Only eye-height and leg-length were correlated in the judging condition for older adults. Also, no relationship could be found in body-scaled factors in the judging condition for the child and adult groups. The disparity between judging and actual crossing conditions was less in the adult group then in the child and older adults groups. This result showed that adults had better perception-action coupling ability, and in particular, range of hip motion was found to be the key predictor. The results also support the findings of earlier research (Konczak, et al., 1992). In the child group, the coupling ability between perception and action was not well-developed, so that they could not match environmental information with their action ability. The disparity of perception-action coupling in older adults group was due to the underestimation of their ability.

Factors	Children		Adults		Older adults	
	Judging	Actual	Judging	Actual	Judging	Actual
Distance of judgment	-----	.008	-----	-.380	-----	.568*
Height	-.114	.079	-.064	.311	.095	.318
Eye-height	-.111	.103	-.419	.274	.561*	.248
Leg-length	-.142	.163	-.420	.415	.551*	.155
Range of motion in hip	.128	.472*	-.007	.543*	.529*	.423*
Muscle strength	-.013	.218	-.139	-.142	.356	.576*

* $p < .05$

Table 1. The correlation among factors and judged and actual crossing

All of the predictors could be categorized into two major portions. It suggested that individuals could judge the environment not only by body-scaled ratio, but also physical fitness factors such as hip flexibility and leg strength. The cumulative explained variances were higher then 66% in three age groups, suggesting that the variance could represent original scores well. These results were in line with the ecological perspective (Stoffregen, Yang, & Bardy, 2005), which indicated that body-scaled ratios were relevant references for individuals to use when judging environmental information.

References

Gallahue, D. L., & Ozmun, J. C. (2006). *Understanding motor development: Infants, children, adolescents, adults* (6th ed.). New York: McGraw-Hill.

Gibson, J. J. (1979). *The ecological approach to visual perception.* Boston: Houghton-Mifflin.

Konczak, J., Meeuwsen, H. J., & Cress, M. E. (1992). Changing affordances in stair climbing: The perception of maximum climbability in young and older adults. *Journal of Experimental Psychology: Human Perception and Performance, 18,* 691-697.

Stoffregen, T. A., Yang, C. M., & Bardy, B. G. (2005). Affordance judgements and nonlocomotor body movement. *Ecological Psychology, 17*(2), 75-104.

Studies in Perception & Action X
E. Charles & L.J. Smart (Eds.)
© 2011 Taylor & Francis Group, LLC

Wheelchair Users' Locomotion Controlled to Fit the Potential Traffic around Hallway Intersections

Makoto Inagami[1], Akiko Hibiya[2], and Ryuzo Ohno[3]

[1]Department of Information Processing, Tokyo Institute of Technology, Japan
[2]Mitsubishi Estate Building Management Co., Ltd., Japan
[3]Department of Built Environment, Tokyo Institute of Technology, Japan

Intelligence tends to be associated with abstract thought, fertile imagination, highly developed languages, and so on; however, locomotion control is also an important and fundamental form of intelligence (Turvey & Shaw, 1995). To move around safely and smoothly, it is necessary to not only avoid visible obstacles but also control locomotion by predicting the situation of currently invisible spaces (e.g., around a blind corner).

This study specifically investigates the behavior of wheelchair users while turning hallway intersections. We assume that they control such daily behavior more prospectively than able-bodied people. The hypothesis is that wheelchair users' locomotion is precisely controlled to fit the probability that hidden pedestrians will appear from behind the corners (i.e., "potential traffic"). Previous studies on wheelchair locomotion suggest that long-term training is necessary for able-bodied participants to move accurately (e.g., Higuchi, Takada, Matsuura, & Imanaka, 2004). Accordingly, our experiment employed three wheelchair users with over ten years' experience (A: 34-year-old woman, B: 42-year-old man, and C: 24-year-old man).

Method

The participants' locomotion was observed under eight conditions that combined two levels of spatial configuration (L- or

T-shaped), viewability (viewable or blind), and the amount of traffic (low or high). Figure 1 illustrates the four hallway intersections used in the experiment. The start line was six meters behind each intersection. With regard to the viewable routes, the walls of the inside corners were equipped with glass windows. The experiment was conducted when there were very few pedestrians, and under low-traffic conditions, the participants moved naturally in accordance with the situation. In contrast, under high-traffic conditions, they watched a video of a heavily trafficked hallway on a laptop computer and then moved under the assumption that they were in the same situation.

During the experiment, an experimenter followed behind the participant and recorded his or her behavior with a video camera. Based on the video images, we measured the planimetric position of the wheelchair, which was
defined as the middle point between the lower ends of the right and left wheels, at 0.4-s intervals. To achieve precise measurements, we placed marks (2-cm-square black stickers) on the floor at 0.3-meter intervals. By connecting the wheelchair positions, we created the participants' locomotion paths (Figure 2).

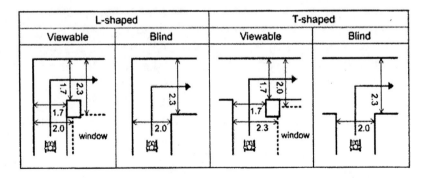

Figure 1. Intersections used as experimental routes. The L-shaped routes, although actually left-hand turns, are horizontally reversed for simplicity. The floor plans are drawn in meters.

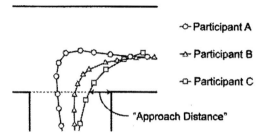

Figure 2. Examples of locomotion paths and an "approach distance."

Results and Discussion

First, we modeled the potential traffic of each experimental condition, which was defined as the relative balance of the probabilities that hidden pedestrians will appear from the right vs. left sides at the intersection. As illustrated in Figure 3a, the probabilities are classified into four levels and represented by the arrows. The blind corners in the high- and low-traffic conditions have three and two arrows, respectively. In each traffic condition, the viewable corners have one arrow, and the outside walls of the L-shaped intersections have no arrow. By contrasting the right and left probabilities of each condition, we obtained the balances of potential traffic. As shown in Figure 3a, the eight conditions are ranked and arranged according to the resultant right/left balances.

Next, we quantified the locomotion paths by measuring the distance to the inside corner of the intersection (i.e., "approach distance," see Figure 2). In this measurement, we modified some data as follows. In view of the difference in entrance width between the viewable and blind intersections (Figure 1), the approach distances for the T-shaped blind route were multiplied by 1.7/2.0. This is because the locomotion paths at the T-shaped intersections seemed to result from the trade-off of the required distances to the inside vs. outside corners, and were therefore thought to be dependent on the entrance width.

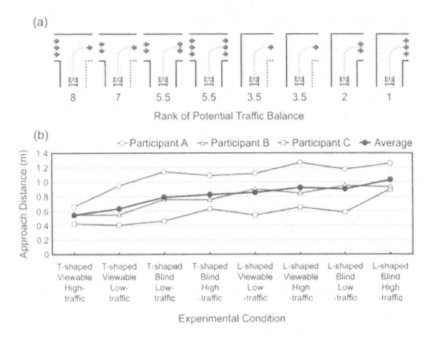

Figure 3. Relationship between the modeled potential traffic (a) and the measured approach distances (b).

Figure 3 shows the relationship between the modeled potential traffic and the measured approach distances. As observed in Figure 3b, the data with respect to the three participants, while showing clear individual differences, share a pattern that slopes upward from left to right. The Kendall's coefficient of concordance indicates that the pattern is significantly consistent across the participants, $W = .83$, $p = .015$. From this result, we averaged the approach distances across the participants (Figure 3b) and examined the correlation with the potential traffic. The Kendall's rank correlation coefficient indicates a significant correspondence between the averaged approach distances and the potential traffic balances, $\tau = .89$, $p = .001$. This result supports our hypothesis that wheelchair users' locomotion is precisely controlled to fit the potential traffic around intersections.

Note that the result does no imply that the participants performed such stochastic calculations and then chose the locomotion paths. In this experiment, the occluded spaces appeared gradually as the participants proceeded. Thus they could not make any action plans in advance. Instead, their locomotion made new information available and, at the same time, the information controlled the locomotion. Macroscopically, the locomotion was guided to fit the "field" of environmental information (Gibson & Crooks, 1938; Kadar & Shaw, 2000). From this point of view, locomotion control is considered to be an environmentally grounded interaction, rather than the execution of an abstract action plan made in the head.

References

Gibson, J. J. & Crooks, L. E. (1938). A theoretical field analysis of automobile-driving. *American Journal of Psychology*, 51 (3), 453-471.
Higuchi, T., Takada, H., Matsuura, Y., & Imanaka, K. (2004). Visual estimation of spatial requirements for locomotion in novice wheelchair users. *Journal of Experimental Psychology: Applied*, 10 (1), 55-66.
Kadar, E. E. & Shaw, R. E. (2000). Toward an ecological field theory of perceptual control of locomotion. *Ecological Psychology*, 12 (2), 141-180.
Turvey, M. T. & Shaw, R. E. (1995). Toward an ecological physics and a physical psychology. In R. L. Solso & D. W. Massaro (Eds.), *The science of the mind: 2001 and beyond* (pp. 144-167). Oxford, New York: Oxford University Press.

Studies in Perception & Action X
E. Charles & L.J. Smart (Eds.)

Load-Induced Gait Transitions in Way-finding

Vivek Kant, Jason M. Gordon, Mohammad Abdolvahab,
M. T. Turvey, and Claudia Carello

Center for the Ecological Study of Perception and Action, University of
Connecticut

In its simplest form, navigation or way-finding is an ability of animals (including humans) to return to the starting point of a journey without using familiar places as landmarks (Etienne & Jeffrey, 2004). Legged navigation does not depend on counting steps or time (Schwartz, 1999; Turvey, Romaniak-Gross, Isenhower, Arzamarski, Harrison, & Carello, 2009). A recent trend in the study of way-finding by legged locomotion conceptualizes the problem in terms of abstract physical systems. The Measurement-Report, or *M-R*, system is considered a "smart perceptual instrument" (cf. Runeson, 1977; Turvey & Carello, 1995), with the implication that the measured units may be abstract in nature. This approach exploits the characterization of legged locomotion in terms of primary and secondary gaits (Golubitsky et al., 1998, 1999). In primary gaits (e.g., hop, walk, run) the component oscillators do the same thing; in secondary gaits (e.g., skip, gallop, hesitation walk) the component oscillators do different things. Under this characterization, the *M-R* instrument is a successful odometer—that is, the measured difference Δd between M and $R \approx 0$—when the measure and report gaits are of the same symmetry class; it is less successful —that is, $\Delta d \neq 0$— when the symmetry classes of measure and report gaits differ (Turvey et al.).

In previous research, a change in gait symmetry was defined by instruction. Participants were asked to perform a particular outbound gait whose symmetry is known and a particular return gait whose symmetry is also known. The instructions controlled whether or not symmetry was broken between the outbound and return gaits. In the research reported here, we attempted to induce a primary to secondary bifurcation in the *M-R* instrument by weighting one leg at the ankle during the *M* phase and removing that weight during the *R* phase. A transition is defined as a change from $\Delta d \approx 0$ to $\Delta d \neq 0$ at some level of load. Across trials, the weight was either increased incrementally or decreased incrementally to allow an evaluation of whether the expected transition was characterized by hysteresis, that is, whether it occurred at a different load level in the increasing and decreasing conditions.

Method

The experiment was conducted on an indoor basketball court measuring approximately 30 m × 15 m. Prior to the experiment, participants received training in straight-line locomotion with eyes closed at a comfortable speed. Typically, three training runs, in which visual feedback was provided at the end, were sufficient. However, in case the participant deviated considerably from straight-line locomotion during the experiment, the trial was discarded and run again later in the session. Figure 1 illustrates the basic task. Walking was the instructed gait for both *M* and *R*. During the measurement phase, an ankle weight was strapped to a participant's dominant leg. The weights, ranging from 0 to 9 kg in .9 kg increments, were increased or decreased steadily across trials. The experiment took approximately 1 hour.

A trial consisted of an outbound traversal to a target distance followed by the reproduction of the distance traveled. Target distances were indicated by an experimenter who accompanied the participant and issued an audible command to stop when the appropriate distance had been reached. During the *M*-phase, the participant moved at a comfortable pace with the ankle weight attached. Another experimenter recorded the duration, number of

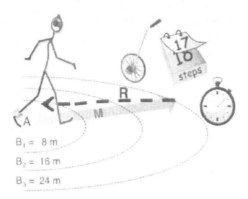

Figure 1. The starting point, A, along with three target distances B_i were marked with tape. Three semi-circles, with radii of B_i measured from A, were taped on the floor to allow participants to stray from straight-line locomotion. Participants were blindfolded and wore noise-cancelling headphones throughout the experiment. A stop-watch was used to measure the duration of each outbound and return trial. An experimenter followed participants with a rotary pedometer to measure the distance traveled on each outbound and return trial.

steps, and the actual distance covered (the participant could stop just short of or just beyond the target radius). The participant was then turned around in a random direction, the weight was removed, and they were asked to reproduce the distance traveled. During the R-phase, participants stopped on their own when they felt that they had reproduced the distance. The distance, duration, and number of steps were again recorded. Upon completion of the trial the experimenter guided the participant back to the starting location, taking a path that varied, in terms of length and heading direction, from trial to trial. Participants were not informed about the number of distances or the actual distances that they were to traverse.

Results and Discussion

As Figure 2 shows, the load manipulation was successful in inducing a transition from $\Delta d \approx 0$ to $\Delta d \neq 0$. This demonstrates a change in symmetry owing to gait dynamics, not just instruction. Moreover, the transition point differed as a function of whether the load was gradually increased (ascending) or gradually decreased (descending). That is, the transition was characterized by hysteresis. These results confirm two guiding assumptions of the modeling of the *M-R* system as a smart perceptual instrument. Namely, so-called primary and secondary gaits truly differ in symmetry (a bifurcation is defined as a change in the number and/or type of attractors), and the *M-R* instrument is nonlinear.

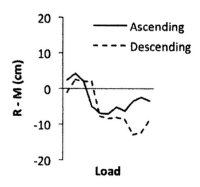

Figure 2. The difference between the distances traversed during report *R* and measure *M*. The shift of $\Delta d = 0$ to $\Delta d \neq 0$ occurred at different values of load between the ascending and descending series.

References

Etienne, A. S., & Jeffrey, K. J. (2004). Path integration in mammals. *Hippocampus, 14,* 180-192.

Haken, H. (1985). Pattern formation and chaos in synergetic systems. *Physica Scripta, 111.*

Golubitsky, M., Stewart, I., Buono, P. L., & Collins, J. J. (1998). A modular network for legged locomotion. *Physica D, 115,* 56–72.

Golubitsky, M., Stewart, I., Buono, P. L., & Collins, J. J. (1999). The role of symmetry in locomotor central pattern generators and animal gaits. *Nature, 401,* 693–695.

Runeson, S. (1977). On the possibility of "smart" perceptual mechanisms. *Scandinavian Journal of Psychology, 18,* 172-179.

Schwartz, M. (1999) Haptic perception of the distance walked when blindfolded. *Journal of Experimental Psychology: Human Perception and Performance, 25,* 852–865.

Turvey, M. T., & Carello, C. (1995). Dynamic touch. In W. Epstein & S. Rogers (Eds.), *Handbook of perception and cognition, Vol. V. Perception of space and motion* (pp. 401–490). San Diego, CA: Academic Press.

Turvey, M. T., Romaniak-Gross, C., Isenhower, R. W., Arzamarski, R., Harrison, S. J., & Carello, C. (2009). Human odometry is gait-symmetry specific. *Proceedings of the Royal Society B, 276,* 4309-4314.

Acknowledgments. The research reported here was supported by National Science Foundation grant BCS-0925373.

Studies in Perception & Action X
E. Charles & L.J. Smart (Eds.)
© 2011 Taylor & Francis Group, LLC

Negative Hysteresis in Affordance Experiments

Stacy M. Lopresti-Goodman[1], & T. D. Frank[2]

[1]Marymount University, Arlington, VA, 22207,
[2]CESPA, University of Connecticut, Storrs, CT, 06269.

To perceive an *affordance* is to perceive what the current layout of surfaces *affords* with respect to one's body size and action capabilities (Gibson, 1979). Affordance experiments have demonstrated that the shift from one mode of behavior to another exhibits the features typical of a self-organized dynamic system (Fitzpatrick et al., 1994; Richardson et al., 2007; van der Kamp et al., 1998), where stable patterns of behavior emerge from the lawful interaction between components of the animal-environment-task system.

For example, the boundary between graspable-with-one-and-two-hands differs experimentally when the object-to-hand-ratio (e.g. pi-number, α) is scaled in an ascending and descending manner: There is hysteresis ($\Delta\alpha$). When the critical value of α for ascending trials (α_{c2}) is larger than that for descending trials (α_{c1}), *positive hysteresis* has occurred. This is typically found in experiments where perception is indexed by selective action (e.g. actually grasping objects) (Lopresti-Goodman et al., 2009; Richardson et al., 2007). When $\alpha_{c1} > \alpha_{c2}$, *negative hysteresis* (e.g. *enhanced contrast*) has occurred, and is typically found when perception is indexed by selective verbal classification (e.g. "two-hands") (Fitzpatrick et al., 1994; Hirose & Nishio, 2001; Richardson et al., 2007). When $\alpha_{c1} = \alpha_{c2}$, a critical point has occurred.

Frank et al. (2009) developed a dynamical model, the Grasping Transition (GT) model, for affordance transitions. The different types of grasping modes represent the system's stable states and may be considered order parameters (ξ) of the dynamic system. The order parameters ξ_1 and ξ_2 represent the generalized amplitudes of the one- and two-hand grasping modes, respectively. $\xi_1 > 0$, $\xi_2 = 0$ defines the one-hand mode, $\xi_2 > 0$, $\xi_1 = 0$ defines the two-hand mode. Then, the grasping behavior is determined by the time evolution of ξ_1 and ξ_2:

$$(1) \quad \dot{\xi_1} = \lambda_1\xi_1 - g\xi_2^2\xi_1 - \xi_1^3, \text{ and } \dot{\xi_2} = \lambda_2\xi_2 - g\xi_1^2\xi_2 - \xi_2^3.$$

λ_1 and λ_2 are the one- and two-hand so called "attention" parameters (Haken, 1991), respectively, corresponding to ξ_1 and ξ_2. α acts as a control parameter. By Eq. (12) in Frank et al. (2009), λ_1 and λ_2 relate linearly to α where β determines the overall size of λ like $\lambda_1 = \beta(1 - \alpha)$ and $\lambda_2 = \lambda_{2,0} + \beta\alpha$.

Parameter values for g in Eq. (1) can be derived from experimental observations of α_{c1} and α_{c2}. Eq. (13) of Frank et al. (2009) yields

$$(2) \quad g = (1 - \alpha_{c1})/(1 - \alpha_{c2}).$$

g represents the strength of the interaction between the two grasping modes, as well as to the stability of the attractors and the hysteresis size ($\Delta\alpha$). This experiment investigated what changes in g are responsible for the hysteresis differences observed in selective action and verbal classification experiments.

Experiment 1

Experiment 1 investigated differences in grasping dynamics where the perception of graspability was indexed by selective action, hereafter referred to as the "action" condition, and when perception is indexed by verbal classification, hereafter referred to as the "perception" condition.

Method

Thirty-two University of Connecticut students participated as partial fulfilment of a course requirement.

Two sets of narrow wooden planks, 2 cm high and 6.5 cm wide, ranging in length from 4.5 to 24.5 cm, in 0.5 cm increments, were used as the objects. These planks were painted black with their ends red. Participants were instructed that they were only permitted to grasp the objects by their red ends (lengthwise).

Each individual participated in two task conditions (action and perception) with three plank presentation sequence trials blocked within each condition (ascending, random and descending), for a total of 6 trials per participant. For each trial, the participant was presented with an experimental object, one at a time, on a small table. For the action trials, participants were asked to grasp, lift, and move the objects from location 1 marked on the table, to location 2, which was marked 30 cm to the right of location 1. For the perception trials, participants kept their eyes closed until the object was placed in location 1. They were then instructed to open their eyes and indicate verbally whether they would use one hand or two hands if asked to grasp and move each object to location 2.

The experiment was a 2 (task: perception, action) × 3 (sequence: ascending, random and descending) within subject design. α_{c2} was calculated as the plank length at which a participant physically transitioned (action) or verbally indicated (perception) they would transition from one- to two-hand grasping (vice versa for α_{c1}), divided by their hand-span. These values were substituted into Eq. (2) to calculate g values for both task conditions.

Results and Discussion

Given the results of previous perception and action affordance experiments (Richardson et al., 2007), we expected moderate positive hysteresis ($\alpha_{c2} > \alpha_{c1}$; $\Delta\alpha > 0$) in the action trials and expected negative hysteresis ($\alpha_{c1} > \alpha_{c2}$; $\Delta\alpha < 0$) in the perception trials. A Univariate ANOVA on the $\Delta\alpha$ values revealed significant differences between the two conditions, $F(1, 31) = 54.08$, $p < .001$, $\eta^2 = 0.64$, with very moderate positive hysteresis, or a critical point, occurring in the action trials ($M_{\Delta\alpha} = 0.01 \pm 0.05$) and negative hysteresis occurring in the perception trials ($M_{\Delta\alpha} = -0.12 \pm 0.10$).

A Repeated Measures ANOVA revealed that the average g value for the action trials ($M = 1.03 \pm 0.15$) was significantly larger than that for the perception trials ($M = 0.71 \pm 0.25$), $F(1, 31) = 48.51$, $p < .001$, $\eta^2 = 0.61$. This suggests that negative hysteresis in the perception trials is the result of decreased interaction of the grasping modes, and decreased stability of their attractors, relative to the modes and attractors in the action condition. It is possible that the differences in dynamics in the perception trials are the result of a lack of feedback about grasping abilities which is obtained while grasping the objects.

Experiment 2

Experiment 2 investigated whether the GT Model could capture the affordance dynamics in an experiment investigating the perception of maximum sit-on-ability. Given this is an investigation of perception, we expected negative hysteresis and expected $g < 1$ due to a decreased interaction between the sit-on-able (ξ_1) and not-sit-on-able (ξ_2) modes.

Method

Twelve participants from the University of Connecticut participated as partial fulfillment for a course requirement.

The experimental apparatus was a 61 cm wide × 136.5 cm high wooden stand with a 2 × 42 × 61 cm wooden seat attached to the front that had a range of mobility of 25 to 100 cm. The seat pan was manually adjusted by the experimenter who was hidden from the participants' view. Participants asked the experimenter to "stop" moving the seat when it reached what was judged to be the maximum height they could sit on without lifting their feet off of the ground.

Individuals participated in 12 trials where the seat pan slowly moved from the ground up (ascending trials) and 12 trials where the seat pan moved from the top of the apparatus down (descending trials), the order of which alternated. α_c was calculated for each trial as the seat height in cm judged to be the maximum height that afforded sitting on, divided by the participant's leg length in cm. The mean α_{c2} and α_{c1} values were calculated as the average α_{c2} and α_{c1} values for all 12 ascending and 12 descending trials, respectively. These values were substituted into Eq. (2) to calculate the g value for this experiment.

Results and Discussion

Given the results of previous experiments investigating the perception of maximum sit-on-ability (Hirose & Nishio, 2001), we expected negative hysteresis ($\alpha_{c1} > \alpha_{c2}$; $\Delta\alpha < 0$). A Repeated Measures ANOVA on the mean α_c values revealed that α_{c1} ($M = 0.87 \pm 0.05$) was significantly larger than α_{c2} ($M = 0.80 \pm 0.05$), $F(1, 11) = 103.67$, $p < .001$, $\eta^2 = 0.90$, suggesting that negative hysteresis occurred ($M_{\Delta\alpha} = -0.07 \pm 0.02$).

Given our expectation of negative hysteresis, we anticipated $g < 1$, which might indicate a weak interaction between, and stability of, the ξ_1 and ξ_2 modes. Our analysis revealed that this was the case ($M_g = 0.63 \pm 0.17$). Interestingly, a qualitative analysis reveals that the g value for maximum sit-on-ability was similar to that found in the perception condition of Experiment 1, which may suggest an invariance of the g parameter dynamics for perception experiments.

Conclusion

As expected, negative hysteresis was observed in both of our perception experiments. The evaluation of the GT model suggests that the negative hysteresis effects observed were the result of weaker interactions between, and a weaker stability of, the two behavioral modes (e.g. $g < 1$). It is possible that the lack of active exploration of the environment in our perception conditions is what led to the weaker interactions and stabilities observed.

References

Fitzpatrick, P., Carello, C., Schmidt, R. C., & Corey, D. (1994). Haptic and visual perception of an affordance for upright posture. *Ecological Psychology, 6(4)*, 265-287.

Frank, T. D., Richardson, M. J., Lopresti-Goodman, S. M., & Turvey, M. T. (2009). Order parameter dynamics of body-scaled hysteresis and mode transitions in grasping behavior. *Journal of Biological Physics, 35*, 127-147.

Gibson, J. J. (1979). *The ecological approach to visual perception.* Boston: Houghton Mifflin.

Haken, H. (1991). *Synergetic computers and cognition.* Springer: Berlin.

Hirose, N., & Nishio, A. (2001). The process of adaptation to perceiving new action capabilities. *Ecological Psychology, 13(1)*, 49-69.

Lopresti-Goodman, S. M., Richardson, M. J., Baron, R. M., Carello, C., & Marsh, K. L. (2009). Task constraints and affordance boundaries. *Motor Control, 13*, 69-83.

Richardson, M. J., Marsh, K.L., & Baron, R. M. (2007). Judging and actualizing intrapersonal and interpersonal affordances. *Journal of Experimental Psychology: Human Perception and Performance, 33*, 845-859.

Van der Kamp, J., Savelsbergh, G. J. P., & Davis, W. E. (1998). Body-scaled ratio as a control parameter for prehension in 5- to 9-year-old children. *Developmental Psychobiology, 33(4)*, 351-361.

Studies in Perception & Action X
E. Charles & L.J. Smart (Eds.)
© 2011 Taylor & Francis Group, LLC

Remembering Affordances for Objects

Leonard S. Mark[1], Di Tong[1], Lin Ye[2]

[1]Miami University (Ohio), [2]Motorola Corporation

Ye, Cardwell, and Mark (2009) showed that the perception of one affordance for an object could interfere with the detection of its other affordances. That study also examined a proposal about the conditions under which people are more likely to notice a second affordance. When the actions supported by the two affordances involved the same grip and hand placement on the object, people were more likely to notice a second affordance for the object than when the two actions entailed different grips. Similarities in how people interacted with an object when performing two goal-directed actions (e.g., *cut-with*, *dig-with*) predicted the likelihood people would notice a second affordance.

If the perception of an object or event entails the perception of the existing affordance structure, we might ask what we remember about objects that we have seen. A typical memory experiment measures verbatim recall for a list of words or pictures. But if perception entails detection of affordances, might people remember the affordances for the objects and events they have witnessed, rather than the object per se, or specific component features? This study examines whether the perception of one of an object's affordances affects the likelihood of recalling (from memory) another of its affordances.

Method

Overview. Thirty-two college students participated in this study for course credit. The experimenters instructed participants that they were going to be shown a series of objects one at a time. For each object they were to indicate whether the object could be used to perform a particular task (e.g., scoop rice). Participants were then told that they would be asked to identify *from memory* which of the objects they had just been shown could be used to perform another task, (e.g., pound crackers). After performing these two tasks, participants used the objects to perform the two actions so that we could analyze how they interacted with the objects.

Objects and affordances. Two pairs of affordances were used: (1) scoop-with/pound-with and (2) cut-with/dig-with. The experimenter used the following descriptions of these affordances: *Scoop-with*: Imagine that you are planning to cook a cup of rice. Which objects are suitable for scooping a cup of rice with? *Pound-with*: An object that you can pound with repeatedly with enough force to break this piece of Melba toast. Pounding entails lifting the object and then lowering it with force in order to break the toast. *Cut-with*: Imagine that you have some Play-Doh and need to cut it into strips. Which objects do you think are suitable for cutting this Play-Doh? *Dig-with*: Imagine that you are going to dig a hole in sand. The size of the hole should be big enough to bury a Ping-Pong ball. In previous work (Ye et el., 2009) a group of people were asked to (a) judge primary use for each of the objects, and (b) whether the object could be used to perform the particular action in a reasonably efficient manner. The objects we selected for this experiment had been judged as (a) not having one of the above affordances as their primary use and (b) able to be used to perform one or more of the above affordances in a reasonably efficient manner. In previous work, we found that people readily recognized the objects as having these affordances when allowed to view and manipulate the object. The order of presentation of the two pairs of affordances was counterbalanced across participants, as was the order of presentation within each pair of affordances.

Task 1. Participants were shown a large table covered with black cloth on which the objects used in the experiment were placed. Each of the objects was hidden from view with a piece of the same black cloth. The experimenter explained to what the first affordance (referred to as *task* or *action*) referred. The experimenter illustrated the action with an object not used in the actual experiment. In the first part of the study, the experimenter revealed each of the objects to the participant one at a time and the participant simply judged whether she/he could use the object to perform the specified action. In this phase of the experiment participants did not perform the action, though they were allowed to pick up and explore the properties of the object if they were unsure about the object.

Task 2. After making judgments about whether each of the objects could be used to perform the first action, participants were asked to look away from the table. The experimenter described the second action and then asked the participant to name (from memory) all of the objects they just saw that could be used to perform the second action.

Task 3. Participants were then instructed to perform both actions using each of the objects that afforded that particular action. Each object was revealed and the participant performed the first action with that object. When the first action had been completed with all of the objects that had been judged to afford that action, participants performed the second action with those same objects. These actions were videotaped and coded with respect to the following criteria: (1) Grip used to hold the object (2-finger, 3-finger, 4-finger, 5-finger, and 2-hand) (Newell et al., 1989); and (2) the location on the object on which the fingers were placed. Two experimenters independently judged each action with respect to these criteria. There was over 95% initial agreement. The experimenters then compared the grips used to perform the two different actions with the same object. When both criteria were met, the *same* grip was said to be used for the two actions. A violation of either criterion led to the actions to be classified as involving a *different* grip.

Analysis. We compiled the judgment, memory and grip data using the method devised by Ye et al. (2009). When a participant judged an object as affording the first action and recalled the object as affording the second action, the object was said to have been remembered as having the second affordance. If the object was recognized as having the first affordance, but was not recalled as having the second affordance, the second affordance was said not to have been remembered. Similarly, the two actions performed with each object could have the *same grip* or *different grips*. Table 1 shows the four resulting possibilities and the total number of objects in each of these categories summed across the 32 participants.

Results and Discussion

Dig–Cut	2nd AFF recalled	2nd AFF not recalled		Pound - Scoop	2nd AFF recalled	2nd AFF not recalled
Same Grip	111*	19		Same Grip	69*	23
Different Grip	56	102*		Different Grip	65	89*

Table 1: Number of Objects in the Four Possible Memory Conditions for Recalling the Second Affordance and Grip Combinations for the Dig-Cut and Pound-Scoop Affordance Pairs. *correct predictions according to Ye et al.'s (2009) proposal.

To analyze the frequency data shown in Table 1, we used the following procedure: Our proposal that participants would be more likely to remember objects with the second affordance when the same grip is used for both actions and less likely to remember an object when a different grip is used, indicates that "correct" predictions may be found in the upper-left and lower-right cells. For each participant we calculated the percentage of correct predictions, normalized these percentages (arcsin transformation) and then performed a t-test to compare the percentage of correct predictions to chance (50% transformed to 1.571). For the dig-cut pair of affordances the untransformed percentage of correct predictions was 74% (SD = 13%), t(31) = 10.36, p < .001); for the scoop-pound affordances, the comparable data were 65% (20%), t(31) = 4.27, p < .001.

Ye et al. (2009) also examined a second prediction. In trying to understand why on some occasions people notice a second affordance and on other occasions they fail to do so, we realized that the hypothesis made a strong prediction that when the same grip was used for the two actions, people should recognize both affordances for that object. This suggests that failure to notice the second affordance for an object when the same grip is used for both actions should rarely obtain. Thus, Ye et al predicted that the errors when both affordances are noticed and the same grip was used to perform both actions (upper-right cell in Table 1) should be rare compared to errors in which different grips were used but both affordances were noticed (lower left-hand cell). This predicted outcome was obtained in both Ye et al.'s original experiment and in the data presented in Table 1.

The results of Ye et al. (2009) showed that the perception of whether an object can be used to perform a goal-directed action entails detecting a nesting of affordances (for grip, hand placement, wield-ability, etc.) that determine how a person can interact with the object. The current findings suggest that the way in which a person perceives he/she can interact with an object shapes what one remembers about what the object affords. Similar ways of interacting with an object facilitate remembering affordances for an object.

References

Newell, K. M., Scully, D. M, Tenenbaum, F., & Hardiman, S. (1989). Body scale and the development of prehension. *Developmental Psychobiology, 22*, 1-13

Ye. L., Cardwell, W., & Mark, L. S. (2009). Perceiving multiple affordances for objects. *Ecological Psychology, 21*, 185-217.

Studies in Perception & Action X
E. Charles & L.J. Smart (Eds.)
© 2011 Taylor & Francis Group, LLC

Judgments of Interior Spaces: The Role of Affordances

Benjamin R. Meagher[1] and Kerry L. Marsh[1]

[1]University of Connecticut

The physical structure of an enclosed space can have a powerful impact on its inhabitants. Being within an environment inadequate for satisfying basic psychological needs can lead to stress, illness, and even death for an organism. Hediger (1955) famously articulated this point for the purposes of designing zoo enclosures. Central to his theory was the animal's need to maintain a *flight zone*, the freedom of movement to create a safe distance between itself and any intruder. Animals held in cages too small, and thus unable to meet this need, are in a constant state of anxiety, which leads inevitably to health problems.

Crowding is a concept with a long history in environmental psychology which accounts for the similarly deleterious effects on humans that result from having inadequate physical space to pursue one's goals and meet one's needs. However, an individual's feeling of spaciousness within a setting is not based solely on the raw, physical dimensions of the enclosure. Rather, numerous findings have found a link between impressions of spaciousness and other, seemingly incidental environmental properties. For example, greater intensity and wider distribution of light leads to increases in perceived spaciousness (Martyniuk, Flynn, Spencer, & Hendrick, 1973). Rectangular rooms are judged to be larger than square rooms (Sadalla & Oxley, 1984), rooms with smooth walls are seen as less spacious than those with bookcases (Stamps & Krishnan, 2006), and greater amounts of visible floor space produce larger impressions of room size (Benedikt & Burnham, 1985).

Despite these varied findings, no single theory has explained the effect these factors have on feelings of spaciousness in a unified way. We propose that the ecological concept of *affordances* fills this theoretical void. Space is perceived in terms of action potentials, and so feelings of spaciousness within an enclosure will depend in part on the wealth of behavioural opportunities it affords. Within this framework, rectangular rooms can be understood as feeling larger because they afford more movement, which allows for greater interpersonal distances. Similarly, bright rooms feel larger because more light increases both the possible actions available to a perceiver, as well as his or her ability to actually detect those possibilities within the setting.

The current research sought to test this functional view of spaciousness directly by altering the affordances within a given room. Furniture was arranged such that the physical structure of the environment either facilitated or inhibited its use. It was hypothesized that a room whose physical features afford more behavioural possibilities would be detected as such by participants and, therefore, be judged as more spacious than a non-functional room, even when the furniture itself was identical.

Method

Eighty-eight undergraduates participated in this experiment. Participants were brought into a 16'8" x 11'2" room, furnished with office furniture in one of three ways: (1) the room was empty, (2) furniture was arranged to be functional, or (3) furniture was arranged so as to limit its functionality (see Figure 1). In the functional condition, the furniture provided both individual and joint work areas, easily enabled the use of different types of wall fixtures, and allowed for uninhibited manoeuvring within the space. In contrast, the non-functional condition limited interaction and made the utilization of the furniture and the room's fixtures (e.g., boards and door) difficult.

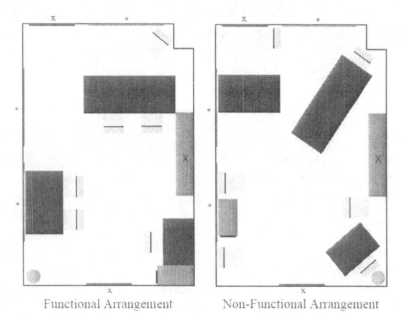

Functional Arrangement   Non-Functional Arrangement

Figure 1. Bird's-eye view of room arrangement. Fixed structures included two white boards, a projector screen, and a foldable partition (*X*). Asterisks denote boards or screen; *x* denotes doors. The manipulated furnishings consisted of two tables, one desk, six chairs, one filing cabinet, and a round wastebasket.

Half the room was unlit when the participant arrived. Upon entering, the experimenter asked the participant to turn on the light on the opposite side of the room, so as to ensure that the participant walked across the entire length of the space. The participant was given one minute alone in the room to look around while the experimenter waited outside. Afterwards, the participant faced the door and completed Likert-type 7-point scales that assessed their impressions of the room on key items and filler items. Composite measures were created by averaging three spatial judgment items (Cramped, Crowded, Spacious, $\Box\Box$= .70) and three items assessing general affective reactions (Adequate, Good, Pleasant, $\Box\Box$ = .72). Additional filler items were also completed (Clean, Comfortable, Old, Well-lighted). Participants were then brought into the hallway and asked to estimate the length and width of the room in feet, using their clipboard as a 1-foot reference.

Results and Discussion

The hypothesis that participants' impressions of a room would be affected by its affordances was tested using one-way ANOVAs. Spatial judgments significantly differed across the three arrangement conditions, $F(2, 85) = 3.42$, $p < .05$. Planned comparisons employing orthogonal contrasts showed that participants presented with the non-functional arrangement judged the room lower on spatial items (i.e., less spacious, $M = 3.63$) than did those in the empty ($M = 4.54$) and functional conditions ($M = 4.32$), $t(85) = 2.52$, $p < .05$. Ratings of the functional and empty rooms did not differ, $t(85) = .52, p = .56$.

Furniture arrangement also had a significant effect on general affective reactions, $F(2, 85) = 4.07$, $p < .05$. As before, planned comparisons using orthogonal contrasts revealed that those in the non-functional condition rated the room less positively than those in the empty and functional conditions ($Ms = 3.00, 3.74,$ and 3.65, respectively), $t(85) = 2.82, p < .01$. The functional and empty room again did not differ, $t(85) = .30$, $p = .76$. Significant effects of condition were found on only one filler item, *clean*, $F(2, 85) = 6.07$, $p < .01$. Participants in the non-functional condition rated their room as less clean than did participants in the empty and functional rooms, $t(85) = 3.01$, $p < .01$, and the functional room was rated moderately cleaner than the empty room, $t(85) = 1.88, p = .06$.

The final measure taken was judgments of the room's size in feet, given by participants immediately upon exiting the room. Two cases were detected as extreme values (3 * IQR) and removed from the analysis. Unlike participants' impressions while in the room, a one-way ANOVA failed to find significant differences in judgments of area between conditions, $F(2, 83) = 1.56$, $p = .22$. Participants had difficulty estimating the length and width of the room from memory. Variability of judgments was high ($SD_{total} = 174.26$), and in all conditions participants substantially overestimated the room's actual area of 186.11 ft² ($M_{\text{non-functional}}$ = 223.07; M_{empty} = 286.17; $M_{\text{functional}}$ = 212.59).

The results of this experiment by and large support the hypothesis that manipulating the affordances of a setting influences the impressions people form about the space. Rooms felt more cramped and were rated more negatively when furniture arrangement afforded fewer possibilities for action. Room size estimates, however, did not differ across conditions. This suggests that subjective impressions may be more sensitive to the presence of affordances than are reconstructions of size from memory. Interestingly, the functional room did not differ from the empty room in terms of these same spatial judgments, despite having less visible floor space available to the perceiver. Therefore, it would seem that occlusion and partitioning need not inherently reduce one's sense of spaciousness, provided these obstructions actually facilitate other types of activity. Taken in sum, these findings argue for the central role affordances play in one's experience of an environment and highlight the need for researchers to better understand the psychological ramifications their presence has on a setting's inhabitants.

References

Benedikt, M. L., & Burnham, C. A. (1985). Perceiving architectural space: From optic arrays to isovists. In W. H. Warren and R. E. Shaw (Eds.), *Persistence and change* (pp. 103-114). Hillsdale, NJ: Lawrence Erlbaum.

Hediger, H. (1955). *The psychology and behavior of animals in zoos and circuses.* New York: Dover.

Martyniuk, O., Flynn, J.E., Spencer, T.J., & Hendrick, C. (1973). Effect of environmental lighting on impression and behavior. In R. Küller (Ed.), *Architectural psychology* (pp. 51-63). Stroudsburg, PA: Dowden, Hutchinson & Ross.

Sadalla, E. K., and Oxley, D. (1976). The perception of room size: The rectangularity illusion. *Environment and Behavior, 16,* 291-306.

Stamps, A. E., & Krishnan, V. V. (2006). Spaciousness and boundary roughness. *Environment & Behavior, 38,* 841-872.

Chapter 4:

Posture

Studies in Perception & Action X
E. Charles & L.J. Smart (Eds.)
© 2011 Taylor & Francis Group, LLC

Posture and Performance of a Precision Task at Sea

Fu-Chen Chen & Thomas A. Stoffregen

University of Minnesota

Mariners must adjust their dynamic body orientation in response to ship motion. Despite this mechanical obligation, mariners also adjust standing posture in response to variations in body configuration (foot placement) and in response to changes in the difficulty of visual tasks performed while standing (e.g., Mayo, Wade, & Stoffregen, 2011; Stoffregen et al., 2011; Yu et al., 2010). In these previous studies, participants have always faced in one direction relative to the ship (athwartship). However, ship motion occurs in 6 degrees of freedom, and differs across degrees of freedom as a function of sailing conditions. Moreover, due to the fact that ships are longer than they are wide, motion in roll will tend to differ from motion in pitch in most situations. Accordingly, postural effects that occur when facing in one direction may differ when facing in another direction. In the present study, one of our goals was to conduct direct comparisons of posture and visually-based performance with participants bodies oriented in different directions relative to the ship.

When the body's coronal plane is perpendicular to the ship's long axis, ship motion in pitch will give rise to compensatory postural activity in the body's sagittal plane. When the body's coronal plane is parallel to the ship's long axis, ship motion in pitch will give rise to compensatory postural activity in the body's coronal plane. Thus, variations in body orientation relative to the ship have consequences for the functionality of postural activity in different body planes. This fact recalls a study by Balasubramaniam, Riley, & Turvey (2000) which was conducted on land. They varied the functional consequences of sway in the body's coronal and sagittal planes by asking participants to perform a visually-based task while standing with the torso either parallel or perpendicular to the line of sight. They found that patterns of sway were related to the difficulty of visual tasks, and that these patterns were deployed on an axis-specific basis, that is, that sway in different body axes was functionally related to the demands of the visual task. We sought to determine whether this effect would be preserved among mariners.

We combined the principle manipulations of Balasubramaniam et al. (2000) with a manipulation of the orientation of the body relative to a ship at sea.

Method

The study was carried out aboard the R/V Thomas G. Thompson, on a cruise from Seattle WA to Honolulu HI. The Thompson was 84 m long with a 16-m beam, displaced 3500 tons, and cruised at 12 knots. The ship was at sea for nine days. Subjects (nine experienced mariners) stood with their body perpendicular (forward) or parallel (athwart) to the ship's long axis. We used the laser pointer task developed by Balasubramaniam et al. (2000), in which participants held a laser pointer in their right hand with the arm straight and the hand held against the right thigh. The laser beam was to be kept within circular targets (black circles) that were presented on a white ground. Targets were 110 from subjects, and were circles of either 2 cm or 4 cm diameter. Targets were placed directly ahead of the subject (front), or 90 degrees to their right (side). For side trials, subjects were asked to turn their head only to face the target. For side trials, we fitted the laser pointer with an angled mirror. Thus, the orientation of the subject's hand was the same in all conditions. The angle between the feet was fixed at 10 degrees, and the heels were 23 cm apart. We used a 2 (body: forward vs. athwart) × 2 (head: front vs. side) × 2 (targets: small vs. large) within-subjects design. Each day, there was one trial (60 s) in each of the eight conditions. Head and torso motion were monitored using a magnetic tracking system. We analyzed positional variability in the AP and ML axes (defined relative to the torso).

Results and Discussion

Due to rough weather we were able to collect data on only two days. In each case the sea state was 7 on the Beaufort scale (Beer, 1997), with a 3-meter swell and winds tearing the crests off waves. In our previous studies the sea state has been less than 4 (Mayo et al., 2011; Stoffregen et al., 2011; Yu et al., 2010). The rough weather meant that subjects found it challenging to maintain stance for 60 s without moving their feet. In about 10% of cases, subjects took a step during a trial (these trials were repeated). Stepping occurred exclusively in athwart conditions. Despite these challenging conditions, like Balasubramaniam et al. (2000), we found that performance at the laser pointer task was good; the beam rarely left the target.

For analysis, we defined AP and ML movement for both the head and torso relative to the torso only. Movement of the torso and head in the AP axis were greater in athwartship than in forward conditions. Movement of head in AP was greater when facing front than when facing side, but movement of the torso in ML was less when facing front than when facing side. Head movement in AP was also affected by an interaction between torso orientation and head orientation (Figure 1). Target size influenced movement of the torso in its ML axis as an interaction with head orientation (Figure 2).

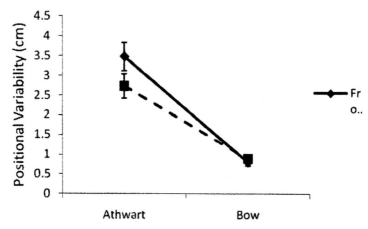

Figure 1. Interaction between body orientation (athwart vs. bow) and head orientation (front vs. side), for movement of the head in the AP axis.

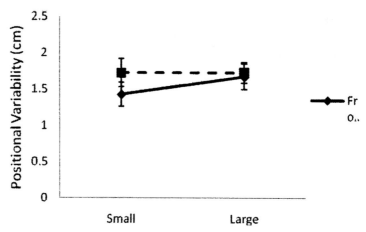

Figure 2. Interaction between orientation of the head (front vs. side) and task difficulty (small vs. large targets), for movement of the torso in the ML axis.

Each independent variable influenced one or more parameters of postural activity. The influence of body orientation (forward vs. athwart) is not surprising. Given the very rough seas, the influence of head orientation (front vs. side) is remarkable. Perhaps more remarkable is the influence of task difficulty (small vs large): The mechanical influence of ship motion did not eliminate subjects' ability to "tune" their sway to the demands of a precision task. Overall, the results are consistent with the hypothesis that postural activity emerges from the simultaneous influence of external conditions (ship motion), body configuration (head orientation), and purely psychological factors (task demand).

References

Balasubramaniam, R., Riley, M. A., & Turvey, M. T. (2000). Specificity of postural sway to the demands of a precision task. *Gait and Posture, 11*, 12-24.

Beer, T. (1997). *Environmental oceanography*. Boca Raton, FL; CRC Press.

Mayo, A. M., Wade, M. G., & Stoffregen, T. A. (2011). Postural effects of the horizon on land and at sea. *Psychological Science, 22*, 118-124.

Stoffregen, T. A., Villard, S., Chen, F.-C., & Yu, Y. (2011). Standing body sway on land and at sea. *Ecological Psychology, 23*, in press.

Yu, Y., Yank, J. R., Katsumata, Y., Villard, S., Kennedy, R. S., & Stoffregen, T. A. (2010). Visual vigilance performance and standing posture at sea. *Aviation, Space, and Environmental Medicine, 81*, 375-382.

Studies in Perception & Action X
E. Charles & L.J. Smart (Eds.)

Influence of Specific Sports Experience on Postural Responses to Optic Flow

Hyun Chae Chung

Kunsan National University, Republic of Korea

Many studies have demonstrated adaptive postural responses during stance to imposed optic flow, using the moving room paradigm (e.g., Lee & Lishman, 1975; Stoffregen, 1985). The purpose of the present experiment was to investigate the influence of specific sports experience on postural responses to imposed optic flow. We compared three different groups: 1. No specific sports experience. 2. Experience with canoeing and rowing. 3. Experience with kum-Do. Kum-Do is a form of fencing that is popular in Korea; it resembles Japanese Kendo. Any form of fencing requires precise control of the dynamic orientation of the entire body. By contrast, canoeing and rowing are preformed while seated and do not make specific demands on control of upright stance.

Method

Thirty two participants of canoeing and rowing (21.7 ± 1.25 yrs), kum-Do (25.3 ± 4.9 yrs), and no specific sports experience (23.4 ± 2.5 years). Participants were asked to maintain erect posture (standing on a force plate) while facing along the axis of room oscillation. Each trial was 30 sec. Using a 2×2 design I co-varied the amplitude (2 cm vs. 5 cm) and frequency (0.1 Hz vs. 0.2 Hz) of room oscillation. I measured motion of the room, and displacement of the of center of pressure in the AP axis (COPap), that is, along the line of sight. For statistical comparisons, 3 (groups) × 2 (frequency) × 2 (amplitude) mixed-measures ANOVA with repeated measures on the last two factors, with Scheffe posthoc were used. All tests were evaluated at $p < .05$

Results and Discussion

Postural responses to room motion varied in response to changes in room motion. I found significant Frequency × Amplitude interactions on the positional variability of the COP, $F_{(1,30)} = 4.31$, $p < .04$, and on the gain of COP motion relative to room motion, $F_{(1,30)} = 22.91$, $p < .0001$. These effects were consistent with the results of previous studies using the moving room paradigm (e.g., Schmuckler, 1997; Stoffregen, 1986).

In addition, there was a significant main effect of Group on mean position of the COP, $F_{(2,30)} = 3.91$, $p < .03$. The Canoe/Rowing group (mean = 4.27, SD = 2.07) differed from the kum-Do group (mean = 6.18, SD = 2.07) and the group with no specific sports experience (mean = 6.50, SD = 2.05). Finally, there was a significant Amplitude × Group interaction on room-COP gain, $F_{(2,30)} = 5.96$, $p < .0006$. Post-hoc tests revealed that gain differed between groups when the room moved 5 cm at 0.1 Hz. The Canoe/Rowing group (mean = 0.14, SD = 0.07) differed from the kum-Do group (mean = 0.26, SD = 0.10) and the group with no specific sports experience (mean = 0.23, SD = 0.07). These results indicate that the effects of room motion on standing posture differed as a function of athletic status, and between different types of athletic activity. Unlike the other two groups, waterbourne athletes are exposed to visible motion of the environment (e.g., ripples on water) that is irrelevant to the stability of their body. It may be, therefore, that canoists and rowers learn to avoid stabilizing posture relative to the visible surface of the water.

References

Lee, D. N., & Lishman, J. R. (1975). Visual proprioceptive control of stance. *Journal of Human Movement Studies, 1*, 87-95.

Schmuckler, M. A. (1997). Children's postural sway in response to low- and high-frequency visual information for oscillation. *Journal of Experimental Psychology: Human Perception and Performance, 23,* 528-545.

Stoffregen, T. A. (1985). Flow structure versus retinal location in the optical control of stance. *Journal of Experimental Psychology: Human Perception and Performance, 11,* 554-565.

Stoffregen, T. A. (1986). The role of optical velocity in the control of stance. *Perception & Psychophysics, 39,* 355-360.

Studies in Perception & Action X
E. Charles & L.J. Smart (Eds.)
© 2011 Taylor & Francis Group, LLC

Postural Expertise and Development: A Cross-Sectional Comparison of Ballet Dancers to Non-Dancers

Sarah E. Cummins-Sebree[1], Adam W. Kiefer[2], Julie A. Weast[3],
Michael A. Riley[3], Kevin Shockley[3], & Jacqui Haas[4]

[1]University of Cincinnati – Raymond Walters College,
[2]Brown University – Department of Cognitive, Linguistic & Psychological
Sciences, [3]University of Cincinnati – Department of Psychology
[4]Cincinnati Ballet Company

Research is mixed on potential differences between adult ballet dancers and non-dancers in elements of basic postural control (cf. Hugel et al., 1999; Kiefer et al., 2007; Schmit et al., 2005). For example, under simple biomechanical and perceptual manipulations, such as when eyes were open versus closed or when standing with feet together or apart, ballet dancers have exhibited both greater sway variability (Kiefer et al., 2007; Michielsen et al., 2007) and no differences in sway variability (Schmit et al.) compared to untrained controls. Such a lack of consensus is revealing of the complexities that are associated with understanding the role of expertise in postural control.

To understand the role of expertise it might be important to first address the question of whether these differences can only be seen in adults who have had extensive years of ballet training, or rather is it possible that early signs of changes in postural control are observable in childhood and/or adolescence for dancers who have had fewer years of training. Though it is commonly accepted that adult-like postural control occurs before adolescence (Shumway-Cook & Woollacott, 2007), it is unclear whether dance training may generalize and contribute to variations in basic postural control prior to adulthood. As part of a larger study, we compared elementary-aged children and adolescents who either had ballet training or no training to determine at what point ballet dancers would begin to exhibit different postural control patterns than non-dancers. To do so, we measured both the variability of center of pressure (COP) time series and used detrended fluctuation analysis (DFA) to quantify COP dynamics.

Method

Thirty ballet dancers (elementary-aged, adolescent, and adult; N = 10/group) and 30 controls matched on age and body-mass index (BMI) participated (Elementary Ballet Age = 8.70 ± 2.13 years, BMI M = 16.45 ± 2.63; Elementary Control Age = 9.10 ± 1.10 years, BMI M = 16.38 ± 3.23; Adolescent Ballet Age = 15.22 ± 1.45 years, BMI M = 19.96 ± 1.56; Adolescent Control Age M = 15.31 ± 0.36 years, BMI M = 20.86 ± 2.09; Adult Ballet Age = 23.50 ± 5.08 years, BMI M = 19.11 ± 0.71; Adult Control Age = 22.17 ± 4.76 years, BMI M = 19.48 ± 1.04). Participants were instructed to stand relaxed during four separate stance (feet together vs. shoulder-width apart) and vision (eyes open vs. closed) conditions totaling 8 trials (two per condition). Each trial lasted 30 s. An AMTI AccuSway+ force platform recorded participants' COP at 100Hz. COP variability measurements in the anterior-posterior (AP) and medial-lateral (ML) directions included standard deviation (SD) and local standard deviation (LSD – the average of SDs for non-overlapping, 1 s data windows). We also analyzed the COP dynamics as quantified by DFA. DFA computes the scaling exponent, α, which provides an index of the structure of the COP trajectory. Larger α values are indicative of a more deterministic (more correlated) variability pattern.

Results and Discussion

Due to the extensive scope of the overall project, we report here effects as they relate to elementary and adolescent participants on the following measures: SD and DFA in the ML direction, and LSD in the AP direction. We focus on these measures to illustrate the variety of differences that occurred within age and dance status groups. There was an effect of age for SD [$F(2,54)$ = 15.65, p <

.001] in the ML plane and for LSD [$F(2,54) = 23.44, p < .001$] in the AP plane; elementary-aged children exhibited more ML variability ($M = 0.208$) compared to adolescents ($M = 0.134$), and they also showed more AP fine-grained variability (LSD) than adolescents ($M = 0.100$ vs. $M = 0.065$, respectively).

Age, dance status, and vision interacted to impact LSD in the AP direction [$F(2,54) = 4.32, p = .02$]. Elementary-aged dancers and non-dancers showed no difference in LSD when their eyes were open ($M = 0.092$ and $M = 0.107$, respectively), but adolescent non-dancers exhibited lower LSD values than dancers when their eyes were open ($M = 0.044$ and $M = 0.060$, respectively). In the ML direction, an interaction occurred between age, dance status, and vision for SD [$F(2,54) = 4.38, p = .02$]. Elementary dancers were less variable with eyes open ($M = 0.182$) compared to eyes closed ($M = 0.239$), but elementary non-dancers' COP was equally variable ($M = 0.216$ eyes open, $M = 0.234$ eyes closed). However, both adolescent dancers and non-dancers were less variable with eyes open ($M = 0.135$ and $M = 0.108$, respectively) than with eyes closed ($M = 0.185$ and $M = 0.138$, respectively). Age, dance status, and stance interacted to influence α [$F(2,54) = 6.65, p = .003$] in the ML direction. Both elementary-aged and adolescent dancers were less deterministic with their feet apart ($M = 1.31$ and 1.36, respectively) than when their feet were together ($M = 1.49$ and 1.48, respectively). Elementary-aged controls also exhibited this pattern (feet apart $M = 1.32$ vs. feet together $M = 1.53$); however, unlike the adolescent dancers, adolescent controls did not exhibit α differences across stance.

How does this compare to adults? When compared with data from Kiefer et al. (2007), adult dancers exhibit less variability (i.e. lower SD) with eyes open than eyes closed in the ML direction, as we see with younger dancers. Adult dancers show less fine-grained variability (i.e. lower LSD) with eyes open compared to eyes closed in the AP direction; however, this is not the case with younger dancers. This may be indicative of a greater reliance on vision by the adult dancers given their development of visual feedback strategies acquired through years of ballet training (cf. Golomer et al., 1999).

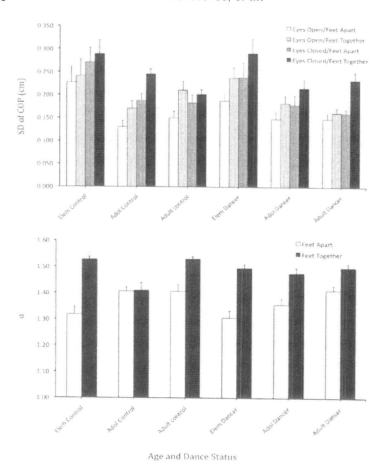

Figure 1. Age × dance status × vision × stance interaction for SD in the ML direction (top) and an age × dance status × stance interaction for α in the ML direction (bottom).

The relation between age, dance status, vision, and stance is a complicated one, as illustrated in Figure 1; there are different patterns for dance status and age combinations where elementary and adult dancers vs. non-dancers seem very different, while adolescent dancers and non-dancers show much more similar variability patterns. Thus, some differences in postural sway measures can be seen with relatively few years of dance training, but other variations in measures do not appear until adulthood.

Specifically, the difference in the developmental trend of COP dynamics for dancers compared to controls, as indexed by α, might suggest that ballet training may be modulating the effect development has on the postural control of adolescents. Teasing apart the relationship between training and age-related, physical developmental changes in dancers' postural sway in future research will be essential to understand the relative contributions of each towards elite postural control.

References

Golomer, E., Cremieux, J., Dupui, P., Isableu, B., & Ohlmann, T. (1999). Visual contribution to self-induced body sway frequencies and visual perception of male professional dancers. *International Journal of Neuroscience, 105*, 15-26.

Hugel, F., Cadopi, M., Kohler, F., & Perrin, P. (1999). Postural control of ballet dancers: A specific use of visual input for artistic purposes. *International Journal of Sports Medicine, 20*, 86-92.

Kiefer, A. W. Multi-segmental postural coordination in professional ballet dancers. Unpublished Dissertation. Retrieved September 21, 2010 from http://etd.ohiolink.edu/view.cgi?acc_num=ucin1250045828

Kiefer, A. W., Cummins-Sebree, S., Riley, M. A., Shockley, K., & Haas, J. G. (2007). Control of posture in professional level ballet dancers. In S. Cummins-Sebree, M. A. Riley, & K. Shockley (Eds.), *Studies in perception & action IX* (pp. 123-126), New York: Lawrence Erlbaum Associates.

Michielsen, M. E., Stins, J. F., Roerdink, M., & Beek, P. J. (2007). Effects of cognition and expertise on postural sway regularity. In S. Cummins-Sebree, M. A. Riley, & K. Shockley (Eds.), *Studies in perception & action IX* (pp. 127-130), New York: Lawrence Erlbaum Associates.

Schmit, J. M., Regis, D. I., & Riley, M. A. (2005). Dynamic patterns of postural sway in ballet dancers and track athletes. *Experimental Brain Research, 163*, 370-378.

Shumway-Cook, A., & Woollacott, M. H. (2007). *Motor Control: Translating Research into Clinical Practice*. Philadelphia, PA: Lippincott Williams & Wilkins.

Acknowledgements. Linda Kohne, Ayesha Ekanayake, Erin Grimes, Sailee Teredesai, Candace Sitton, and David Knapp assisted on this project. We thank the Cincinnati Ballet Company, Lincoln Elementary School, and Hamilton Freshman School for their participation in this project. Supported by NSF grants BCS-0926662, and BCS-0728743.

Studies in Perception & Action X
E. Charles & L.J. Smart (Eds.)
© 2011 Taylor & Francis Group, LLC

Visual Vigilance Tasks Influence Stance Width

Anthony M. Mayo, Jenna E. Urbain, & Thomas A. Stoffregen

University of Minnesota

When asked to stand comfortably, people typically position their feet so that their stance width (the distance between the midline of the heels) is about 17 cm (McIlroy & Maki, 1997). This placement is a choice, and it can vary across situations. As one example, we may choose a wider stance when lifting a heavy object. As another example, mariners choose wider stance width when at sea than on land (Stoffregen et al., 2009). In several studies conducted on land, researchers have controlled stance width (rather than allowing participants to select it), and have found that stance width influences the magnitude of body sway during stance on land (Day et al., 1993; Mouzat et al., 2004; Stoffregen, Chen, Yu, & Villard, 2011). When stance width is in the range from 0 – 30 cm, the magnitude of sway tends to be negatively correlated with stance width. Similar effects have been observed during stance at sea (Stoffregen et al., 2011; Stoffregen, Villard, & Yu, 2009). Stance width can also influence the performance of visual tasks that are engaged in during stance. Yu et al. (2010) found that stance width influenced the performance of visual vigilance tasks at sea: Performance of a demanding vigilance task was best when stance width was 17 cm, and was worse when stance width was narrower (5 cm), or wider (30 cm). For Yu et al., stance width was an independent variable. If stance width can influence visual performance, we wondered whether participants would adjust their stance width as a function of the difficulty of visual tasks, so as to maximize visual performance. Thus, in this study we treated stance width as a dependent variable.

Method

We manipulated the difficulty of a visual signal detection vigilance task. Pairs of vertical lines were presented on a video monitor for 200 ms at the rate of one pair per second. In most pairs, the lines were of the same length, and no response was required. In 33% of pairs the two lines were of different length; for each of these *critical signals* participants were to press a response key (on a handheld wireless mouse) as quickly as possible. In the Easy condition, changes in line length occurred only in one end of one line, whereas in the Hard condition changes occurred in any of four positions (one of two ends on each line). There were 10 trials in each condition presented in alternating order over successive trials, and each trial lasted 60 s. We monitored head and torso movements using a magnetic tracking system (Fastrak, Polhemus, Inc., Cochester, VT). Participants were required to place their feet on pairs of lines on the floor (one line for each foot). Lines for the left foot were at a constant angle of 10 degrees relative to lines for the right foot (i.e., we controlled stance angle). There were ten lines for the left foot and ten for the right. For each foot, lines were separated by 2.0 cm. The minimum distance between left and right lines (and, therefore, the minimum stance width) was 5.0 cm, while the maximum was 45.0 cm. For each trial, participants chose on which lines to place their feet, that is, they chose their own stance width. Participants were required to sit down after each trial, thereby ensuring that stance width would be chosen anew for each trial.

Results and Discussion

We analyzed vigilance performance in terms of d' (Ehrenstein & Ehrenstein, 1999), which is a weighted sum of hits (correct button presses), false alarms (incorrect button presses) and misses (absent button presses). We also analyzed self-selected stance width, and postural activity. As expected, d' differed between the Easy (mean = 4.32) and Hard (mean = 1.27) tasks, confirming that the Hard task was hard and the Easy task was easy. Measures of body sway did not differ between the Easy and Hard task. However, participants chose wider stance when performing the Hard task (mean = 22.07 cm) than when performing the Easy task (mean = 21.58 cm), $F_{(1,9)}$ = 5.63, p = 0.033.

Yu et al. (2010) controlled stance width during performance of visual vigilance tasks. They found that the positional variability of sway was greater during performance of an easy vigilance task than during performance of a hard vigilance task. In the present study, we found no differences in sway between hard and easy tasks, but we did find a difference in self-selected stance width. As noted above, wider stance width tends to reduce the magnitude of body sway. Given this, it may be that task-specific variations in stance width in the present study were intended (albeit unconsciously) to support performance of the easy and hard vigilance tasks. This possibility highlights a gap in the literature—prior to the present study, there has been no research in which the kinematics of body sway were measured when participants were free to select their own stance width. We know that stance width influences body sway when stance width is under experimental control, but we do not know whether the same is true when stance width is under participants' own control.

The fact that participants modulated their stance width as a function of the difficulty of visual vigilance tasks is consistent with the hypothesis that there can be functional integration between posture (in this case, body configuration) and visual performance (Riccio & Stoffregen, 1988).

References

Day, B. L., Steiger, M. J., Thompson PD, Marsen CD. (1993). Effects of vision and stance width on human body motion when standing: implications for afferent control of lateral sway. *Journal of Physiology, 469,* 479 – 99.

Ehrenstein, W. H., & Ehrenstein, A. (1999). Psychophysical methods . In: U. Windhorst and H. Johansson (Eds.), *Modern techniques in neuroscience research* (pp. 1211 – 1241). New York: Springer.

McIlroy, W. E., & Maki, B. E. (1997). Preferred placement of the feet during quiet stance: development of a standardized foot placement for balance testing. *Clinical Biomechanics, 12*, 66 – 70.

Mouzat, A., Dabonneville, M., Bertrand, P. (2004). The effect of feet position on orthostatic posture in a female sample group . *Neuroscience Letters, 365*, 79 – 82.

Riccio, G. E., & Stoffregen, T. A. (1988). Affordances as constraints on the control of stance. *Human Movement Science, 7*, 265-300.

Stoffregen, T. A., Chen, F.-C., Yu, Y., & Villard, S. (2009). Stance width and angle at sea: Effects of sea state and body orientation. *Aviation, Space, and Environmental Medicine, 80*, 845-849.

Stoffregen, T. A., Villard, S., Chen, F.-C., & Yu, Y. (2011). Standing body sway on land and at sea. *Ecological Psychology, 23*, in press.

Stoffregen, T. A., Villard, S., & Yu, Y. (2009). Body sway at sea for two visual tasks and three stance widths. *Aviation, Space, and Environmental Medicine, 80*, 1039-1043.

Yu, Y., Yank, J. R., Katsumata, Y., Villard, S., Kennedy, R. S., & Stoffregen, T. A. (2010). Visual vigilance performance and standing posture at sea. *Aviation, Space, and Environmental Medicine, 81*, 375-382.

Studies in Perception & Action X
E. Charles & L.J. Smart (Eds.)
© 2011 Taylor & Francis Group, LLC

Mode Analyses on the Kinematical Structure of Basic Movements and Residual Patterns in Human Locomotion

Nanase Takata, Sadahiro Senda, Kazuki Nakai
and Katsuyoshi Tsujita

Department of Biomedical Engineering, Osaka Institute of Technology

Human locomotion control is typical of a multi-body system control that may be specific for periodic and stable motion patterns of locomotion. During rhythmic and steady motion such as straight walking, many joints and muscles are organized into a collective unit that is controlled as though it has fewer degrees of freedom (DOFs), even though it still needs to retain the necessary flexibility for adapting to changes in the environment. In this study, we investigated human locomotion by mode analyses using singular value decomposition. From motion-captured data of human locomotion, we extracted common basic movements and residual modes, and analyzed kinematical structures. The results show that there are basic movements whose proportion of variance is significant, and those are common to all the test subjects. The residual modes involve personal peculiarities or symptoms of motor dysfunction in locomotion. We can note that by utilizing the results, we may expect to identify personal traits and run diagnostic check systems for applications.

Method

Human locomotion on a treadmill is measured with an optical motion capture system. The motion capture system in this study is composed of six cameras with a frame rate at 100[Hz] and 34 markers attached to the human body (shown in Figure 1). Ten healthy subjects (five males and five females, 1.47-1.77 m) volunteered for the experiments. Measured data on test subjects' motions are transformed to joint angle vectors of the 18 DOF skeleton models (Figure 2). The motion pattern matrix consists of the obtained time series of joint angle vectors as follows:

$$A = \begin{pmatrix} \theta_1(t) & \cdots & \theta_N(t) \end{pmatrix}, \quad A \in \mathfrak{R}^{18 \times N}$$

The motion pattern matrix is decomposed to motion components with the SVD (Singular Value Decomposition) method as follows:

$$A = U\Sigma V^*$$

where Σ consists of singular values. U and V^* are composed of mode vectors relating time-dependent motion patterns and distribution functions to joint angles, respectively. We can figure out which mode is significant by checking the singular values. From the decomposed motion components, we investigated the kinematical structure and discrepancy of the basic movements and the residual motion patterns in human locomotion.

Results and Discussion

The results show that there are two major periodical modes whose values of proportion of variance are significant (Figures 3

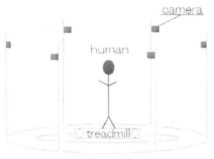
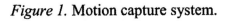
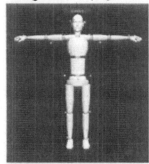

Figure 1. Motion capture system.   *Figure 2.* Human skeleton model with 18 joints and 34 markers.

and 4). These modes are common to all the test subjects. The cumulative proportion of variance of these two major modes is greater than 75% in every test subject's data. As well, these common major modes are quite stable periodic motion patterns and are robust against the variance of locomotion conditions such as walking speed, inclination of the ground, disturbances, etc. That means these periodic modes construct invariant limit cycles on

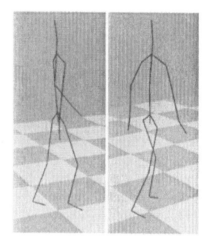 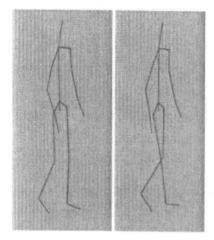

Figure 3. The most significant mode. Arms and legs are periodically swinging. Opposite-side arms and legs are in phase. The left arm and right leg are in phase.

Figure 4. The secondly significant mode. Arms and trunk are almost still. Knees periodically bending in antiphase.

phase space. On the other hand, we investigated the locomotion of subjects whose knees on one side were physically constrained with knee supporters. In those cases, the two major modes also observed and correlation coefficients between the major modes in usual locomotion and in constrained locomotion are almost equal to 1.0; that means a high correlation where there is almost no difference. But the residual higher modes, especially the third mode or ones higher, have quite a large difference in correlation coefficients between the cases of usual locomotion and constrained locomotion.

We can note that the results show these two major modes are essential basic movements in human locomotion. As well, higher-order modes whose values of proportion of variance are small are the residual modes that involve personal peculiarities or symptoms of motor dysfunction in locomotion. It is expected that by utilizing the results, we will be able to identify personal traits and run diagnostic check systems for applications.

References

Bernstein, N. (1967). *The co-ordination and regulation of movements.* Oxford:Pergamon.

Grillner, S. (1985). Neurobiological bases of rhythmic motor acts in vertebrates. *Science, 228*, 143-149

Ivanenko, Y.P., Cappellini, G., Dominici, N., Poppele, R.E., & Lacquaniti F. (2005a). Coordination of locomotion with voluntary movements in humans. *J Neuroscience 25*,7238 –7253.

Ivanenko, Y.P., Dominici, N., Cappellini, G., & Lacquaniti, F. (2005b). Kinematics in newly walking toddlers does not depend upon postural stability. *J Neurophysiology 94*,754 –763.

Kelso, J.A.S. (1997). *Dynamic patterns: The Self-Organization of Brain and Behavior (Complex Adaptive Systems)*, MIT Press.

Mishima, K., Kanata, S., Nakanishi, H., Sawaragi, T. & Horiguchi, Y. (2010). Extraction of Similarities and Differences in Human Behavior using Singular Value Decomposition, *Proc. of The 11th IFAC/IFIP/ IFORS/IEA Symp. on Analysis, Design,and Evaluation of Human-Machine Systems.*

Taga, G., Yamaguchi, Y., & Shimizu, H. (1991). Self-organized control of Bipedal locomotion by neural oscillators in unpredictable environment, *Biological Cybernetics, 65*, 147-159.

Taga, G. (1994). Emergence of bipedal locomotion through entrainment among the neuro-musculo-skeletal system and the environment. *Physica D, 75*, 190-208.

Rossignol, S., Dubic, R. & Gossard, J.P. (2006). Dynamic sensorimotor interaction in locomotion. *Physiol. Rev., 86*, 89-154

Acknowledgements. This work was partially supported by a Grant-in-Aid for Scientific Research (C) No. 22500416 from the Japan Society for the Promotion of Science (JSPS).

Studies in Perception & Action X
E. Charles & L.J. Smart (Eds.)
© 2011 Taylor & Francis Group, LLC

Chapter 5:

Human Factors

Studies in Perception & Action X
E. Charles & L.J. Smart (Eds.)
© 2011 Taylor & Francis Group, LLC

Interaction Between Voluntary and Automatic Control of Grip Force when Manipulating an Object

Frédéric Danion

Movement Science Institute, Université de la Méditerranée & CNRS, FRANCE

Humans and other primates demonstrate an exquisite ability to finely grade fingertip forces. In this study I consider two motor behaviours in which accurate grip force control is crucial: handling objects and squeezing them. When transporting hand-held objects, our grip force (GF) is largely determined by automatic and predictive mechanisms that prevent the object from slipping under the influence of movement dependent load force (Westling & Johansson, 1984). The term predictive refers to the fact that GF is modulated in synchrony, or slightly ahead of load force (LF), whereas the term automatic refers to the observation that the GF-LF coupling is apparently not open to voluntary influence (Flanagan & Wing, 1995). In contrast, when squeezing objects, GF can be under voluntary control and this ability is largely exploited in force tracking tasks. The goal of the current study was to explore the extent to which automatic and voluntary control of GF can coexist simultaneously (or possibly interfere) during a combined task that both requires to squeeze and transport an object.

Method

Subjects were instructed to hold a light object between the thumb and index finger (see top of Figure 1). It contained a single force sensor that measured the fingertip force applied perpendicularly to the sensor's surface. The object was attached to an elastic cord such that the minimum GF to prevent slip of the object increased linearly as a function of movement amplitude (i.e., load force, LF). Another force sensor was placed at the end of the elastic cord so as to determine LF. Force signals were collected at 1,000 Hz.

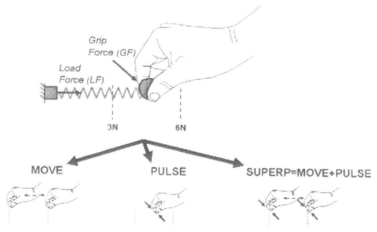

Figure 1. Schematic illustration of the set-up and experimental conditions.

The bottom of Figure 1 illustrates the three different tasks that were investigated. MOVE and PULSE were used to investigate independently automatic and voluntary GF control. During MOVE, the task was to oscillate the instrumented object between two targets distant by 10 cm (at LF=3 and 6 N). Participants were instructed to synchronize movement reversals in the vicinity of the targets with the beeps of a metronome. During PULSE, the task consisted in producing rhythmical GF pulse onto the instrumented object, while maintaining the object immobile between the two targets (i.e. LF = 4.5 N). Participants were instructed to produce one pulse at each beep of the metronome. During SUPERP, subjects had to perform simultaneously the MOVE and PULSE tasks. This means that, while oscillating the object, subjects had to generate one pulse at each target. Altogether, during SUPERP, voluntary GF modulations had to be performed at twice the movement frequency. For each task, metronome frequency was tested between 1.2 and 4 Hz.

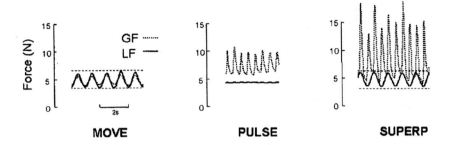

Figure 2. Representative force signals in each experimental condition.

Results and Discussion

Typical data from one subject are presented in Figure 2 (metronome = 2.0 Hz). Visual inspection of data during MOVE (left side) shows that GF and LF varied in synchrony and with rather similar amplitude. This view is supported by significant coefficients of correlation between these two signals for all subjects and all movement frequencies (R>0.6, p<0.001). Further temporal analyses showed that, on average, GF was preceding LF by 37±15 ms, thereby confirming the feedforward nature of GF adjustments (Flanagan, Vetter, Johansson, & Wolpert, 2003; Danion & Sarlegna, 2007). During PULSE, according to the instruction of squeezing, voluntary GF modulation was performed at twice the frequency of the metronome while the amplitude of LF modulation was close to zero (<0.1 N). During SUPERP, the task became somewhat more difficult because subjects had now to simultaneously squeeze and oscillate the object. Nevertheless, the example provided in Figure 2 (right side) shows that the subject was able to complete this task, namely to oscillate the object at 1.0 Hz, while making voluntary GF modulations at 2.0 Hz. Additional analyses showed that the GF-LF correlation was not significant (0.2<R<-0.2, p>0.05), suggesting that voluntary GF modulations can overrule the well established GF-LF coupling.

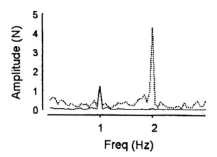

Figure 3. Power spectral analysis of GF and LF force signals in representative trial during SUPERP.

To further investigate the issue of GF-LF coupling during SUPERP, power spectral analyses were conducted. A typical example is presented in Figure 3 (metronome = 2.0 Hz). The results showed that GF carried two peaks: one peak at twice the frequency of movement (consistent with the instruction of squeezing at each movement reversal), and another one coinciding with the LF peak frequency. To explore whether this second GF peak was the expression of a functional GF-LF coupling, phase analyses were conducted. Results showed that during slow arm movements one component of GF was indeed oscillating in phase with LF. However, as movement frequency increased, the asynchrony between GF and LF was found to build up, reaching up to 160 ms during 2.0 Hz oscillatory movements. This suggests that during fast oscillatory movements, an automatic component of GF is still operating, but does no longer provide a functional coupling between GF and LF.

Overall, those results may be interpreted as evidence that voluntary and automatic (predictive) GF control can be superimposed smoothly during slow arm movements, but the risk of interference increases for faster movements. At a more general level, those results are compatible with brain imaging studies showing that automatic and voluntary GF control are mediated by partly distinct neural substrates (e.g. Kawato et al., 2003).

References

Danion, F., & Sarlegna, F. R. (2007). Can the human brain predict the consequences of arm movement corrections when transporting an object? Hints from grip force adjustments. *The Journal of Neuroscience, 27*(47), 12839-12843.

Flanagan, J. R., & Wing, A. M. (1995). The stability of precision grip forces during cyclic arm movements with a hand-held load. *Experimental Brain Research 105*(3), 455-464.

Flanagan, J. R., Vetter, P., Johansson, R. S., & Wolpert, D. M. (2003). Prediction precedes control in motor learning. *Current biology, 13*(2), 146-150.

Kawato, M., Kuroda, T., Imamizu, H., Nakano, E., Miyauchi, S., & Yoshioka, T. (2003). Internal forward models in the cerebellum: fMRI study on grip force and load force coupling. *Progress in Brain Research, 142*, 171-188.

Westling, G., & Johansson, R. S. (1984). Factors influencing the force control during precision grip. *Experimental Brain Research, 53*(2), 277-284.

Studies in Perception & Action X
E. Charles & L.J. Smart (Eds.)
© 2011 Taylor & Francis Group, LLC

Regulating Rotation Speed in Wheel Throwing: Effects of Mass and Shape

Enora Gandon, Frédéric Pous, Thelma Coyle
Franck Buloup, and Reinoud J. Bootsma

*Institut des Sciences du Mouvement E.J. Marey (UMR 6233),
Université de la Méditerranée, Marseille, France*

In throwing a ceramic vessel on a rotating wheel, two main phases can be distinguished. During the pre-forming phase the potter centers the mass of clay on the wheel and subsequently sets the stage for the forming process by opening (hollowing) the centered lump of clay. During the forming phase pulling the clay brings out the initial form as the vessel rises from its base, while the final form is acquired during the thinning process. All along the potter combines the manually exerted pressures with the wheel's rotational energy to plastically deform the clay. By exploiting the wheel's rotational energy, the emergence of wheel throwing marks a breakpoint in the evolution of ceramic techniques (Roux & Courty, 1998). In the framework of our ongoing research program into potters' wheel-throwing skills, we analyse the combined effects of manual pressure and energy dissipation through the resultants effects on the clay in terms of the geometrical and mechanical characteristics of the vessels produced (e.g., Gandon et al., 2011). In the present contribution, we focus on the control of rotation speed.

On a self-driven wheel the dissipation of rotational energy inevitably leads to a slowing down of the rotation speed, with the amount of speed lost depending on the wheel's moment of inertia. During the energy-consuming throwing process the potter therefore has to insert energy into the system. A stick-wheel requires the potter to interrupt the throwing process in order to accelerate the wheel with the help of a hand-held stick. Because of this process-disrupting characteristic, a stick-wheel typically has a large moment of inertia allowing minimization of the loss of rotation speed. A foot-operated kick-wheel, on the other hand, allows the potter to insert energy while continuing the throwing activity. Given skilled potters' capacity to effectively separate foot and hand movements, one may reasonably expect the regulation of rotation speed to be close to optimal for reasons of energy efficiency.

Because wheel throwing is a bimanual skill, the purposeful deformation of the clay is achieved by coordinating both the tangential and axial pressures exerted at the clay-hand interfaces. During centering the hands are placed on either side of the lump of clay, pushing inward. Hollowing is performed with the thumbs placed near the centre pushing downward and outward while the fingers of both hands remain on the outside. During pulling and thinning one hand is placed on the inside and the other the outside, exerting theirs opposing pressures on the common wall. In order to gently deform the clay and maintaining axial symmetry, friction at the interfaces has to be small and stable. This requirement sets the minimal linear speed with which the clay must pass between the hands. Given that the stability of the hands cannot be perfect, one may also expect an upper limit on the linear speed, beyond which the potter can no longer control the shaping process. Thus, we expect the potter to regulate the wheel's rotation speed so as to maintain the linear speed with which the clay passes between the hands within certain boundaries. Linear speed could be a key functional variable in the control of wheel-throwing (Bernstein, 1967; Turvey, 1990). To our knowledge, the control of wheel rotation speed in throwing has not been addressed experimentally. The only information we have found is Hulthen's (1974) suggestion that the minimum linear speed required to produce wheel-thrown pottery would be 0.7 m/s.

Our experimental requirement to produce vessels of different mass and form implies that the vessels will differ in diameter. This leads to the following operational hypotheses. During the pre-forming phase the larger mass (of larger diameter) should reveal a lower rotation speed, without any influence of the final form requirements. During the forming phase, rotation speed should be lower than during the pre-forming phase, with vessels of larger diameter revealing lower rotation speed.

Method

Six professional male potters (31.3 ± 4.5 yrs of age) with a kick-wheel throwing experience of 16.5 years (± 6.4 yrs) participated in the experiment that took place in a traditional pottery workshop in the village of Jahanjirabad (India). All used the same low-inertia kick-wheel.

Participants were asked to reproduce four different model forms (cylinder, bowl, sphere and vase) using two different quantities of clay (0.75 and 2.25 kg), for a total of eight experimental conditions. They produced five vessels in each condition. Wheel rotation speed was measured during each session by means of a magnet fixed to the lower side of the rotating wheel and a sensor (NI USB-6008, National Instruments). Acquisition of rotation speed was synchronized with video recordings allowing the start and end points of the different phases to be identified. We focused on durations and rotation speeds during the pre-forming phase (Phase 1: centering and hollowing) and the forming phase (Phase 2: pulling and thinning).

Results and Discussion

As can be seen from Fig. 1, Phase 1 was shorter than Phase 2 (29.3 and 77,1 s, respectively; $F(1, 5) = 76.5$, $p < .001$). During both phases throwing the 2.25-kg mass took longer than throwing the 0.75-kg mass ($F(1, 5) = 41.1$, $p < .001$). A Form x Phase interaction ($F(3, 15) = 40.1$, $p < .001$) indicated that Form did not affect the duration of Phase 1. In Phase 2, the cylinder took longer to throw than the sphere and vase that in turn took longer than the bowl (p's < .05).

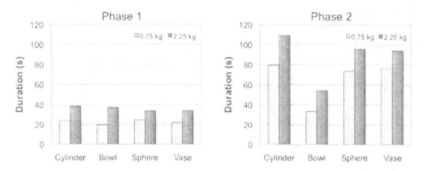

Figure 1. Throwing duration as a function of Phase, Mass, and Form.

Rotation speed was considerably higher ($F(1, 5) = 271.2$, $p <$ .001) during the Phase 1 (120 rot/min) than during Phase 2 (86 rot/min). As shown in Fig. 2, Mass systematically affected the speed of rotation ($F(1, 5) = 73.4$, $p < .001$) during both phases, with the larger masses being thrown at lower rotation speeds. A Form x Mass x Phase interaction ($F(3, 15) = 3.4$, $p < .05$) indicated that Form affected rotation speed only during the second phase, with bowl having a smaller rotation speed than the other forms.

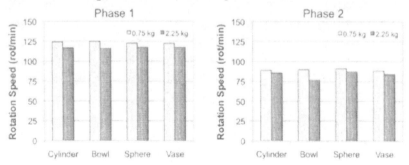

Figure 2. Rotation speed as a function of Phase, Mass, and Form.

Estimating linear speed based on each vessel's diameter at the end of Phases 1 and 2, indicated that linear speed remained between 0.3 and 1.2 m/s. As can be seen from a comparison between Figures 2 and 3, the lower rotation speed observed for larger masses should not be uniquely attributed to the associated larger diameters: linear speed was higher for the larger masses $(F(1, 5) = 55.7, p < .001)$. This effect of Mass might be explained by the necessarily thicker walls of the 2.25-kg vessels (see Gandon et al., in press), requiring less precision on the part of the potter. A Form x Mass x Phase interaction $(F(3, 15) = 3.7, p < .05)$ indicated that Form affected the linear speed only during Phase 2, with the bowl having a higher linear speed than the other forms.

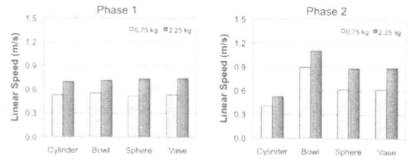

Figure 3. Linear speed as a function of Phase, Mass, and Form.

Larger masses of clay consistently showed higher linear speeds, during both phases of throwing. Still, as expected, rotation speed decreased during throwing to compensate for the vessel's increasing size, allowing the linear speed with which the clay passes between the potter's hands to remain within certain boundaries. Indeed, without the observed change in rotation speed, linear speed would have increased by more than 85%. The average linear speed observed (0.68 m/s) was close to Hulthen' (1974) estimation. Yet the range was relatively large, varying between 0.36 and 1.52 m/s.

The bowl was the most common form thrown by our potters during their daily activity. Interestingly, for this particular form, the duration of pulling and thinning phase was shortest while linear speed was highest. Overall, the present results suggest that the effects of mass and form on linear speed are related to the precision requirement on the pressures exerted.

References

Bernstein, N.A. (1967). The Coordination and Regulation of Movements. Pergamon Press, London.

Gandon, E., Casanova, R., Sainton, P, Coyle, T., Roux, V., Bril, B., & Bootsma, R.J., (2011), A proxy of potters' throwing skill: ceramic vessels considered in terms of mechanical stress, *Journal of Archaeological Science*, 38: 1080-1089.

Hulthen, B. (1974). On documentation of pottery. *Acta Archaeologica Lundensia (Lund).*

Roux, V., & Courty, M. A. (1998). Identification of wheel-fashioning methods: technological analysis of 4th – 3rd millennium BC oriental ceramics. *Journal of Archaeological Science, 25,* 747-763.

Turvey, M.T. (1990). Coordination. *American Psychologist, 45,* 938-953.

Studies in Perception & Action X
E. Charles & L.J. Smart (Eds.)
© 2011 Taylor & Francis Group, LLC

Postural Control While Reading in Unstable Visual Environment

Chia-Chun Huang and Chih-Mei Yang

Department of Physical Education, National Taiwan Normal University

The uncomfortable response to unstable environments called motion sickness has been described as the negative effect of provocative motion or apparent motion of an environment on a human (Flanagan, May, & Dobie, 2004). People become ill in situations where they fail to adapt appropriately to the motion of transportations, such as produced by cars and buses. In particular, motion sickness arises more often while reading a book or watching a video while being transported. Riccio and Stoffregen (1991) proposed postural instability theory and argued that the prolonged postural instability induced by maladaptation to the environment occurred prior to motion sickness. Thus postural sway could be regarded as an indicator of susceptibility of motion sickness (Smart, Pagulayan, & Stoffregen, 1998; Stoffregen & Smart, 1998). "Visually induced motion sickness" (VIMS) is used to describe motion sickness occurring in situations of imposed visual motion without body motion. VIMS has been observed in the cases of moving rooms (Stoffregen & Smart, 1998), flight simulators (Stoffregen, Hettinger, Haas, Roe, & Smart, 2000), and console video games (Stoffregen, Faugloire, Yoshida, Flanagan, & Merhi, 2008). The result of the studies above showed that individuals who become motion sick exhibit higher postural sway and head-environment coupling.

Optical flow, the continuous change of optical array produced by motion of animals or the environment of an animal (Gibson, 1979), is important information for postural control. The moving room technique has been recruited to produce optical flow that would cause perception of self-motion, and further induce postural response (e.g., Lee & Aronson, 1974; Stoffregen, Hove, Schmit, & Bardy, 2006). Postural sway could be reduced in order to achieve supra-postural tasks such as reading-like visual searching (Stoffregen, Pagulayan, Bardy, & Hittinger, 2000).

In sum, the possibility of higher occurrence of motion sickness while reading in transportations might be related to higher postural instability. Furthermore, reading could be regarded as a supra-postural task which would induce postural sway reduction, but it is unknown what role optical flow plays in postural control when reading. The purpose of the present study was to investigate the effects of dynamic visual environment and presentation of reading targets on postural control while sitting and standing.

Method

Sixteen young adults served as participants voluntarily. They had normal or corrected to normal vision, with no reported vestibular dysfunction.

The optical flow was generated by a moving room, comprised of three walls and a ceiling covered with marble-like pattern paper, 2.4 m on a side. The motion of room was 0.2 Hz oscillation with amplitude of 4 cm. The reading targets were eight Chinese articles in black, 12 pt, Times New Roman font, printed with 2 columns on A4 size white paper which were pasted on foam core boards. Targets were fixed on an adjustable tripod or held by two hands by the participant 50cm away in front of the participant.

The independent variables were (1) room motion in moving and stationary; (2) presentation of targets in fixed, hand-held, and no target; and (3) posture in standing and sitting. The three independent variables constitute twelve conditions, one trial for each condition, 50 seconds per trial. Participants were asked to stand normally or to sit on a stool, facing alone the line of room motion, 1.5 m away from the frontal wall. They read the articles in fixed and hand-held target trials and gazed a point mark on the frontal wall in no-target trials. Polhemus Liberty magnetic tracking system and Motion Monitor software were used to detect and collect the position and motion of moving room as well as participants' head, trunk (the 7th cervical), and thumb of right hand.

The dependent variables were (1) postural sway, obtained from calculated SD of positions of head in anterior-posterior and lateral axes; (2) head-room coupling, the cross correlation between head and room motions in the anterior-posterior axis; and (3) head-trunk coupling, the cross correlation between head and trunk motions in the anterior-posterior axis.

Results and Discussion

Motion Sickness

All of the participants were remained well in this study and they all completed the experiments. Two of the participants reported never being motion sick in the past, but 14 participants reported having been motion sick in the past. Twelve of the 14 participants' experience of motion sickness occurred before they were 14 years old; the other two participants were motion sick recently.

Postural Sway

Separate 2 (room motion) × 3 (target) × 2 (posture) repeated measure ANOVAs were performed to analyze postural sway data in the AP and ML axes. The analysis revealed an significant interaction between posture and target ($F(2,28) = 9.68, p < .05, \eta_p^2 = .41$). As *figure 1* shows, in seated posture, sway was larger in hand-hold target trials than in fixed target and no target trials. Standing postural sway was larger in hand-held target and no target than in fixed target trials. Across viewing conditions, postural sway while standing was larger than when sitting.

In lateral axis, the analysis revealed significant main effects of posture ($F(2,28) = 5.535, p < .05, \eta_p^2 = .283$) and target ($F(2,28) = 30.295, p < .05, \eta_p^2 = .648$). Postural sway was larger while reading the hand-held target and smaller while sitting on a stool.

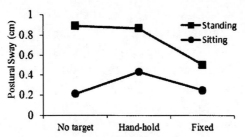

Figure 1. Interaction between stance type and target on postural sway in anterior-posterior axis.

Head-room Coupling

A 3 (target) × 2 (posture) repeated measure ANOVA was performed to analyze the coefficient of cross correlation between motions of head and room. The result revealed significant main effects of target ($F(2,28) = 53.250$, $p < .05$, $\eta_p^2 = .80$) and posture ($F(2,28) = 3.928$, $p < .05$, $\eta_p^2 = .22$). Individuals' sway less coupled with visual environment in sitting and hand-hold target trials.

Head-trunk Coupling

A 2 (room motion) ×3 (target) × 2 (posture) repeated measure ANOVA revealed a significant interaction between room motion and target ($F(2,28) = 6.95$, $p < .05$, $\eta_p^2 = .33$). The correlation between head and trunk in sitting was lower when the room was moving then when it was stationary. Nevertheless, head-trunk coupling in standing was equally high across motion conditions.

Discussion

Postural sway decreased while reading fixed target. This result confirms that people modulate their postural sway in supra-postural task (Stoffregen et al., 2000). However, postural sway increased when the target was held by two hands. It is possible that higher sway was allowed while reading hand-held targets because the range of stimulation on the retina is easier to maintain. Furthermore, the larger variability in postural sway while reading hand-held targets might relate to the decoupling of the individual and his environment.

Notably, postural sway was not influenced by room motion. It might because participants had easily perceived the pattern of regular oscillation of moving room and adapted to the perturbative visual environment. However, the visual effect might be not revealed on the amount of postural sway, but might be revealed on the structure of postural control. Head-trunk coupling could be explained as neck control that is influenced by the interaction between room motion and postural sway. Specifically, neck adjustment was higher when the individual was sitting in the unstable visual environment.

In conclusion, postural sway and the coupling of head and visual environment (optic flow) were influenced by the manner of presentation of the target and the type of posture employed. The effect of the visual perturbation was revealed solely in measures of neck control. Postural sway was not become unstable while reading in unstable visual environment. The result above could not directly support the prediction of postural instability theory (Riccio & Stoffregen, 1991). However, the effect of interaction between optic flow and surface of support on postural stability while reading might be the critical issue. In order to unveil the causes and mechanisms of motion sickness while reading in transportation, it is still necessary to investigate the issues about how posture is controlled while performing tasks like reading in other types of unstable environments.

References

Flanagan, M. B., May, J. G., & Dobie, T. G. (2004). The role of vection, eye movements and postural instability in the etiology of motion sickness. *Journal of Vestibular Research, 14*, 335-346.

Gibson, J. J. (1979). *The ecological approach to visual perception*. Hillsdale, NJ: Lawrence Erlbaum Associates.

Lee, D. M., & Aronson, E. (1974). Visual proprioceptive control of standing in human infants. *Perception & Psychophysics, 15*, 529-532.

Riccio, G. E., & Stoffregen, T. A. (1991). An ecological theory of motion sickness and postural instability. *Ecological Psychology, 3*, 195-240.

Smart, L. J., Pagulayan, R., & Stoffregen, T. A. (1998). Self-induced motion sickness in unperturbed stance. Brain Research Bulletin, 47, 449-457.

Stoffregen, T. A., & Smart, L. J. (1998). Postural instability precedes motion sickness. *Brain Research Bulletin, 47*, 437-448.

Stoffregen, T. A., Faugloire, E., Yoshida, K., Flanagan, M. B., & Merhi, O. (2008). Motion sickness and postural sway in console video games. *Human Factors, 50*, 322-331.

Stoffregen, T. A., Hettinger, L. J., Haas, M. W., Roe, M. M., & Smart, L. J. (2000). Postural instability and motion sickness in a fixed-base flight simulator. *Human Factors, 42*, 458–469.

Stoffregen, T. A., Hove, P., Schmit, J., & Bardy, B. G. (2006). Voluntary and involuntary postural responses to imposed optic flow. *Motor Control, 10*, 24-33.

Stoffregen, T. A., Pagulayan, R. J., Bardy, B. G., & Hettinger, L. J. (2000). Modulating postural control to facilitate visual performance. *Human Movement Science, 19*, 203-220

Studies in Perception & Action X
E. Charles & L.J. Smart (Eds.)
© 2011 Taylor & Francis Group, LLC

Layout of the Ground Surface in Daily Environments: An Ecological Approach to Natural Scene Statistics

Makoto Inagami and Hirohiko Kaneko

Department of Information Processing, Tokyo Institute of Technology, Japan

Natural scene statistics is an approach to perception that measures various physical characteristics of our surrounding environment (e.g., Geisler, 2008). This approach aims at uncovering the relationships between probabilistic regularities in the environment and our perceptual properties. Recent successful studies include work on visual space conducted by Yang and Purves (2003), who measured radial distances using a 3D laser scanner at multiple locations in a forest and at a university campus. Their analyses revealed that the characteristics of the measured distances could explain several anomalies in distance perception. For example, they found that the probability distribution of distances peaked at around 3 m, a finding that could explain a phenomenon wherein objects in an impoverished setting (e.g., in the dark) are perceived to be 2–4 m away—so-called specific distance tendency (e.g., Gogel, 1969). On the basis of similar findings, Yang and Purves have argued that perception is statistical inference based on environmental regularities and the Bayesian framework. This is the fundamental theory in natural scene statistics.

Gibson's ecological approach also focuses on the environment to understand perceptual abilities. Gibson (1950) proposed the "ground theory" of space perception, according to which space is veridically perceived with a continuous surface or an array of adjoining surfaces as a background. For example, the ground provides definitive information to perceive the distances of the objects on its surface. Recent experiments have also demonstrated that the ground enables accurate distance perception (Wu, Ooi, & He, 2004). The ecological approach insists that perception requires no inferential process because of the richness of environmental information.

As mentioned so far, the two approaches, despite placing equal emphasis on the environment, have developed crucially different theories of perception. Obtaining a better understanding of perception requires resolution of this inconsistency. The overall purpose of this study is to discuss natural scene statistics from an ecological perspective. By analyzing spatial measurements obtained in daily environments, we examine the reproducibility of the above- cited distance distribution and then investigate the layout of the ground and other lower surfaces.

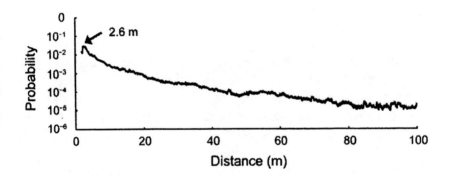

Figure 1. Probability distribution of the measured distances to the surrounding environments.

Method

We sampled 17 measuring environments from those routinely experienced by author one. Two of them were indoor environments, which were measured at the center of his room and the laboratory where he works. The other 15 environments fell along the outdoor route regularly taken by him via his bicycle. They environments were selected in a manner such that he passes through them at approximately two-minute intervals. The route was in a suburban area and included a park and a university campus.

In each environment, a 3D laser scanner (RIEGL LMS-Z210i) measured the radial distances to the surrounding surfaces. The measuring point was set at a level of 1.5 m above the ground as normal eye level. The environment was scanned at a resolution of 0.2° within the area subtending 360° horizontally × 80° (±40°) vertically. The device can typically detect surfaces at distances of 2–200 m with an accuracy of ±25 mm. The measured data included distances that did not fall within range, which were then eliminated by us.

Results and Discussion

First, we examined the probability distribution of all distances measured. As shown in Figure 1, the probability peaks at 2.6 m and decreases approximately exponentially with distance. This result is almost consistent with that obtained by Yang and Purves (2003). Accordingly, the result supports their argument that the probability distribution is commonly obtained when multiple environments are measured, and also confirms that the specific distance tendency is attributed to statistical inference based on the distribution.

To investigate the distribution in greater detail, we next calculated percentiles of the measured distances for each elevation angle. As observed in Figure 2, the distances are asymmetrically distributed with respect to eye level. The surfaces below eye level are more narrowly distributed, being bounded at a level around the ground (height = −1.5 m). To understand the contribution of such lower surfaces to space perception, we considered the situation of perceiving the distance to the surface distributed with respect to eye level. The surfaces below eye level are more narrowly distributed, being bounded at a level around the ground (height = −1.5 m). To understand the contribution of such lower surfaces to

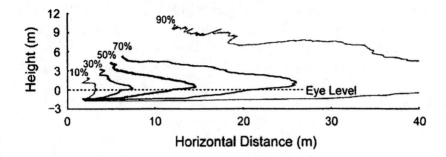

Figure 2. Percentiles of the distances measured for each elevation angle (the range of ±40° around eye level). The vertical and horizontal axes represent the height relative to eye level and the horizontal distance, respectively.

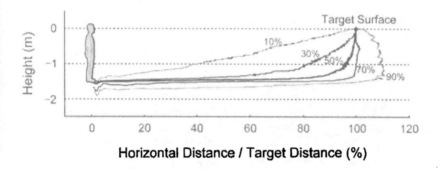

Figure 3. Distribution of lower surfaces in distance perception at eye level. The horizontal axis represents the percentage of the horizontal distance in the target distance (i.e., the measured eye-level distance) for each azimuth.

space perception, we considered the situation of perceiving the distance to the surface being at eye level (i.e., target surface). Figure 3 illustrates the distribution of surfaces between the standpoint and the target, where the horizontal distance is standardized as the proportion to target distance for each azimuth. The 50th percentile (i.e., median) indicates the most typical case, in which the ground extends from the standpoint to near the target. The distribution shows that 80% of the lower surfaces are present in the area between the 10th and 90th percentiles. This result suggests that in daily environments, we perceive distances basically along the ground and other lower surfaces.

To sum up, the present results correspond with Yang and Purves' (2003) finding and, on the other hand, show that daily environments typically provide the ground and other lower surfaces. These results suggest that in impoverished settings with little or no supplementary information, objects could be perceived to be at a specific distance as a result of statistical inference; however, when distances are perceived in daily environments, the definite information provided by the surfaces is important as Gibson (1950) argued.

References

Geisler, W. S. (2008). Visual perception and the statistical properties of natural scenes. *Annual Review of Psychology, 59*, 167–192.

Gibson, J. J. (1950). *The perception of the visual world.* Boston: Houghton Mifflin Company.

Gogel, W. C. (1969). The sensing of retinal size. *Vision Research, 9* (9), 1079–1094.

Wu, B., Ooi, T. L., & He, Z. J. (2004). Perceiving distance accurately by a directional process of integrating ground information. *Nature, 428,* 73–77.

Yang, Z. & Purves, D. (2003). A statistical explanation of visual space. *Nature Neuroscience, 6* (6), 632–640.

Studies in Perception & Action X
E. Charles & L.J. Smart (Eds.)
© 2011 Taylor & Francis Group, LLC

A Study on Driving Behavior from an Ecological Approach in Car-following Situations

Takayuki Kondoh[1,2], Nobuhiro Furuyama[2,3], Yousuke Akatsu[1],
Yoshihiro Miyake[2]

[1]Nissan Motor Co., Ltd, [2]Tokyo Institute of Technology,
[3]National Institute of Informatics

Gibson & Crooks (1938) argued that a driver chooses a path with fewer risks in their discussion on the Field of Safe Travel. Based on this idea, we attempt to quantify the risk feelings in car-following situations (Kondoh, et al., 2008). Risk feelings can be expressed in terms of τ (defined as distance headway divided by relative velocity) and THW (THW: defined as distance headway divided by host car velocity) in the following way (a and b are constants):

$$RiskFeelings = \frac{a}{\tau} + \frac{b}{THW} \qquad (1)$$

The following information is how we derived this formula. To formalize the risk feelings in a car-following situation, latent risk feelings, and overt risk feelings should be considered. Latent risk feelings refer to the risk feelings one obtains from the unpredictable behavior of the lead car. For example, even when the distance headway of the lead car is extremely short (such as 50cm), there would be no collision as long as the relative velocity between the lead car and the host car is zero. This would sound ridiculous, and in fact drivers would spontaneously avoid following the lead car with such a limited distance headway for the possible deceleration of the lead car. In the above-mentioned equation, the latent risk feelings are represented as an inverse of THW. Meanwhile, the overt risk feelings refer to the feelings one has when the lead car is approaching the host car, and if this situation continues, these cars shall collide with one another. In Eq. (1), the overt risk feelings are represented as an inverse of τ. In Study 1, using a fixed-based driving simulator that allowed the experimental conditions to be stably generated, the car-following experiment was conducted to quantify the drivers' risk perception. Study 2 describes the driver's behavior in stable car following situations on real-world express highway in Japan in terms of $1/\tau$ and THW.

Study 1: Quantification of Risk Feelings

Using the magnitude estimation method, we quantified the risk feelings of the participants driving a driving simulator vehicle in a car-following situation. The ME method is a procedure for formulating the relationship between human perception and the intensity of a stimulus by having a subject directly express the magnitude of the perceived sensation. There were ten male participants in this experiment. When the lead car approaches, τ and THW decreases. The image of the lead car disappeared when τ and THW decreased to the given point, for which we wanted the driver to evaluate their risk feelings.

Figure 1 shows the subjective risk feelings and quantification of risk feelings. For the subjective risk feelings, the size of the circle and the enclosed number indicate the relative magnitude of the perception of risk at each point in relation to the perceived risk at THW = 1 (The values are the average ratings of all the participants). The following points can be made: i) The larger the value of $1/\tau$, the greater the driver's risk feelings, ii) When THW is small, the contribution of $1/\tau$ becomes relatively small, and the risk feelings are more or less the same regardless of $1/\tau$, and iii) The smaller the THW value, the greater the driver's risk feelings.

Regarding the quantification of the risk feelings, the values of constants a and b in Eq. (1) that would fit the experimental results mentioned above were identified to be $a = 5$ and $b = 1$, and the contour lines calculated with those results are shown in the figure for the perception of risk on the $1/\tau$ -THW phase plain. We conducted Study 2 to more fully understand the relationship between the subjective risk feelings and quantification of risk feelings.

Study 2: Driving Behavior Analyzed in Terms of τ and THW

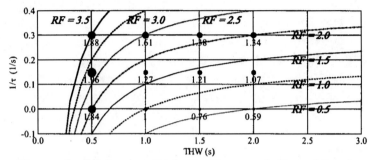

Figure 1. Subjective Risk Feelings and Quantification of Risk Feelings

This study describes the driver's behavior in stable car-following situations in terms of τ and THW without any cut-in by other vehicles. The experiment was conducted on a highway in Japan with a moderate vehicle density. The total distance traveled was approximately 460 km and the amount of time spent was approximately five hours. The test vehicle was an ordinary sedan installed with measurement equipment to record data under the following conditions. The driver's behavior was analyzed in terms of τ and THW. Ten male participants (average age= 45.2) took part in this experiment. They were nonprofessional drivers, and all had driving experiences of no less than 12 years. They were each instructed to drive safely as usual, to keep to the left-most lane where lane changes are not prohibited, and take breaks if necessary.

Figure 2(a) shows one cycle of a behavior pattern: 1) Stable following (τ = approx. 0), where the driver keeps the gas pedal pressed; ii) the lead car approaches (i.e., τ is positive) and the GasOff (cross) of the host car takes place (If the lead car nonetheless keeps approaching despite the GasOff, BrakeOn (circle) and BrakeOff (asterisk) follows); iii) as the lead car drives away from the host car (i.e., τ is negative), the GasOn (square) takes place; and iv) the stable car-following situation is obtained once again (τ = approx. 0). The trajectory moves counter-clockwise on the $1/\tau$-THW phase plain.

Figure 2(b) shows multiple car-following driving cycles and the operations that make changes on the $1/\tau$-THW phase plane. The THW mode value of this driver was 1.2 s. Accordingly, we can assume that the driver meant to keep this as the target THW, where ☐equals zero (marked with # in the figure).

Figures 2(c)-(d) show the driving patterns of the GasOffs (cross) and BrakeOns (circle) for the representative drivers on the one hand, and, on the other, the contour plots of the iso-percentile of duration that include the observed trajectory on the $1/$☐THW phase plane (The observed trajectories themselves are not shown) in the car-following situation for each participant. For example, in the case of Fig. 2(c), within the contour line of 90%tile (the most outer line), the host car stays in this area of the $1/$☐THW phase plane for 160 minutes because the extracted driving duration of this driver was 178 minutes. A quick glance at the panels in Figs. 2(c) and (d) reveal that the heights and widths of the area surrounded by the contour line are different. This suggests that the distributions of τ and THW differ among the participants, and that different drivers react differently to the approach of the lead car. The THW mode values were also different among the participants. Despite these differences, the following can be observed for all the participants: BrakeOns seem to depend less on τ alone when the THW is below 1, and does seem to depend on τ when the THW is greater than 1. The drivers C (Fig. 2 (c)) and I (Fig. 2(d)) rather clearly exhibited this pattern. This last point is exactly what Study 1 would predict, suggesting the validity of the framework invoking both τ and THW for a real-world environment. In conclusion, this paper demonstrated: a) that the risk feelings of the driver in the car-following situation can be quantified with τ and THW, and b) the drivers individual differences as well as their common behavioral patterns can be described when the car-following scenes are depicted on the $1/\tau$-THW phase plain. These points suggest that we can describe the driving behavior in a car-following situation more sufficiently by including THW in the τ theory proposed by Lee (1976).

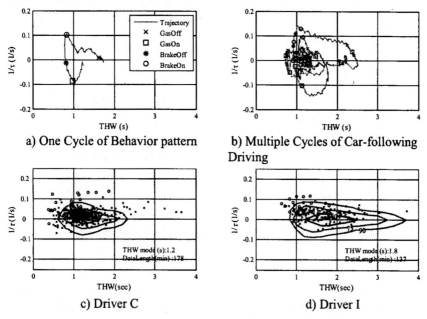

a) One Cycle of Behavior pattern

b) Multiple Cycles of Car-following Driving

c) Driver C

d) Driver I

Figure 2. Driving Behavior in Car-following Situations

References

J. J. Gibson & L. E. Crooks (1938). A theoretical field-analysis of automobile-driving, *Amer. J. Psychol., vol. 51, no. 3,* 453–471.

Lee, D. N. (1976). A theory of visual control of braking based on information about time-to-collision. *Perception, 5,* 437–459.

Kondoh, T., Yamamura T., Kitazaki T., Kuge N., & Bore E. R. (2008). Identification of visual cues and quantification of drivers' perception of proximity risk to the lead vehicle in car-Following situations. *Journal of Mechanical Systems for Transportation and Logistics, vol. 1, no. 2,* 170-180.

Kondoh, T., Furuayama, N., Akatsu, Y., & Miyake, Y. (2011). An ecological approach to characterizing driving behavior in car-following situations from the viewpoint of☐ and THW. *IEEE Transactions on Systems, Man, and Cybernetics --- Part A: Systems and Humans.* (in prep.)

Acknowledgements. We wish to thank Mr. Nobuyuki Kuge at Nissan Motor, Co. Ltd. for his useful comments.

Studies in Perception & Action X
E. Charles & L.J. Smart (Eds.)
© 2011 Taylor & Francis Group, LLC

Readiness-to-hand, Unreadiness-to-hand, and Multifractality

Lin Nie[1] Dobromir G. Dotov[1] Anthony Chemero.[2]

[1]University of Connecticut, Storrs, Connecticut [2] Franklin & Marshall College, Lancaster, Pennsylvania

In a recent set of experiments (Dotov, Nie, & Chemero, 2010), we provided evidence for the transition in experience from readiness-to-hand to unreadiness-to-hand proposed by phenomenological philosopher Martin Heidegger. In these experiments, we generated and then temporarily disrupted an interaction-dominant system that spans a human participant, a computer mouse, and a task performed on the computer screen. Past research suggested that 1/f-like scaling infers the presence of an interaction-dominant system as opposed to component-dominant. We focused on detecting long-range correlation as indexed by the Hurst exponent, $.5 < H < 1$, a characteristic of processes exhibiting 1/f-like scaling. We found long-range correlation in the hand-mouse movements with both proper mouse and the perturbed mouse, but the scaling coefficient decreased significantly during the perturbation (see Figure 1). In this paper, we subjected our previous data to a more rigorous and necessary reanalysis using
wavelet transform modulus maxima method. We attempted to show that human-mouse system displays multifractal scaling indexed by a spectrum of local Hurst exponents, and, so, is interaction dominant in a stronger sense

Increasing evidence has shown that single scaling exponent is insufficient to characterize behaviors of noisy processes (Mandelbrot, 1986; Ivanova & Ausloos, 1999; Ivanov et al., 1999), might in fact result from a component-dominant system (Thornton and Gilden, 2005; Torre and Wagenmakers, 2009), and that multifractality is sufficient as an indicator that a system is interaction dominant (Ihlen & Vereijken, 2010). For example, in the context of self-regulated biological signals, healthy heart-beat was shown to exhibit multifractal temporal scaling (Ivanov et al, 1999) and the span of Hurst exponent h reduced during perturbation-like periods such as congestive heart failure (Ivanov et al., 1999) and certain medicated interferences with normal heart-beat regulation (Amaral et al., 2001) .

Method

Participants (N=6 in Experiment 1, undergraduates) were told that the experiment was to investigate their motor control behaviours by their performance on two simultaneous cognitive tasks. They played a video game that asked them to use a computer mouse to steer a target object to a designated area on the screen (see Figure 2), while verbally counting numbers backwards by three. To ensure participants' capability of taking effective control over the target while counting at the same time, the experimenter demonstrated doing both tasks to the participants and allowed them to practice with no mouse perturbation. Once enough practice trials were guaranteed, six experimental trials followed. The task was designed so that its mechanics resembles pole-balancing on the finger (Treffner & Kelso, 1999). The properly functioning computer mouse played the role of Heidegger's ready-to-hand tool; approximately thirty seconds into each trial, an unexpected perturbation in the mapping between mouse movement and the pointer visible on the monitor was induced to trigger the transition into unreadiness-to-hand represented by the malfunctioning mouse. Experiment 2 (N=13, undergraduates) shared the design of Experiment 1 except that instead of capturing motion-data by using a optical infrared system , we audio-taped the counting task to obtain their counting rate.

Results and Discussion

Figure 3 summarizes the findings of the current study. The average spread of the fractal spectrum, $h_{max} - h_{min}$, was higher for the section before the perturbation ($M = .236$, $SD = .013$) than for the one containing the perturbation ($M = .202$, $SD = .008$) or the one following it ($M = .199$, $SD = .007$). As expected if the experiment has induced an interaction-dominant system that includes the mouse, the perturbation resulted in a drop in the multifractal spectrum. This effect was supported; however, it lasted well into the remaining of the trial, something we did not predict. We supposed this had to do with the taxing nature of the experiment as several participants had reported.

A two-way Repeated Measures ANOVA was performed with perturbation and trial number as factors. The main effect of perturbation was significant, $F(2, 10) = 4.22$, $p < .05$, $\eta^2 = .45$, while the effect of trial was not significant, $F(5, 25) = .73$, $p = .60$. Therefore the possible interpretation to ascribe the observed effect to a function of time and variables such as fatigue and learning was not supported. The interaction between the two factors was not significant either, $F(10, 50) = .54$, $p = .86$.

We wish to stress that the multifractal spectrum taken as a whole supports the idea of an interaction-dominant system and is hard to explain by alternative models. For this reason it is more interesting to focus on it and changes induced by perturbation rather than try to explain specific values of h or identify the source of scaling for each and every part of the parameter range. In this vein, our results support our general hypothesis of an interaction-based coupling between tool and user that leads them to becoming an interaction-dominant system that operates smoothly before the perturbation of the coupling and continues to function, albeit less fluidly, during and after the perturbation. Interestingly, according to the monofractal DFA analysis h "reverted" relatively quickly to its pre-perturbation level whereas a lasting effect of perturbation can only be seen in the multifractal range of h exponents. This pattern resembles the aforementioned data regarding heart beat dynamics in that only a multifractal analysis is subtle enough to detect some cardiac conditions (Ivanov et al., 1999; Amaral et al., 2001).

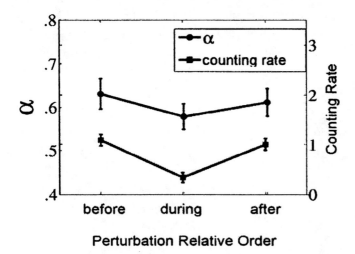

Figure 1. Means of the main measures used in the two experiments. Counting rates are averaged across consecutive 6-second-long blocks. Error bars are standard errors.

Multifractal analysis was adopted to better distinguish between genuinely interaction-dominant systems and other models that generate $1/f$ scaling; it also allowed behavior on longer and larger scales that has an anti-persistent character into the analysis. Liebovitch and Yang (1997) pointed out that the characteristic cross-over scaling behavior of fractal signals recorded from continuous biological motion is a somewhat trivial feature of the experimental paradigm. The significant mass of the body segments necessarily leads to positive correlations over short intervals while the physical constraints on the range of motion leads to negative correlations at longer scales. In our results, the presence of both positive and negative correlations in the signal is not surprising given the frequently observed anti-persistent character of biological limb motion at longer time scales (Liebovitch & Yang, 1997), and the fact that here we use a longer analysis window of 15 seconds. On the other hand, we cannot not reject the possibility that as in other paradigms there are meaningful sources of scaling exponents of the movement data in addition to such features. The multifractal formalism is thus useful in our study because it can reveal all exponents without presupposing which scale of behavior is the relevant one and allows the behavior to be viewed in its full complexity.

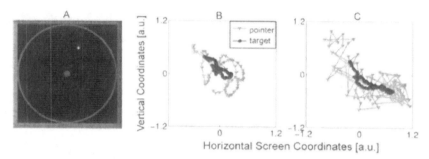

Figure 2 The visual playground environment. A single frame (a) captured during the course of a trial is shown and visible inside it are the pen, the grey center, and blue and green circles for the target and pointer objects, respectively. Representative pointer and target object trajectories on the screen from three-second excerpts with a normally behaving (b) and impaired (c) mouse are portrayed.

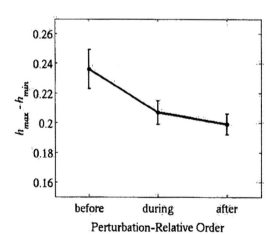

Figure 3 Averages of the multifractal spectrum range scores ($h_{max} - h_{mean}$) as a function of perturbation-relative order. Error bars are standard errors.

References

Amarnal, L. A., Ivanov, P. C., Aoyagi, N., Hidaka, I., Tomono, S., Goldberger, A. L., Stanley, H. E., & Yamamoto, Y. (2001). Behavioral-independent features of complex heartbeat dynamics. *Physical Review Letters, 86*(26), 6026-6029

Dotov DG, Nie L, Chemero A (2010) A Demonstration of the transition from ready-to-hand to unready-to-hand. *PLoS ONE 5*(3): e9433. doi:10.1371/journal.pone.0009433

Ihlen, E. A. F. & Vereijken, B. (2010). Interaction-dominant dynamics in human cognition: beyond 1/f α fluctuation. *Journal of Experimental Psychology: General, 139*(3), 436-463.

Ivanov, P. C., Amaral, L. A. N., Goldberger, A. L., Havlin, S., Rosenblum, M. G., Struzik, Z., & Stanley, H. E. (1999). Multifractality in human heartbeat dynamics. *Nature, 399*, 461-465.

Ivanova, K. & Ausloos, M. (1999). Low-order variability Diagrams for short-range correlation evidence in financial data: BGL-USD exchange rate, Dow Jones industrial average, gold ounce price. *Physica A: Statistical and Theoretical Physics, 265*(1), 279-291.

Liebovitch, L. S., & Yang, W. (1997). Transition from persistent to antipersistent correlation in biological systems. *Physical Review E, 56*(4), 4557-4566.

Mandelbrot. (1983). *The Fractal Geometry of Nature.* New York, NY: W. H. Freeman.

Thornton, T.L. & Gilden, D.L. (2005). Provenance of correlations in psychological data. *Psychonomic Bulletin & Review, 12*(3), 409-441.

Torre, K. & Wagenmakers, E.J. (2009). Theories and models for $1/f^{\beta}$ noise in human movement science. *Human Movement Science, 28*(3), 297-318.

Treffner P. and Kelso, J.A.S. (1999). Dynamic encounters: long memory during functional stabilization. *Ecological Psychology, 11*, 103–138

Studies in Perception & Action X
E. Charles & L.J. Smart (Eds.)
© 2011 Taylor & Francis Group, LLC

Dynamics of Asymmetric Bimanual Coordination in Dexterous Tool-use

Tetsushi Nonaka[1], Blandine Bril[2]

[1]Research Institute of Health and Welfare, Kibi International University, Japan
[2] Groupe de Recherche Apprentissage et Contexte, École des Hautes Études en Sciences Sociales, France

The current study is one of the series of experimental studies on dexterity of stone beads craftsmen in India (Biryukova & Bril, 2008; Bril, Roux, & Dietrich, 2005; Roux, et al., 1995). Craftsmen produce stone flakes of different profiles in such a way to shape the stone into a specific form (Bril et al., 2005). With one hand, which we call the *postural hand*, the craftsman holds a piece of stone between his fingers and places the stone against the pointed tip of an iron bar. With the other hand, which we call the *hammering hand*, the craftsman strikes the piece with the hammer so that a stone flake is fractured from the point of contact with the iron bar (*Figure 1A*). Our research was designed to investigate bimanual coordination in a goal-directed tool-use task in which the two hands' activities are asymmetrical and highly specialized (Nonaka & Bril, in press).

Method

Participants were recruited from two classes of workshops. HQ consisted of six expert craftsmen from the higher quality workshops. LQ consisted of six craftsmen from the lower quality workshops.

The task consisted of shaping a parallelepiped-shaped roughout, made of two different materials (carnelian stone and glass) into an ellipsoidal preform. Two phases in the process of shaping an ellipsoidal preform—calibration and within each 30-second sequence, mean amplitudes of the hammering hand and mean resultant velocities of the postural hand at each frame within each 30-second sequence were calculated. CRQA was performed to quantify the dynamics of the bimanual movement coordination (*Figure 2*). For CRQA, a delay of 18 data points (0.3 seconds), 8 dimensions, and a radius of 34% of the mean distance separating points in reconstructed space were used as input parameters to compute the indexes of repeatability of states (*%CREC*), stability (*CL_{max}*), and determinism (*%CDET*) of the dynamics of bimanual coordination.

A   B

Calibration   Fluting

Figure 1. A: Typical posture and movement of craftsmen. B: Two sub-goals of an ellipsoidal bead production: calibration and fluting. fluting—were studied (*Figure 1B*). The first 30-second sequences of calibration (standardization of crests to prepare for fluting) and fluting (detachment of long crests) were extracted from each trial. In total, 108 calibration and 113 fluting sequences contributed to the analysis.

Results and Discussion

Bimanual coordination. An ANOVA on *%CREC* found a significant interaction between sub-goal and group, $F_{(1,204)}=14.84$, $p < .001$. A post-hoc analysis indicated that only for HQ, the proportion of shared activity in reconstructed phase space (*%CREC*) was greater during fluting compared to calibration, $p <$ .001 (*Figure 3A*). An ANOVA on CL_{max} found a main effect of sub-goal, $F_{(1,204)}=7.61$, $p < .01$, as well as an interaction between sub-goal and group, $F_{(1,204)}=10.53$, $p < .01$. A post-hoc analysis indicated that only for HQ, the dynamics of shared activity in reconstructed phase space (CL_{max}) was less sensitive to perturbations during fluting compared to calibration, $p < .001$ (*Figure 3B*). The dynamics of shared activity (*%CDET*) were more predictable for HQ compared to LQ, $F_{(1,10)}=5.06$, $p < .05$ (*Figure 3C*).

Unilateral movement. An ANOVA on mean hammering amplitudes found significant main effects for sub-goal, $F_{(1,203)} = 9.08$, $p < .01$, and raw material, $F_{(1, 203)} = 103.45$, $p < .001$. An interaction between these two factors, $F_{(1, 203)} =8.40$, $p < .01$, and the three-way interaction, $F_{(1, 203)} = 4.65$, $p < .05$ were also significant. A post-hoc analysis revealed that craftsmen from both groups oscillated their hammering hands with greater amplitude when stone was used than when glass was used, $p <. 001$ (*Figure 3D*). In the ANOVA on mean resultant velocity of the postural hand, a main effect was obtained for sub-goal, $F_{(1, 204)} = 9.8$, $p < .01$. Sub-goal and raw material both exhibited interactions with group: sub-goal by group, $F_{(1, 204)} = 7.45$, $p < .01$,

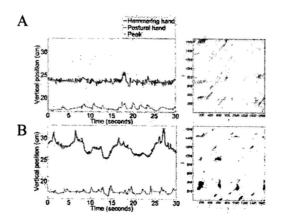

Figure 2. Sample time series data and cross recurrence plots of the two hands during: (A) calibration and (B) fluting of a craftsman from HQ.

and raw material by group, $F_{(1, 205)} = 6.21$, p < .05. The three-way interaction was also significant, $F_{(1, 204)} = 9.21$, $p < .01$. As shown in *Figure 3E*, the velocity of the postural hands of LQ was significantly lower than that of all the comparable conditions, $p <$ .05.

A linear regression revealed that as the amplitude of the hammering movement (M_{ah}) increased, the mean resultant velocity of the postural hand (M_{vp}) also reliably increased for LQ, $F_{(1, 110)} =$ 104.97, $p < .001$, $r^2=.49$, $M_{vp}=.09*M_{ah}+1.59$, but this was not the case for HQ (*Figure 3F*). These results imply that the velocity of the postural hand of the craftsmen from HQ was relatively independent of the kinetic energy transmitted by the hammer, which may be indicative of an aspect of dexterity of HQ.

CRQA found a significantly greater %*CDET* for HQ than for LQ (*Figure 3C*). High %*CDET* indicates that deterministic rules are present in the dynamics of shared states between the two movement trajectories in the reconstructed phase space. Given the fact that the velocity of the postural hand was not reliably related to the amplitude of the hammering movement in HQ (*Figure 3F*), the possibility that the greater amount of observed deterministic structure of the dynamics of bimanual coordination in HQ compared to LQ stems from the perturbation caused by the mechanical impact may be excluded. One remaining possibility is that such regularity of the displacement of the two hands in HQ emerged from the control of bimanual action, in which the activity of the postural hand to position and orient the object to be hit and that of the hammering hand to deliver a blow are coupled in a coherent manner.

Only in HQ, greater degree of shared activity of the two hands (greater %*CREC*) was found when they were fluting than when they were calibrating (*Figure 3A*), and the trajectories diverged less over time (longer CL_{max}) during fluting than during calibration (*Figure 3B*). These results suggest that only in HQ, switches in the sub-goal affected the dynamics of bimanual coordination, in such a way to decrease the noise magnitude and the sensitivity to perturbation during fluting. Fluting is said to be the most critical phase in stone bead production, as subtle disruptions in fluting may result in failure of the entire task (Roux et al., 1995).On the other hand, calibration, a process of standardization of the uneven surfaces to make available the affordances for fluting, requires

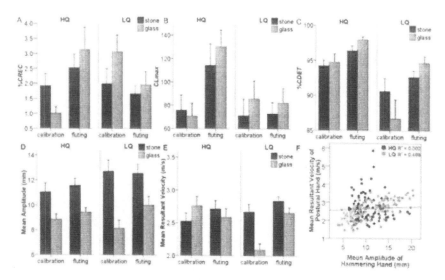

Figure 3. Means of dependent measures calculated for each 30-second sequence: (A) $\%CREC$, (B) CL_{max}, (C) $\%CDET$, (D) mean amplitude of the hammering hand, (E) mean resultant velocity of the postural hand, and (F) mean resultant velocities of the postural hand in each 30-second sequence as a function of mean amplitude of the hammering hand.

flexibility. The characteristics of HQ craftsmen where the dynamics of bimanual coordination is more stable and less noisy during fluting compared to calibration specify such different functional requirements of sub-goals.

References

Biryukova, E. V., & Bril, B. (2008). Organization of goal-directed action at a high level of motor skill: the case of stone knapping in India. *Motor Control, 12(3)*, 181-209.

Bril, B., Roux, V., & Dietrich, G. (2005). Stone Knapping: Khambhat (India), a Unique Opportunity? In B. Bril & V. Roux (Eds.), *Stone knapping: the necessary conditions for a uniquely hominin behavior* (pp. 53-71). Cambridge: McDonald Institute for Archaeological Research.

Nonaka, T. & Bril, B. (in press). Nesting of asymmetric functions in skilled bimanual action: Dynamics of hammering behavior of bead craftsmen. *Human Movement Science*, doi:10.1016/j.humov.2010.08.013.

Roux, V., Bril, B., & Dietrich, G. (1995). Skills and Learning Difficulties Involved in Stone Knapping: The Case of Stone-Bead Knapping in Khamphat, India. *World Archaeology, 27(1)*, 63-87.

Acknowledgements. This research was funded by the European Commission (Sixth Framework Programme Project 29065 HANDTOMOUTH), and the French Ministère délégué à la recherche et aux nouvelles technologies (ACI TTT P7802 n° 02 2 0440).

Studies in Perception & Action X
E. Charles & L.J. Smart (Eds.)

Low Vision Aids in Young Visually Impaired Children: Prospects from Motor Control

J. Schurink [1,2], R.F.A. Cox [1,2], F.N. Boonstra [2]

[1] Behavioural Science Institute, Radboud University Nijmegen, The Netherlands
[2] Bartiméus Institute, Zeist, The Netherlands

Exploration and perception with a low vision aid (LVA), such as a magnifier, is more complex than without LVA. However, for children with a visual impairment the use of a LVA is indispensible in many tasks. To understand how these children use and learn to use LVAs, we must focus on the specific coordination and control problems such aids entail. For instance, the distances between eye, LVA and object are critical for a sharp and stable image. In general, a child has to coordinate movements of body, head, eyes, and hands appropriately during the task. Successful performance on a LVA-mediated task, therefore, requires quite advanced motor planning and control. Since these abilities are still fully developing in (young) children, this of course influences task performance.

In order to address the complexity of LVA use in visually impaired children a conceptual framework was recently introduced (Figure 1; Schurink et al., 2011). Within this framework, LVA use is effectively and fully described by the dynamic interrelations that hold between the characteristics of the LVA, the specific requirements of the task at hand, and the exploratory and goal-directed movements made by the a particular user. More specifically, a child's task performance with a LVA is constrained by three reciprocal relations: the Child-to-Task relation, the Child-to-LVA relation, and the LVA-to-Task relation. The latter relation expresses the (potential) LVA-task match, and has been labelled 'topology' in tool use (Smitsman, Cox & Bongers, 2005).

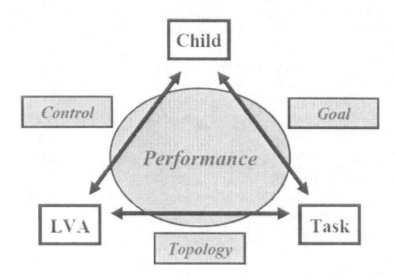

Figure 1. A schematic representation of the interrelated system of child, low vision aid (LVA), and task, which together define LVA-mediated task performance.

As said, handling a LVA entail specific motor control and coordination problems related to the exploratory and goal-directed movements necessary in a tasks. For this to be possible, basic abilities such as eye-hand coordination and fine-motor skills are needed. However, it has been shown that visually impaired children have delays in motor development (e.g. Houwen, Visscher, Lemmink, & Hartman, 2008; Reimer, Cox, Boonstra, & Smits-Engelsman, 2008). As a result, this might negatively influence their ability to use a LVA, in ways we still know very little about. To learn more about this, we need a thorough investigation of children's motor performance in LVA-mediated tasks.

In the present study we focussed on the constraints entailed by the Child-to-LVA and Child-to-Task relation, involving control-related and goal-related information. A specific set-up and objects were chosen so as to resemble relevant aspects of LVA-mediated tasks, without actual including a LVA at this point. Characteristics of the LVA-object, such as size and shape, were varied, as well as requirements of the task, such as distance, accuracy, and type of movement. We studied how children's individual capacities for action in relation to these aspects determines task performance. Only part of the data gathered in this study will be reported here.

Method

Visually impaired children (N=56) and normally sighted children (N=57) participated in this study. Mean age in both groups was 6.2 years (SD: 1.3; range: 4 to 8). The visually impaired children all had a visual acuity between 0.05 and 0.4.

Children had to perform rhythmical aiming movements with an object over the surface of a digitizer (Wacom, Saitama, Japan; type 21ux), which was placed horizontally in front of the child. The digitizer displayed two circles ($\varnothing$ 2.5 cm), which acted as the target locations. Children were asked to move between these targets as accurately and fast as possible, using two types of objects. One object had the dimensions of a dome magnifier ($\varnothing$ 4.5 cm; height 4.0 cm), the other one the dimensions of a stand magnifier ($\varnothing$ 5.0 cm; height 4.8 cm). Both such magnifiers are highly common for children in this age range.

Two types of movements (cyclic and discrete), in two orientations (azimuthal and radial), and over two distances (10 and 20 cm) had to be performed, in a random order. This had to be done with and without visible information about the target location: In the cyclic condition, after the start signal, children moved the object between the (visible) targets for 5 seconds, after which the targets disappeared and children continued for 5seconds. In the discrete condition, children had to make 10 strokes with, followed by 10 without targets visible. In the latter condition there was a start signal before each individual stroke.

Results and Discussion

Table I shows the overall results in both groups. With respect to the movement time of the goal directed movements, visually impaired children performed the movements slower than their normally sighted peers. These differences were significant in all cyclic conditions (all *p's* < .001) but not in the discrete conditions. Accuracy was defined as the distance between the centre of the target and the end-point of the movement. We found significant differences in accuracy between the visually impaired children and their normally sighted peers, but only in the discrete conditions with the object resembling the stand magnifier.

	Visually impaired children (N=56)				Normally sighted children (N=57)			
	Target		Object		Target		Object	
	Visible	Not visible	Stand	Dome	Visible	Not visible	Stand	Dome
Movement time (s)	.77	.99	0.91	0.85	.69	.85	0.80	0.75
Accuracy (mm)	22	28	25	24	22	27	25	24

Table I: Dependent variables for each vision groups as a function of object and type movement.

As mentioned, movements were first performed with targets visible and then with targets invisible. Both visually impaired children and normally sighted children moved slower and less accurate when the targets were not visible (*p* < .001).Also, children had to perform the movements with two objects resembling the dome and stand magnifier (see Table I). In general, we found that children were faster with the dome-like object (*p* < .001). Furthermore, visually impaired children were more accurate with the dome-like object compared to the stand-like object (*p* < .01).

As a preliminary conclusion, visually impaired children seemed to have specific differences in motor control when performing manual rhythmical aiming movements with an object, compared to their normally sighted peers. This was demonstrated either by lower speed or accuracy, depending on the type of movement they had to perform and the type of object. A dome magnifier seems more suitable for performing fast and accurate movements than the stand magnifier.

The motor-control differences revealed by the set up of this experiment might help us to get a better insight into the abilities of visually impaired children to use and learn to use a LVA.

References

Houwen, S., Visscher, C., Lemmink, K. A. P. M. , & Hartman, E. (2008). Motor skill performance of school-age children with visual impairments. *Developmental Medicine & Child Neurology, 50,* 139–145.

Reimer, A. M., Smits-Engelsman, B. C. M., & Siemonsma-Boom, M. (1999). Manual skills in blind and visually impaired children between 6 and 12 years of age. *Journal of Visual Impairment Blindness, 93,* 643–658.

Schurink, J., Cox, R.F.A., Cillessen, A.H.N., van Rens, G.H.M.B., & Boonstra, F.N. (2011). Low vision aids for visually impaired children A perception-action perspective. *Research in Developmental Disabilities, 32,* 871–882.

Smitsman, A.W., Cox, R.F.A., & Bongers, R.M. (2005). Action dynamics in tool use. In B. Brill & V. Roux (Eds.), *Knapping Stone: The necessary conditions for a uniquely hominid behavior?* (pp. 129-147). Cambridge: McDonald Institute.

Studies in Perception & Action X
E. Charles & L.J. Smart (Eds.)
© 2011 Taylor & Francis Group, LLC

Activities of Designing Architectural Environments: An Ecological Perspective

Hiroki Seki[1]

[1]The University of Tokyo

To understand continuity and changes in the built environment, it is necessary to understand the relationship between two fundamental activities—designing the architectural environment and living or dwelling in the environment.

Each of these activities has been examined from the perspective of the human–environment relationship in fields such as architectural planning and psychology as well as in studies of environmental behavior. These investigations have revealed the mutuality between humans and the environment and have developed practical suggestions for building a user-centered environment by using keywords such as "environmental transition" or "behavior settings" for the activities of living in the environment and "communication" or "workshops" with architects and inhabitants for the activities of designing the environment. However, the designing activity by itself has not been fully examined from the human–environment relationship perspective— that is, the relationship between architects and the environment during the processes of designing. Recently, some theoretical suggestions have been presented regarding this issue. Ingold (2000) pointed out the possibilities of understanding the activities of designing architectural environment from the human– environment relationship perspective on the basis of reviewing works in psychology, anthropology, and architectural studies that considered the relationships between humans and the built environment. In addition, he presented a monistic perspective, called the "dwelling perspective," for understanding the two abovementioned activities in terms of the human–environment relationship.

Given this background, this paper describes the detailed observations of the actual processes of architectural design, performed by professional architects. This study aims to examine the human–environment relationship embedded in the activities of designing and planning an architectural environment.

Method

Six cases of designing and planning by five Japanese professional architects were observed. Figure 1 indicates the basic building information for each case. Each case was investigated using an interview survey (90–120 min at a time, two or three times per case) and the surveys about all the materials that were made during the designing activities, such as sketches, drawings, blueprints, and models.

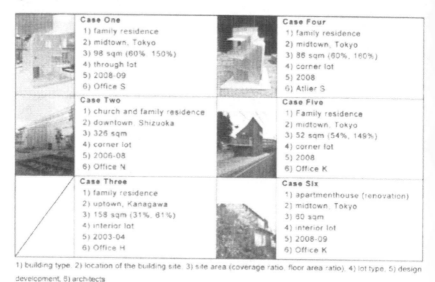

1) building type. 2) location of the building site. 3) site area (coverage ratio, floor area ratio). 4) lot type. 5) design development. 6) architects

Figure 1. Basic building information for each six cases.

Results and Discussion

The following results were obtained.

1) No architect in the study began designing on the basis of the images that they already held and had decided to try in advance. All began by confirming the properties of the building site such as possible approaches from the paths or views from the location.

2) The process of designing tended to proceed even after the architects presented more than one proposal that met the given conditions. Figure 2 shows a part of the process in Case 4. In this case, a suitable proposal was presented in b004, 14 days after the client's initial request. As shown in this figure, however, the designing activities did not stop. Furthermore, the designing process after b004 proceeded on the basis of the same part of roofing that had been the key in the former designing process, because of the need to comply with legal restrictions. The activities of designing architectures typically proceed under complex conditions that include client needs, formal and environmental constraints of the building site, and legal restrictions. However, all the architects in this study were able to create several suitable proposals in a short duration (e.g., on the day the client made his request or one day after). Moreover, they seemed to have no difficulty drafting proposals that met the conditions. This shows that designing activities are undertaken with additional aims other than to present proposals that merely meet the given conditions.

3) If the aim is not necessarily to present a proposal that meets the given conditions, what drives the processes of designing activities? In this study, it was also observed that the architects developed some proposals in more depth than others. According to the architects, these proposals not only met the given conditions but also identified the possibilities that were not noticeable in the beginning. One architect expressed this possibility as "the principle (to generate an architectural design unique to this site)." In all cases except one, the architect mentioned having discovered something close to this "principle." In Case 4, as shown in Figure 2, the architect referred to the principle as "mushroom-ness (being like a mushroom)," which he recognized in b006.

4) The interview surveys revealed that the architects thought of the designing activities as "finding" or "looking for carefully," not as "computing" or "calculating." Following the discoveries of the abovementioned "principles," the designing processes tended to converge.

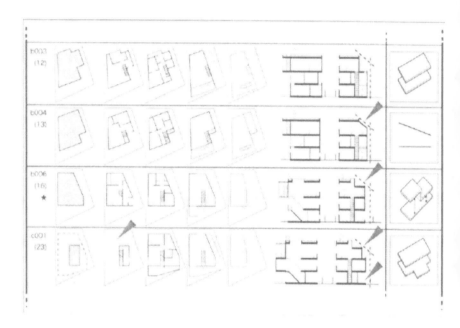

Figure 2. A part of the proposal flow investigated in Case 4. In this case, the architect presented 10 proposals in all. He met the given conditions in b004; however, he continued his designing by following six more proposals. And he discovered "mushroom-ness" in b006. (The general arrangement, plans, sections, and the patterns of arrangement are indicated from the left. Arrows show the point of major arrangement, and dotted lines show the legal restrictions on the site. The numbers in parentheses indicate the days after the beginning of the designing activities.)

These results seem to indicate the possibilities of understanding the activities of architectural designing as a method for picking-up and realizing the potentials of architectures that are intrinsic to the building site, not as activities of the architects that are based on mere esthetics and self-centeredness or calculations. This issue is worth discussing in connection with the perspective of human–environment relationships, especially with the concept of an "ecological resource and its usage," introduced in the ecological psychology by James Gibson (1986).

References

Ingold, T. (2000). The perception of the environment: Essays on Livelihood, Dwelling and Skill. Routledge.

Gibson, J.J. (1986). The ecological approach to visual perception. Lawrence Erlbaum Associates, Inc., Hillsdale, NJ.

Studies in Perception & Action X
E. Charles & L.J. Smart (Eds.)
© 2011 Taylor & Francis Group, LLC

Effect of Backrest and Seat-base Support of Driver's Seat on Braking

Seiji Totsuka[1], Hiroshi Inou[1], Mamoru Sawada[1],
& Hiroyuki Mishima[2]

[1]*DENSO* CORPORATION, Japan, [2]Waseda University, Tokyo, Japan.

When moving our limbs, we normally maintain a persistent orientation relative to the environment. This continuous orienting activity, also known as "posture," supports body weight, balances the external forces acting on the trunk and limbs, and keeps the perceptual systems tuned to the available information (Reed, 1988).

The condition of the support surface will have powerful effects on postural control (Stoffregen & Riccio, 1988). Therefore, the car seat, which is the support surface for a driver, will also play an important role in maintaining his/her posture in operating a vehicle.

Nomura et al. developed a seating system called the "Optimized Seating System (OSS)," and showed that a well-adjusted seat improved not only the dynamic balancing activity of postural control but also the performatory action ("reaching") of a handicapped person (Nomura, Muraguchi, Chiba, Inou, Fujita, Sawada, & Mishima, 2009).

In this study, we focused on the surface shape of a car seat that supports a driver's posture, its effect on operating (especially braking) a vehicle, and differences in its effect between a skilled and unskilled driver.

Method

One skilled and one unskilled driver participated in the experiment. The skilled driver had 26 years of experience as a test driver for *DENSO*. The unskilled driver had 5 years of experience as a weekend driver. Experiments were performed in a test track at the *DENSO* Abashiri Test Center (Hokkaido, Japan). On a long straight track, participants were asked to sit on an ordinary seat or a custom-made seat (Figure 1), drive a vehicle at 60 km/h, and then brake as hard as possible to stop the vehicle. Measurements were obtained for the 2D pressure distribution (XSENSOR Technology, XSENSOR system) on the driver's seat and the acceleration (as an index of the force) applied to the brake pedal.

Figure 1. Custom-made seat used in the experiment.

The design features of the custom-made seat were as follows. First, the counteracting force caused by the driver's braking activity was supported by the lower part of the backrest at the ilium. Second, the bowl-shaped seat-base supported not only the ischium but also the thigh.

Results and Discussion

The 2D pressure distributions of each driver when seated on the ordinary seat are shown in Figure 2. In the case of the unskilled driver, the pressure distribution of the seat-base almost completely faded away while braking (Figure 2-D). This was because the unskilled driver's hip was lifted by the counteracting force transmitted through the leg from the brake pedal.

The acceleration applied to the brake pedal for each driver while braking on the ordinary seat is shown in Figure 3. The skilled driver kept a constant braking force while braking, whereas the unskilled driver could not.

Correspondingly, the acceleration applied to the brake pedal for each driver while braking on the custom-made seat is shown in Figure 4. In contrast to Figure 3-B, the unskilled driver was able to maintain the maximum braking power for a longer time in the custom-made seat.

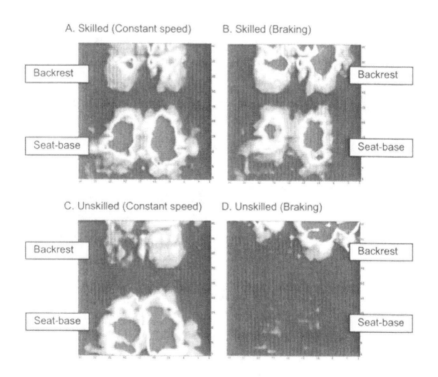

Figure 2. 2D pressure distribution on the ordinary seat for each driver.

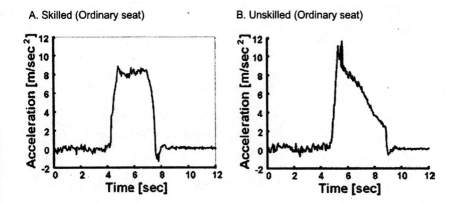

Figure 3. Acceleration applied to the brake pedal (Ordinary seat condition).

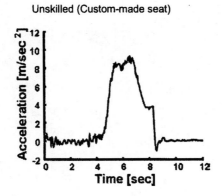

Figure 4. Acceleration applied to the brake pedal (Unskilled driver; Custom-made seat condition).

These results showed that a well-adjusted seat could afford coordination that realized the dynamic stability of posture as well as a greater degree of freedom of the body, even for a less-skilled driver. A well-adjusted seat for a support surface will improve not only static activities but also dynamic ones such as driving, and have the potential to enhance the Quality of Driving.

References

Hisako Nomura, Ken'ichi Muraguchi, Kunihiko Chiba, Hiroshi Inou, Mitsuru Fujita, Mamoru Sawada, & Hiroyuki Mishima. (July 14, 2009). *Posture supported by a well-adjusted seating system creates virtuous perception-action cycles.* Oral presentation at the 15th International Conference on Perception-Action, University of Minnesota, Minneapolis.

Reed, E.S. (1988). Applying the theory of action systems to the study of motor skills. In Meijer, O.G., Roth, K. (Eds.), *Complex Movement Behaviour: The Motor-Action Controversy.* Elsevier, Amsterdam.

Stoffregen, T. A., and Riccio, G. E. (1988). An ecological theory of orientation and the vestibular system. *Psychological Review, 95,* 3-14.

Studies in Perception & Action X
E. Charles & L.J. Smart (Eds.)
© 2011 Taylor & Francis Group, LLC

Manual Wielding and the Dynamics of Liquids

Ken Yoshida & Thomas A. Stoffregen

University of Minnesota

Perception of object length arising from manual wielding is powerfully influenced by the inertia tensor of wielded objects (e.g., Solomon & Turvey, 1988). In solid objects the inertia tensor is a fixed quantity which can be computed, and whose responses to torques are stable. By contrast, when we lift a glass to drink, we are wielding (in addition to the glass) a liquid, whose dynamics (including the inertia tensor) vary as a function of movement. In this study we asked whether judgments of object length during manual wielding would be influenced by the presence of liquid mass in the wielded object.

Method

Ten undergraduate students (5 men, 5 women) participated in the study. Participants wielded wooden dowels (1.25 cm diameter) that were 90 cm in length. We attached weight to rods in five different locations (L1 = 23 cm, L2 = 34 cm, L3 = 46 cm, L4 = 57 cm, and L5 = 69 cm, measured from the handheld end). The weight were either solid ball (180 g) or were plastic spheres (40 g) with filled halfway with water (140 g). All weights had same total mass (180 g) and dimension (10 cm diameter sphere).

Our method was similar to that of Solomon and Turvey (1988). The participant was seated on a height adjustable stool and placed his or her right arm through a hole in a black curtain. The table was placed in the other side of curtain, and the participant was asked to adjust the arm position so the wrist was aligned with the edge of the table. Once the participant adjusted the arm position, he or she was asked to fix the elbow against the table. Throughout the experiment, the rod was occluded from the participant's view. A square of gray cardboard, 60 cm × 125 cm, was attached to the dolly, and the dolly was connected to the ropes and pulley system. There was no audible sloshing. Subjects were asked to judge the maximum distance reachable with the rod in each condition, and to express their judgments by using the rope to slide the dolly to the appropriate position. Each condition was repeated three times, totalling 30 trials, and the order of conditions were randomized and counterbalanced.

Results and Discussion

For the solid weight, the average perceived lengths for L1, L2, L3, L4, and L5 were, 60.9 cm, 69.5 cm, 75.9 cm, 81.4 cm, and 88.7 cm respectively. Average perceived lengths for liquid weight were 57.8 cm, 65.5 cm, 70.5 cm, 78.4 cm, and 88.7 cm respectively. We conducted a 2 (solid vs. liquid) × 5 (weight position) ANOVA on the judgment data. The main effect of weight position was significant, $F(4, 36) = 31.95, p < .001$. There were no other significant effects. The result with the solid weights replicated those of Solomon & Turvey (1988). The absence of a main effect for solid vs. liquid and the absence of a significant interaction between weight location and material suggests that perception of length was influenced by the location of both liquid and solid weights. The inertia tensor might be invoked to explain the results with solid weights, but it is not clear that the same could be true when the weights were liquid. The results raise new questions about the information that supports perception of length in manual wielding.

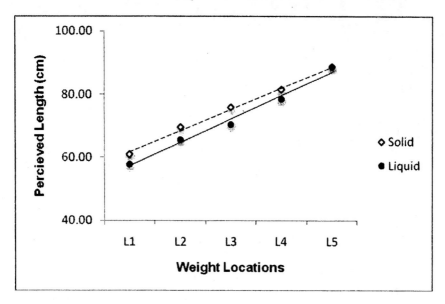

Figure 1. Perceived length for five different weight locations. L1 = 23 cm, L2 = 34 cm, L3 = 46 cm, L4 = 57 cm, and L5 = 69 cm. Dash line indicates trend for the solid weight conditions, and solid line indicates trend for the liquid weight condition. The slope and intercept of liner regression for solid condition was $y = 7.6x + 49.8$, and for liquid condition was $y = 6.7x + 55$.

References

Solomon, H. Y., & Turvey, M. T. (1988). Haptically perceiving the distances reachable with hand-held objects. *Journal of Experimental Psychology: Human Perception and Performance, 14*, 404-427.

Studies in Perception & Action X
E. Charles & L.J. Smart (Eds.)
© 2011 Taylor & Francis Group, LLC

Author Index

A

Abdolvahab, M. 122, 162
Akatsu, Y. 234, 239
Alleoni, B. N. 59
Amazeen, E. L. 59, 62-3, 76
Athreya, D. N. 63

B

Bardy, B. G. 116, 140, 144, 155-6, 223, 227
Barrientos, A. 9
Bennett, S. J. 110-2, 114-5
Bhat, A. 98, 102
Blau, J. J. C. 25, 27, 29
Boonstra, F. N. 30, 253-4, 257
Bootsma, R. J. 117-8, 120, 216, 221
Bosman, A. M. T. 128, 133
Boyadjian, A. 71-2, 74-5
Bril, B. 221, 247, 252, 257
Buloup, F. 216

C

Carello, C. 25, 29, 76, 81, 140, 144, 162, 166, 173
Chaminade, T. 104-5, 108-9
Charles, E. P. 2, 5
Chang, C.-H. 140
Chemero, A. 15-6, 18, 240, 245
Chen, C.-Y. 151
Chen, F.-C. 187, 191, 201, 204
Chung, H. C. 192
Coppin, P. 36

Coyle, T. 216, 221
Cox, R. F. A. 30, 128, 133, 253-4, 257
Cummins-Sebree, S. E. 195, 199

D

Danion, F. 211, 213, 215
Davis, T. J. 146
De Clercq, D. 110, 112, 115
Díaz, A. 9, 13
Dixon, J. 98
Dotov, D. G. 15, 240, 245

E

Engan, Ø. 19

F

Fine, J. 76
Forner-Cordero, A. 48, 52
Frank, T. D. 168-9, 173
Furuyama, N. 89

G

Gandon, E. 216, 220-1
Garcia, V. D. 48
Gifford, T. 98
Gordon, J. M. 25, 162

H

Haas, J. 195, 199
Hasselman, F. 128, 133
Heugas, A-M. 82, 86
Hibiya, A. 157

Author Index